Raising Wrenns

a memoir

BY

MAL WRENN CORBIN

Raising Wrenns, published January, 2024
Editorial and proofreading services: Cath Lauria; Katie Barger
Interior layout and cover design: Howard Johnson
Front cover artwork: Roberta Zeta
Photo Credits: Author photo: Maura Longueil
Interior artwork (part openers): designed by Freepik.com, (chapter openers): feather image: Flaticon.com
Pencil sketch of wren: © Hannah Longmuir

 **SDP Publishing**

Published by SDP Publishing, an imprint of SDP Publishing Solutions, LLC.

The scenarios in this book reflect the memories of the author and that of select family members and friends. **To protect the privacy of certain individuals, names and identifying details have been changed.**

Content Guidance: This book contains subject matter that might be troubling to some readers including, but not limited to, references to childhood trauma, domestic violence, addiction, sexual abuse, and suicide. Please read with care.

To obtain permission(s) to use material from this work, please submit an email request with subject line: SDP Publishing Permissions Department to: Email: info@SDPPublishing.com.

ISBN-13 (print): 979-8-9882715-6-7

ISBN-13 (ebook): 979-8-9885439-0-9

Library of Congress Control Number: 2023919339

Printed in the United States of America

DEDICATION

To my dear son, Jack, my own sweet baby wren. I treasure you and love watching you fly, free bird. And, to Lisa, I am lucky to call you sister.

ACKNOWLEDGMENTS

Thank you to Danielle Wolffe for helping me take what was in my heart and weaving it into this beautifully complicated story.

My deepest gratitude to those that took on the role of family, sometimes providing a soft place to rest my head even for just a night. You showed me what a healthy, happy home life can be.

And, finally, profound thanks to my husband, Greg, for believing in me when I couldn't. You set me free and are the reason I was able to open my heart up to the past and put my story down on paper.

I love you more than words can express.

TABLE OF CONTENTS

PROLOGUE

It is no accident that my family's namesake is the wren. Wrens are scrappy little birds renowned for the way they flitter from place to place, building shallow rooted nests wherever they land: in old leather boots, sawed off soup cans, cardboard boxes, or old drain pipes. Wrens are the dumpster divers of the avian world, picking delicacies like caterpillar larvae and beetle meat out of thorny scrub; gnawing down on pebbles and mud. Wrens are sharp-beaked scavengers. They scurry quickly like mice. They are driftless.

My family are diminutive, crafty people with an instinctive talent for making ourselves invisible and for quick-witted flight. By the time landlords came to enforce the evictions, all they found was rented furniture and piles of garbage. We pecked at the food other people wouldn't touch; we ate potato chip crumbs from between couch cushions, government cheese, hot dogs charred over cigarette lighters, and waited in line at the soup kitchen.

The wren has a specific piercing song that tends to agitate humans. My dad also liked to croon off-colored tunes, half-remembered lyrics passed between men in cruddy bars, where mirrors hide behind plastic containers of year-old pickled eggs. Random listeners passing by may have assumed those songs were coming from tone-deaf men, but my father bellowed them with fierce Irish pride, calling out to the free-spirited birds our ancestors held sacred.

The Irish wren is one of few birds heard in the winter, when the snow buries porches and the bird's body heat plummets. Wren families often roost together to keep warm. This is like the way my twin brother and sister and I used to snuggle together in one bed, especially when the heat and electricity had been shut off. We learned to hug each other's bodies lightly, my sister and I ready to jump onto the floor if my brother peed the bed.

Poets romanticized the wren for its heartfelt ability to build a home wherever it went. I think they underestimated the memory loss and chaos that occurs from such a crash landing. It might have been nice to have been a wren if we'd had more room to travel, if our parents had coasted on the wind to somewhere exotic; perhaps to the Irish or Swedish lands my parents' people came from. But we never flew farther than the two square miles of triple-decker houses we perched in after they'd been abandoned by former factory workers in the Main South neighborhood of Worcester. We lingered there in between worlds with half-slitted eyes, stuck in those blocks like they were a glue trap. We didn't step too hard because we knew these places might tear up parts of our feet or our bellies. But we never left them.

There was something off in Worcester. It was the place we blamed for everything. The lack of jobs and the shitty houses with windows like loose teeth we had to duct tape in the winter were all circumstances of living in Worcester.

In Main South people didn't fuss with ambition. They nursed beers in dark, sorrowful bars that smelled like giant ashtrays. They sat on the stoops talking trash and chucking smoldering cigarettes on the sidewalk. They were the working class, the factory workers and bricklayers who lost their jobs when the city started going to hell, who ate fish on Fridays and smudged their foreheads with soot on Ash Wednesdays, who sunk their tiny butts onto barstools and poured vodka onto pavement as they toasted the loss of their friends to knife fights and cirrhosis.

My father rarely spoke of his immediate family, whose alcoholic roots twined through their bodies and showed themselves in the burst capillaries on some of their faces. He prided himself on his hearty ancestors—the ones who traced their heritage to those who immigrated before the potato famine and dug their spades into rock to build the Blackstone Canal, Main Street, and who laid track for the railroads that turned Worcester from farmland into a city after the famine in 1845.

When my parents were married at City Hall on Halloween 1973, when trick or treaters roamed the streets in costumes and bums set fires in trash cans, my mom was already four months pregnant with me. I was born the following February.

My mother wanted to name me Danielle, but my father insisted they name me Marilyn, the name of the wife of a friend whom he was not-so-secretly madly in love with. The leap of leprechaun logic that makes you name your daughter after your fantasy wife would escape most folks, but I guess it made sense to my dad at the time.

I believe the twins, my brother Davey and sister Lisa who were born just over a year later, may have been the result of an equally dumbfounding sensibility—a race my father decided to have with his brother over who could have more children. Our existence in any official capacity was short-lived. Our parents never kept anything: not furniture, clothing, birth certificates, or social security cards. I've never so much as seen a photograph of the twins as babies. We didn't go to doctors or dentists, and our report cards lingered on kitchen tables for so long that by the time my father signed them they were stained from coffee rims and cigarette ash.

We rarely spoke about anything important.

After I left Worcester, I found it difficult to remember much about the city. It was as if my memories were somehow still stuck there, clapping between the drafty houses. I didn't want to go back there to breathe in the chemical-laced air, to peck in the rubble for shards of all the bad things that happened, or to have to eat spoiled food again. It wasn't a matter of cowardice. I just didn't see the point of paying such close attention. If I went back there, I'd be faced with who I really am.

I would have stayed outside and airborne forever if I could help it, if the people I'd loved hadn't remained in that glue trap so long that they started losing parts of their hearts and their bodies.

Tragedies occurred.

Funerals stuck.

One by one, they called me back.

Some ancient people believed that the feathers of the wren could save a person from drowning. Sailors took them with them when they went out to sea.

Those feathers were of no use in a place that was landlocked.

PART 1

Losing Davey

Chapter 1

Religious Candles & Buzz Cuts

Year: 2018, Age: 44

The chain-link fence is dented and completely bowed out from the weight of my brother's body after he jumped from the roof of his apartment building. A long line of white, chalky powder trails through the asphalt, the kind of chemical that cleaners use to sop blood.

"Are we going to eat something soon?" my mother whines from the back of the car, her breathing thick as if the act of getting her plump body squished in the seat was still exhausting her.

As usual there is no sun in Worcester. The clouds glow like there's a smoldering cigarette behind them. In the corner of the concrete lot is a memorial David's girlfriend Mary set up. Four tall, cylindrical, religious dollar store candles sit on the concrete, half burned. They surround a handmade wooden cross.

RIP DAVID. WE WILL MISS YOU; the sign reads.

Davey. He had just turned forty-three, but for some reason my brother's childhood name returns to me. I think back to ten-year-old Davey with his light brown hair buzzed off, our parent's concession to the need for an occasional haircut. When it grew out, it made cowlicks on the back of his head in silly crooked spikes. Davey putting water in his cornflakes because we couldn't afford milk, or smushing cockroaches in the kitchen with bare feet. Davey with hazel eyes that resembled my own, always lit up with laughter.

My husband, Greg, pulls me back to the present, "We'll get lunch later," he responds from the driver's seat so that I don't have to. My husband can have cynical views on the world, opinions he purses his lips at from a distance. He has occasionally noted that he doesn't understand how people can mooch off the system. At the same time, he has an inordinate amount of patience, even sympathy for my mother.

I look at the building my brother lived in. Merrick Street is the sty of Main South, and that's saying something. It's one of those buildings that ends up worse than those that have been abandoned. It looks practically post-apocalyptic. Some of the windows are boarded up. There's trash strewn all over the lot and graffiti on the door. It's dotted with sallow-skinned people who have given up on themselves, who have been using so long you can smell it coming out of their pores, who have chalky, unbrushed tongues and no longer eat or sleep, living like rats.

It makes me so sad to know that this is where my brother spent his final days.

I don't know what I'm expecting to find here. Maybe I'm seeking out proof, not necessarily about how it happened or why, but that it did. Maybe I hoped that returning to the place of my brother's suicide will make it real for me.

"You think I'll make it to BINGO tonight?" my mother blurts out.

Inside I'm rolling my eyes. I tap my husband on the leg as I peek at him, an attempt to make eye contact, looking for clues that his reaction is the same as mine.

I don't want my mom to notice.

I glance through the rearview mirror at her, trying to figure out what's going on in her mind. Is she really so addled? Is she seriously concerned about BINGO, or is that just her way of dissociating from what's happening? Is it possible that deep down, she is heartbroken over the death of her only son?

I examine my mother's face, which is so different than it was when I was growing up. She's in her late sixties now, but seems so much older to me. Her lips look fuller since she's gotten the dentures. She no longer slurs the way she did when she and my father were both missing most of their teeth. Her dirty blonde hair is still not washed regularly, though, and she still toddles when she walks.

"Which one did Mary tell you was the apartment?" I ask my sister.

"I don't know. The top one?" Her voice is crushed roses and sweet-tarts, the high-pitched voice of a little girl.

"Left or right?

"Right," she guesses.

I look to the third floor and top story of the brown house, its paint peeling away. The two windows on the left and right are each equally non-descript with no evidence of human habitation. I follow the windows down the side of the building and onto the porch sagging under the weight of some junk, including an upended sink, an oil drum, and metal cans.

A guy passes by my side of the car then turns the corner.

He joins some people standing in a pack. One of them dances around like he's having a spasm. The others have squinty eyes and cigarettes dangling from their lips. They watch him, laughing.

I take my hand from my thigh and press it into my lap. My heart is beating a little faster.

I look up the house to the pitched roof. The angle is so steep I still can't understand how Davey could have deliberately tossed himself off it.

That's what the police report says, though. That's the story his girlfriend Mary told the police.

Memories from thirty-plus years ago flood my mind: Davey and me wearing socks on our hands and having snowball fights in the yard; Davey and me having a war over whether we would watch cartoons or MTV; Davey and me catching grasshoppers in the overgrown weeds of an abandoned lot.

Davey getting beaten by my mother's boyfriend.

Davey being shuttled away to foster care.

"Mary said they were evicted maybe twenty times before they found this place," my mother says with judgement in her voice.

We'd been evicted seven times before I was ten.

You did this to him, I want to scream at my mother. *You did this.*

I don't though.

She's still my mother. I've always done my best to treat her with some respect, as if that would somehow align us with normalcy.

Truthfully, I don't know how much I can really hold her at fault. I remember Davey as a sweet little boy, but I haven't seen my brother in fifteen years. He had his escape, a chance for a new life, but he'd returned, barreling through the inky streets toward my mother, toward her boyfriends and dealers, toward Main South in the magnetic way that we all did as children, like the ducks who return to Crystal Lake in the spring.

I only know the rudiments of what happened between my mother and Davey after that point. They had been slumming together. They did lines of coke in the living room. He'd sell her his ADHD meds at a buck a pill. They'd fight and she'd call the welfare office on him with reports of fraud in an effort to shut down his "benefit checks." Good ole' fashioned family dysfunction.

The only way people get out of Worcester is in a body bag, people used to say.

We've only been back in Worcester for a day, but already I can feel it on me, clinging to me like a second skin. It isn't me sitting in the car here, the Mal lucky enough to go to college and even to graduate school, who wears suits to meetings with clients in her corporate job. I am not the mother of a beautiful, well-cared-for, fourteen-year-old boy with light brown hair and the cautious intelligence of Alex P. Keaton. I am not the wife of a wonderful man.

Instead, I am that dirty little welfare kid eating at the picnic tables at the Mustard Seed soup kitchen, the scraggly haired, knobby kneed girl who always felt compelled to apologize for her existence.

I glance at Greg. His kind hazel eyes express only concern for me, but I'm afraid he's reaching his limit. He's been cooped up in the car shuttling my crazy, broken family around all day, no doubt scientifically dissecting the evidence of the stories I've shared with him, stories that occasionally rotted inside me like bad fruit and cause my words to sour. In those moments he worked extra hard to prove to me all the reasons why I deserved to be loved.

Still, it's one thing to listen and another to see. My husband, who is rarely judgmental, who rarely talks badly about anyone, called Worcester a shit hole. He called it a wasteland. But I can tell these words aren't adequate for him to describe it. I notice how he walks around Worcester with his forehead cinched and his head slightly bent toward the concrete, as if it physically hurts him to be here.

A car pulls up in front of us and parks. It's a long black beater car with one of the rearview mirrors held on by gray duct tape. I look up at the brown building again—the broken glass in the yard among gnarled bare branched shrubs, the sealed-in, quiet sadness. The building is still. Dim lights are on in several windows.

Greg gasps and I turn my gaze back to the car parked in front of us, noticing a guy in the driver's seat holding up something like a tray that's no bigger than a notebook, then leaning over, his head popping up and down like he's bobbing for apples. His arms move and the guy next to him does the same thing.

"Jesus. It's broad daylight," my husband says quietly, more to himself than to anyone in the car.

"Zero hesitation. Zero concern. It's like we are invisible. Or worse, like that is natural," he says.

Greg looks at me.

I nod. He turns the key and we pull out, slowly, the rubber tires slapping against pavement.

Chapter

Factories & Ghosts

Year: 2018, Age: 44

The houses we pass are all the same: triple-deckers with pitched roofs and crooked siding, the yellowing window shades half-cocked so you can almost, but not quite, peek into empty rooms. In a few there are lights, in one a flickering blue screen.

The houses have a presence. It is heavy. It is old. It's more than that, though. The houses look practically indignant, the way dying house plants can look, as if they retain memory of the years when they were cared for by people who gave a damn.

It's difficult to see them in the afternoon.

"It's so small," I whisper to Greg, though I'm not certain any words have actually come out of my mouth.

"Main South. It's small," I say.

He hears me this time and pats me on the knee. His lips curve upwards slightly. I'm suddenly thankful for this connection we have that's become so engrained over the last few years it feels practically telepathic.

"Apparently, the Main South neighborhood of Worcester is 1.8 miles in totality," he says.

I want to laugh at Greg's inability to be figurative.

Instead, I glance toward the window, catching a glimpse of my face—the mascara-separated lashes, the hazel eyes.

"I had a lucky rabbit's foot. It was electric blue. I managed to take it every time that we moved. Never any farther than these blocks, though," I say.

My mother sighs loudly. I interpret that this sound isn't intended to deflect blame off herself. It's more frustration that we're not yet done with the events of the day, not yet back to her BINGO.

In front of us, a cluster of brown leaves rises and spirals in the wind.

The sagging porches are empty. I don't remember them being empty in the past. Someone was always there, eyeing the street.

Maybe this place isn't that bad.

I'm an outsider now, and it's nearly impossible to explain Main South to an outsider. It's impossible to explain we were just one of a hoard of scrappy families who made do with scratch tickets, welfare, food stamps, and the occasional day job. We weren't the only ones who puddle-jumped our apartments.

I yawn, run spread fingers across the back of my head, and yank through a few knots in my hair. The hazy light makes my eyes squint.

The geography of the day is more exhausting than anything else.

We roll up slowly under the cracked, white concrete freeway. Two thin guys missing their teeth waver on the sidewalk in front of the old greasy spoon. They examine us. Then they nod in that sweetly comical, nearly familial way everyone has been looking at us today, whether they're begging for change on the sidewalk or standing in front of a cash register unable to work it. It's almost like they know they're here by default, in a place where people shouldn't belong.

My husband coasts down the street and up a big hill.

The back of my head aches as if someone whacked it with a rock.

I wonder again if that sense of unbelonging, the impulse toward flight, is endemic to Main South itself.

It was originally pastureland bought by an abolitionist to tap into industry, but soon after the purchase the owner left the land unseeded and moved to Kentucky to fight slavery. The dilapidated Victorian mansions now sequestered into apartments once housed the owners of nearby factories that manufactured products like corsets and wire and looms. The crumbling triple-deckers we bounced between housed the workers who started to flee in the 50s as, one by one, the factories shut down.

Perhaps the buildings haunted us. When you live in a place other people have left behind after tragedy, it messes with your equilibrium.

The air seems clotted. It clings. This may have had something to do with the Blackstone River, which emerged on the center of Main, slunk underground, and eventually let out near a canal. That canal may have connected us to the rest of the Eastern Seaboard, but it was walled up at the turn of the century.

Somehow, I know that the mystery begins on these streets, where the ghosts of former corset factories, hookers, addicts, and nutty old men who'd lost half their siblings to disease or to war and had drunk themselves into the grave walked. Maybe those ghosts swooped down and snatched up some of the memories of those of us who remained.

"Slow down here, I recognize it," Lisa screams from the back seat.

There is a sign on this one, crooked and green with white writing.

OREAD

I run down the eviction list in my mind.

"Oread. Mom. Yes. Is this one of the ones we lived on—Oread Street?"

"Oread. Yeah, we lived there," my mom responds, ending her "there" with an upturned curl of disgust, as if she is tired of answering my questions. She's deliberately being stingy with her answers.

It's partly the repetition that bothers her. My mother's world centers around her television and hermitting in her apartment, surrounded by the blaring of Jerry Springer and *Press Your Luck*. She played the part of being sad in front of her building mates when they learned of her son's passing, but I can't determine whether or not his death really affects her.

It baffles me that she hasn't cried, not once. I haven't seen anything remotely resembling sorrow, acknowledgement, or even admission of what happened, not even an honest frown. Is she in there?

I look out at the streets, gray and metal, and three-decker houses.

Davey and I used to sit on the steps of those houses, waiting for our parents to stop fighting. That waiting always felt like an eternity, or maybe the fighting just carried on for that long.

By the time Davey became an adult, it must have been too late. He was one of the people on the glue trap. I don't know exactly how it happened, and why it never happened to me.

"Wow, we lived on Oread and Hollywood and Benefit Street and Chelsea, and Benefit was really just across the street from Oread," I say, mentally ticking the names off in my head.

"Yes, Mal. We lived all those places too, I think," Mom says.

We turn the corner. Lisa lets out a strange sound, almost like a yelp.

"Stop here Greg, right here, the tan house with that white lattice gate on the right," Lisa says.

My husband careens toward the spot.

"We lived here. Didn't we, Mal?" my sister asks.

I turn around and look at her. Nobody in my family is a giant, but Lisa is the smallest. She's barely four feet eleven inches tall, and is sometimes still mistaken for a child. She has the same small facial features and strawberry blonde hair as she did when we were kids. She keeps scratching her arm.

I turn back toward the front, looking out the side window for a street sign.

"Illinois Street," Greg says.

"Yes, that's it. Remember, Mal? That's the park where you took us to look for food when they left us alone and we were all hungry."

I listen for an objection from my mother. She is quiet. Through the rearview, I see her staring blankly straight ahead.

Chapter 3

The Hunter

Year: 1980, Mal—6 years old;
The Twins—5 years old

We're in the living room. This is one of those apartments we haven't yet hustled any furniture for. There's a reddish-brown shag rug. The twins are playing on the dirty clothes pile near the kitchen, climbing up and then jumping off the top of it like it's a hill. They screech, the twins. They're five years old.

I'm six. I sit on the floor near the window. My mother closed and locked it before she left. Something is wrong. There's something wrong. There's something wicked wacky about the way the twins play—the way that they screech makes me feel like the windows will break. It's something like the way we all get after we've eaten too much candy, only I am pretty sure we haven't had anything to eat in a long time.

It's hot and the air is crammy. The whole place is stinky. It really stinks. It stinks bad, like a pee-pee, like the way it gets when Davey wets the bed. It stinks like dirty, like old BO in clothes.

It stinks because of the laundry pile. But also because I don't know how to get our shirts over our heads, so we are still wearing the same ones from the other day.

"When's Mom coming back?" Davey whines.

"Shut up," Lisa says.

"Don't backtalk," I say.

"When'd she go?"

I don't know how long our mom has been gone. A lot of times Dad is gone, but not usually Mom.

I sometimes hear the sounds changing out the window. When there are more cars and people it is day. When it is quieter, it is night.

At first, we went back to the bed we shared in our room to sleep. But then we decided it would be better if we just stayed in the living room. So, we brought Davey's Superman pillowcase, Lisa's purple one, my red one, and all of the blankets into the living room and slept in piles like puppies, napping whenever we felt like it. It was less scary then, because it was like we were having a party.

On the floor next to all the blankets and pillows are the pots and pans and wooden spoons I brought out so we could bang on them.

Next to that is Lisa's stuffed animal, a fish made out of purple yarn that my mom brought home from the Salvation Army.

"My head hurts."

"I'm hungry."

The twin's mousy noises nip at me.

I don't feel so good, but I don't know *how*. It is like there are two me's now. There is the Mal who stands in one spot, and the fuzzy Mal that stands right next to her, stomping and rubbing.

There is something weird about the next to me Mal. Her skin is all prickeldy.

And she's almost gonna throw up.

"When's Mom coming back?" Davey asks.

"Where did she go anyhow?" Lisa says.

"Why isn't she back yet?" I don't know the answer to his question.

"I think it's been two days," Davey continues.

"Three."

"Two. No, maybe four."

I'm the big sister. It's my job to do something.

I stand up by the crooked pull shades and peek out. It's bright daylight outside. Everything looks regular. A man is buffing his long blue car. It doesn't have any rust on it. Sun is shining on a little piece of grass in some dirt where the ants live. A woman with short sleeves is standing on the stoop across from us and picking up a rolled-up newspaper. There are comics in it.

I know what we have to do. We have to wait until the woman goes back inside, until the man drives away in his car.

"Davey and Lisa, get your jackets okay, just in case. We're going on an adventure."

The twins are like little baby chicks taking turns pecking at me with their questions.

"Where, Mal?"

"Where, Malaren?" Davey parrots Lisa.

"To Crystal Park. To look for the birds in the lake. We can play there."

"We're not allawed!" Davey clasps his hands over his mouth with equal parts excitement and fear.

"Yeah, Mom said to wait inside until she come back."

"It's okay. She didn't know she'd hafta be gone so long when she said that. It's okay. I'm the older sister. You hafta listen to me. I'm in charge."

I am a hunter. I'm a hunter big sister. As a hunter big sister, it is very important to be secret. To be sly about what you are hunting. I am sly.

Davey and Lisa walk in front of me, holding hands in their twin way. They are both skinny and lopey the way they walk, kind of like our dad. They're bent a little bit into each other like flower stalk heads, making it look like they are one body—some strange lake creature with four hands and two real long skinny arms.

"It's pretty here. This is fun," I say.

"It's pretty," Lisa repeats.

I am sly. I keep a secret. My lips are sealed even to Davey and Lisa. The secret I don't tell them is the thing I'm hunting. I am hunting food.

"You guys. Stay close," I say.

They slow down a little. I'm surprised they're actually listening to me.

There's a lot of grass in the park. Bright green grass. There are a lot of trees. Trees as tall as a giant with pretty leaves. I like the bright orange ones best.

The hunter looks closely—on the ground, behind the bushes and trees. Nobody left a picnic here lately. There are no garbage cans.

"Stay to the right," I yell at the twins.

"Crystal Lake is this way, Mal."

"The lake's this way."

"Let's go to the playground first. The kid's playground. Do you know where it is?"

"I do, falwalah me," Davey says.

Our dad always says Davey has a good sense of direction. Even if he's only been in a place once, he always knows how to get back there. It always surprises me how he finds things. Once Mom sent us off to get Dad at Moynihan's Pub and I thought we were lost, but Davey surprised me and showed me exactly where to cross.

The park is quiet. There are no people here but us. We're walking like phantom ghosts. It's good that nobody is here to see us. We're not allowed to be here alone. We ourselves are a secret, too.

I follow the twins through something like a tunnel, a tunnel of trees with a narrow, dirty path we walk on. Dust is in our face, cool on our cheeks. We are walking and walking and walking down a dirt path, a dirt path I really don't know. Davey knows the way. Davey knows where we are headed.

He starts running, dragging Lisa behind him. I follow. He stops and then runs to the middle of a field.

"I knewd it. You see. Look on that hill, see where the big rocks are. That's where we eat the McDonald's with Dad."

"You found it, Davey. Great!" I say.

I remember the hill. I remember sitting there and our dad joking with us and telling stories while we curled up and ate our Happy Meals. I remember so good, I can almost taste the way that it was: the soft bun with the top that cracked when you bit it, the hot and chewy burger with cheese. I remember the crispy French fries, and the sweet orange drink we had as our soda.

I remember why we are here.

"Let's stop here," Lisa says.

"Nuh-uh. Okay, we have a job to do. We have to get to the playground."

"Why the playground, I'm tired. It's nice right here," Lisa says.

I think about the playground. It had trash cans in it, the place where parents sometimes throw out the ends of the food.

"No, playground's better. Tell Lisa, Davey. We are on a adventure— first the playground and then the lake. Playground. "Playground," I shout.

"Playgwand," Davey repeats.

When we come out on the other side of the hill, we run down it quick-quick so we don't fall. Davey picks up a big stick and is holding it in his hand, swinging around and around with it, whooping and yelling. Lisa laughs but stands carefully on the edge of the hill, like she's afraid to get dirty. I stand between them, watching, charting our course.

The park feels different without our parents here. For one thing it's much, much bigger, and there is a lot of air. The air tastes good. After being inside for so long with the stink-rot smell, like a pee-pee and maybe a mouse who is dead trapped inside the wall, the air tastes so good. I eat it and eat it like it is a Happy Meal cheeseburger from McDonald's.

Also, it is more crooked here somehow. Like maybe it is a different kind of planet where only kids can exist. Slowly, I skip down the hill and join Davey. As he hoots and hollers running around with his stick, I hold my hands out, spread my fingers, and twirl around and around like a plane.

I don't know how long we're on the hill in this secret place. I don't know how long I'm swinging around like an airplane while Davey is moving his stick.

I finally stop, dizzy. Then the world spins even though I am not moving. The other Me stands there with the butterflies all around her, holding her head.

"Mal, Mal, Marilyn," Lisa screeches.

When I look up there is a man standing there. A man that is so tall he leaves a shadow on the hill. I can see his face, too—he has weird yellow skin like an alien, and his front tooth is cracked. He is holding his face strange as he talks, like he has just sucked a lemon ball.

"What are you kids doing here by yasel? Dwana sparklyer?"

I can't understand what he is saying, the words knocking against his teeth.

He puts his hand on my shoulder. His nails are thick and crusty and bent. It's more like a paw.

"Get offa me," I say, shaking my shoulder.

"You leave my sistah alone!" Davey says and starts heading toward him with the stick, swinging it wildly.

Suddenly, I know the tasty air is magic. It bubbles like soda fizz around my head. I know that this is a kid's place and that we are magic here, and we don't have to worry about this man because we can run.

"No, Lisa, Davey, run! Let's go!" I scream.

Without knowing how we do it, we all run as one body, flying down the hill, our hearts pumping in our chests like bird wings. We run with our knees in the air like they showed me in gym glass, a giant dinosaur bird creature with three heads, forty-seven suckers, and a thousand skinny legs.

We fly down the hill, past the tunnel we emerged from, to the place where the air changes and starts to taste like lake. We run slower then, with our knees bouncing, our sneakers pounding the hollow dirt. And then, like we share one giant brain, we decide at once together to stop.

I put my hand on my heart. My brother bends over slightly. Lisa makes loud wheezing sounds.

"Oh, my gawd, that was close!" Davey says.

"He coudata murdered us," I say.

"He's gahne," Lisa says.

As the big sister hunter, I scan the distance behind us, look back to where we came from. The woods are big and hot behind us, so hot something jelly pulses in the air.

And I know Lisa is right. The alien man has not followed us. There is nobody around.

Chapter 4

Landlords & Ladies

Year: 1980, Mal—6 years old;
The Twins—5 years old

Somebody is knocking on the door. We tried to ignore them, but they will not stop. At first the knock sounded friendly—it wasn't loud at least, but knocking wasn't the usual thing where we lived. If someone wanted to see you, they just walked inside.

Then the knocks got louder, kind of angry, like the way the landlord does it when he knows we're in there and my mom and dad put their fingers to their lips to tell us "shhhh, be quiet!" but at the same time we're all starting to crack up.

The knocking is scary without our mom and dad here, though. It could be a robber, or even a monster, who is only knocking to warn us that in a little while he'll break the door down to get in.

"Mal, what's happening?" Davey asks. He's standing near the kitchen with one hand over his face. Lisa is holding his other hand. The twins are frozen, having a staring contest with me.

I'm not stupid. I know better than that. I can never win at a staring contest with four eyes on two.

"I'll check," I say.

I peek out the dirty window shade so carefully, grabbing an edge that's already torn. The shade tears even more and it makes me mad. I don't know if I'm mad because I messed up, or because I've been spotted by the ladies. I decide to give the shade a quick tug anyway so that it sticks in the middle of the window. Then I look out.

"They're ladies."

They're standing out front. One is holding the metal door, the one that booms, with her back. There's one brown woman and one tan woman. They're wearing dresses and look fancy, with very neat hair and holding pocketbooks. They aren't from Main South. That's a sure bet. My father wouldn't like them.

One sees me looking at her and waves. The other one is holding a paper bag. I remember one time when our old dog, Sheeba, ran away. My dad went out to find her and brought a bologna sandwich with him in a bag that looked just like that.

She waves faster, like she's a bird. She's silly. I laugh.

"They ah nice. Let's go see," I say.

We never did find any leftover cheeseburger Happy Meal bits at Crystal Park.

The twins look at me like I am crazy.

"I thought we aren't supposed to let anyone in," Lisa says.

The longer they stand there, the more the neighbors get to stare. It's one of the rules of living here.

The ladies have stopped knocking. They are both staring at the window, waving and making a motion with their hands like they are pulling back the air. They look gentle, nice like my nana and my teacher in kindergarten in the school.

"Yeah. But I like them."

Chapter 5

Salisbury Steak & Gardening Snakes

Year: 1980, Mal—6 years old;
The Twins—5 years old

We're sitting at the kitchen table with the ones the ladies told us are fawstah parents. This means we will stay with them for a while, just until our parents return from wherever. We're having Salisbury steak and eggs. It's a kind of food I've never tasted before, on a real clean table. We can eat as much as we want. The best part about it is we're having this food for breakfast, and early, when the sun is just starting to come out on the farm.

"How did you sleep last night, kids? Mal, Davey, Lisa?" the fawstah mom asks. Her name is Laverne but she lets us call her L because Laverne is so hard to get out of your mouth. She is so nice: a woman who is as tall as a giant with big arms and soft boobies. She likes to hug us all the time.

She says our names because we aren't the only kids there in the kitchen.

Our fawstah parents have four of their own children; two girls who are ten and twelve, a boy who is eight, and one who is a teenager. It's hard for me to remember their names. They've already finished their breakfast and are cleaning up their dirty dishes, getting ready to head outside.

"Good," Lisa and Davey say together. The way that they do.

"Good," I say right after, but that is a fib. The fawstah parents put Davey in the top bunk above me, so sometimes I wake up scared he's going to pee the bed and it will fall down over my head.

"Can we go play with Reynold and Trudy today?" Lisa asks.

"Of course. You may go play with the goats, and in the sandbox, if you finish your breakfast and do your chores. Lisa, you haven't touched your steak."

Lisa is moving a piece of the meat around with her fork, frowning while she does it. Lisa has always been the littlest of all of us, and she's suspicious of food.

I look out the window, which has poofy white curtains that you can see through in the sun. There is a rusty green bug car in the driveway, and beyond that long green fields and round flat circles of dirt. It's pretty outside—there's lots of room to run around. It's the summer, so we don't even have to go to school.

"Eat five bites, Lisa. Five bites and then I'll let you go play."

Davey taps Lisa on the shoulder a few times. She shrugs him away.

Davey loves to play outside with the animals.

"Maybe we can find the gardening snake again," Davey says.

"Yeah," I say.

The two girls laugh though, and I can feel my face turning red. Yesterday we found a long green snake in the yard. It was scary, because we never saw anything like that before. We only yelled just a little and held onto each other. Then we were able to follow it around.

"Garter snake," L says. "There are plenty of them. Just remember what I told you to be careful not to step on them because it will hurt them."

"But they don't want to hurt us. Right, L?" Davey says.

The girls giggle again.

"Marilyn. Are you okay, sweetie? You haven't touched your milk."

I look at the glass. I love the milk that we get to drink here. It is so thick and cold and a little sweet, and somehow the goats and cows pee it out. But my ear hurts every time I swallow.

It feels like I've had a bad earache almost since I came to the farm. It hurts inside my ears, which are red. L says they're raw. It makes it hard to listen, even to what I'm thinking about myself.

"Is your ear still bothering you?"

"Still hurts," I say.

"Aw, sweetie. I'm so sorry you don't feel well. What do you say after breakfast we go to the bathroom and I warm up some drops to put in it?"

I nod because I'm trying to be polite and because L told me the drops are important, that they're the medicine that will fix up my ear. It feels good when she holds my head to the side and drops the warm liquid in. But I always want to cry when she's doing it. It makes me feel bad somehow, like I'm not supposed to be too happy that a stranger is taking care of me.

I still don't know where my mom went.

Chapter

Corollas & Caterpillars

Year: 1980, Mal—6 years old;
The Twins—5 years old

Me and Davey are sitting in our social worker's Corolla. In my lap, I hold my caterpillar in a mason jar with the lid screwed on. It's a plump, hairy caterpillar, and there's some grass and a twig in there. I love the caterpillar. I caught him myself. Ever since then he's been with me, crawling around in the jar. I know that he can sense me and that he understands me. He's proud of me. More than that, he's good luck. As long as I bring the caterpillar back to Worcester safely, me and Davey will be safe, too.

The lady driving the Corolla is nice. I had to beg her, but then she said it was okay to bring the caterpillar in the car as long as I keep him sealed in the jar.

It's strange to be going home. It's stranger because Lisa is missing.

Our Aunt Marybeth took her. Two days before we left, too. Lisa was adahpted. Aunt Marybeth didn't want me and Davey though. Just Lisa, maybe because she's cuter than us.

It's okay because we're going back to our old house. With our mom and dad.

I'm both excited and nervous to see my mom and dad again. I've tried to remember the last time we saw them. My dad left before my mom. After my mom left, we were in the house, and then we went to the park. After that we got taken away to the farm. I hope she isn't mad we left the house.

"We were hungry, Mom. We were looking for food," I think of telling her.

I turn around quick and look at Davey in the back seat. He's gotten taller, and wider; he's not as scrawny as he was when we first came to the farm. Our fawstah parents let him keep his long hair because they said they respected his privacy. But he's gotten wilder since he's been away, too. There are more times when he goes quiet, especially when the adults are talking.

I look at my caterpillar. He is still, clinging to the bottom of the jar.

I'm worried about him. Even though I poked holes in the top of the jar, I worry that he doesn't have enough air to breathe.

I don't know why I do it. I don't know what makes me do it. But I unscrew the jar, just to peek in there and make sure he's okay. I put the metal ring and stick the top on the seat beside me and peek inside.

I take him out. I'm extra careful, letting him climb from my pointer finger and up to my wrist. He tickles me. Then I hold my hand onto my cheek, and he crawls over my face and then my shoulder, down my shirt and onto my stomach, then onto my legs. Then he drops. Somehow, he drops from my lap to the seat. And then he is gone.

I look into the dark space by my legs where he fell. I don't see him.

I tip my head toward the back seat, my mind empty for a second. Davey's face looks worried; I can tell from the way his white skin pinches between his eyes. He didn't notice the caterpillar, though. He's in his own world, maybe worrying about our mom and dad. Or about Lisa.

I remember there's something other than Davey, than Lisa, than even about coming home to worry about.

The caterpillar is gone.

Inside, I freak out. I look in the seat pocket, in the bucket on the floor, on the gear shift, and toward the back again where Davey is sitting. I imagine its furry body, the speckles of gold in what the farm lady told me were the cilla on his back. I imagine him all furry and plump, but I can't see him.

It's my fault. All the bad things that could happen because of the caterpillar's escape flood my brain. I look at the woman who's driving the Corolla, her eyes focused only on the windshield. If she knew the caterpillar had escaped, would she be mad? Would she turn around the car and refuse to bring us to see our parents? Would she send us back to the farm, or to some other place, some long gray kid prison on the end of the town? Would I be in trouble, somehow?

I imagine all the places the caterpillar could be. Could he be crawling around near Davey, or even worse, by the social worker's feet? Would she push on the pedals or slam on the brakes and smush him?

My stomach hurts.

I'm sorry little caterpillar. Come back and I will take good care of you, I promise!

"Mal, I seeeeee him," Davey sings behind me.

I don't turn around.

It surprises me that Davey knows what happened, that he was watching, and that he didn't say anything at all.

It's the way he used to be with Lisa.

"Mal, I goooooottttt him fer ya," he says.

The next thing I know Davey is holding the caterpillar between his fingers and gently pinching him toward me on my forearm, sneakily, against the door on the right side of the car where we both are sitting. It climbs up my forearm. Quickly, I take my left hand, nip it between my thumb and my forefinger, and put it back into the jar.

PART **2**

Losing Lisa

House Wrens

House wrens are the most common kind of wren in the northeastern United States. They are brown and almost pitifully nondescript, lacking any real markings. Their innate strength is in their song, which vibrates with high, piercing, trilling intensity. It then trails off intermittently, as if the frenzy of song exhausted all the wren's energy, until it pipes up again. Their voices are gigantean for their midget bodies: ten times more powerful than a cockerel if matched against them weight for weight. Their tunes are always complex—most males have a playlist of at least twenty-five songs, and some have been recorded to have nearly 200. Perhaps the complications of their shrill, unyielding song are part of their own avian brand of a Napoleon complex—the way they overcompensate for their puny plainness.

Their songs are indecipherable to most outsiders, the way the men's speech was to us children when my mother sent us to the bar to fetch my father in the throes of one of his benders. All the men's words were at once fascinating and completely nonsensical, a slurred secret language they blathered while we sat on our stools drinking milk or orange soda in a cup, gnawing on nuts and stale raisins. We knew they liked us and appreciated that we were there, occasionally nodding at us as if we were cute dogs or starting to speak to us and then dismissing the notion, as if suddenly realizing we weren't capable of understanding.

Chapter 7

Crusty T-shirts, Hot Dogs, & The King

Year: 1981, Mal—6 years old;
Davey—5 years old

The lights are always dim in the house on Oberlin Street, as if the bulbs themselves somehow know the score and are preparing to go dormant for when the electricity is later shut off, like a plant that senses it's about to lose its source of sunlight or water. Huge paintings on velvet hang on the wall. One is a creepy, dark, wooded landscape. Another is my father's prized Elvis Presley painting, the King sporting his jet-black Pompadour, a hairstyle my father says is named after some old French king's secret girlfriend.

My dad sits in the rust-colored armchair, his short legs stretched out on the ottoman in front of him. His stringy, muscled arms flex in his white Fruit of the Loom undershirt, and a Marlboro smolders to ash in the tray on the card table next to him. His face is bathed in matchlight blue from the flickering cartoon on the television, illuminating his own gray-turning-chartreuse eye from the barfight the previous night.

His five-foot four-inch body heaves on the chair as his nearly toothless mouth twists in laughter. One hand clutches a Schlitz beer; the sweet, off-tasting liquid and cartoon make him giggle.

My mother is sitting at the kitchen table, with its curved metal lady's legs and red plastic top, the one we'll leave behind on the filthy linoleum the next time we're evicted. Stinky gnarled socks and undies and crusty old t-shirts are piled up on the floor, sitting on the counter, and pressed against the lime green walls. Although a roach might snack on a crumb or the congealed ketchup on the dirty counters, there's likely little food left—maybe a small hunk of government cheese and two hotdogs in the fridge, a box of corn flakes, and a tub of Quaker oats in the cabinet.

"Hey, Mom? What's for supper?" I ask.

"Shit on a shingle!" she says. She loves to kid with us like that. But I never know what she means by a "shingle."

The only thing on the table is a one-thousand-piece puzzle of a farm-house. My mom's tongue pokes out of her mouth slightly as she works on it. It's a sign she's trying hard to concentrate.

Davey elbows me a bit in the stomach. He is laughing without making any sound, pointing at my dad's feet, which are stretched out and resting on the square couch part.

"So," I whisper and knock him lightly on the arm.

"One shoe. Only one shoe," he mouths.

I shake my head in a grown-up way to make him be quiet. I really don't need to. Our mom and dad might hear us, but they don't listen.

"Mal," he says.

I ignore him. I'm sitting cross-legged, pointing my legs away from him. The bottom of my feet are dirty. I don't like my pink nightgown.

"Mal."

I look at him cut-eyed. It doesn't bother him. He comes too close to me, cups his hands around my ear, and whispers loudly.

"Mom was doing the same puzzle before we left," he says.

I shake my head no and shove him away. It hurts his feelings and I feel bad, but there are no takebacks from shoving. I think Davey and I have been back from the foster house a few months. Even though this is a different apartment, things are exactly as if we'd never been gone.

"Mal. Honey, go get me another beah, will yah?" Dad says.

"I'll get it," Davey jumps in, but his voice is so squeaky and small no-body heard him.

I tap Davey on the shoulder.

"I gaht it. I'll be right back," I say.

I hop up and pad over to the kitchen. On the way, I stop behind my mom to see the puzzle she is doing. She is concentrating really hard, making the far edge of the puzzle on the right—the curved pieces. The farmhouse is half done—there's a windmill and a lot of pretty fall colors. I watch her face for a second. It looks a little waxy, like the candles that drip when they light them at church. And it's so still, except that there's one little muscle toward her mouth that jumps a bit. I want to touch it to see if it stops.

Instead, I go to the refrigerator and open it. There isn't anything in there but some sweet and sour sauces from the Chicken McNuggets Happy Meal at Mickey D's that we got one of the first days me and Davey came back from the fawstah home in the country, plus some mustard and my dad's Tall Boy Schlitz's beers with the red stripe across the front. There are six plastic rings and only two beers still attached to them. I pull one out gently, making sure I don't shake it up, and run toward my dad. The floor is crusty and rough things poke my feet as I go.

My dad is sitting in his chair, still watching the cartoons. I stand there a few seconds before he knows I'm there. Then I pull hard, but carefully, on the metal tab until it cracks open. I did it right. It doesn't spill over, but I hear the bubbles rising inside.

"Your beer, Dad," I say.

He looks at me and smiles, the funny way that he does at night with his missing teeth—they almost disappear in the dark. I smile back and hand him the beer. He takes a sip, then leans back in the chair, resting his head on the pilly, worn fabric.

"Thanks kiddo," he says and half-pinches my cheek. My face turns red.

"What do you think we try to get some ice cream tomorrow? Maybe we can borrow Mr. Rich's car?"

He looks at me. I nod my head. "Yes!" I yell.

He laughs. I love the sound it makes when he's laughing.

"Ice cream!" Davey yells from the floor. It annoys me that he's been listening to us. But then my dad winks and my face gets red again.

I hold onto the arm of his chair until my dad turns back to the television set.

I head back over to the pile of newspapers Davey is sitting on. I sit down with him, listening until the sounds in the night change. The wind whizzing through the open flap of the plastic sheeting on our windows makes a humming sound, like a kazoo at school. The television gets all staticky. When I listen really closely, I can hear the sound of my mom popping puzzle pieces into place.

I lie back down. Davey lies down, too, resting his head on my belly. I let him even though the bones in his head are sharp and heavy. My dad is talking over the television. His words are all mixed up; it sounds like he's chewing pebbles. I'm still hungry and imagine the barfy smell of the hot dog we split earlier, and the crunchy part where Davey cooked it under the cigarette lighter. I drift off to sleep, between the sound of the cartoon animal bleeping and the funny rhythm of Dad's pebble-words.

When I wake up, my neck hurts from sleeping funny on the newspapers. It's so dark now, even the air. It's quiet, too. The quiet is strange.

There's something I am supposed to remember.

Davey's head feels heavy on my belly. I touch the side of his head near his eye. His eyes open, long eyelashes tickling my hand.

"Get up. You're hurting me," I say.

He groans and moves over to the side of the paper, curling up like a baby. I don't move yet.

I turn on my side and raise myself up on my elbow, looking toward the living room. My dad is still sitting on the chair, but the television is off. My mom has come into the room. She is standing behind him near the window twitching like a firefly. She's holding a record in her hand.

I watch my mom open the top of the suitcase that holds the blue record player. She opens the top of the record case and peels out a record. She is slow, the way that she does it: licking her fingers like a cat, putting the folder down carefully on the table in front of us, walking over to the player, turning it on, then moving the arm of the record player and the needle onto the record groove. She does this like a beautiful dance.

Her pretty, dirty blonde hair is still uncombed.

I think about bringing her my barrette, the one with the braided ribbons and the plastic beads that my friend Lilac and I made at her house.

I'd like her to have it, but I don't want my mother to have her feelings hurt.

I push my feet out farther in front of me.

The record player comes on, then, making its funny grumbly noise.

My dad lights a cigarette.

Then the King's voice fills the living room. It's soothing to all of us. That voice, the way he strum-hums his songs, it's more steady than any place. It's a kind of comfort, a kind of love.

"It's Blue Christmas. I know this one," I say.

Davey hums softly.

"Bingo kiddo. Good call, it's almahst Christmas," my dad slurs.

The music is magic. It lifts everyone's mood. My mom is half dancing in the kitchen, sashaying her big, handsome hips from side to side. My dad is rubbing the scruff on his face. Davey has his ear in the crook of his arm but is humming too.

With the music we are quiet together. With this music, it feels safe.

I feel a little sad. I ball my hand to a fist and press it to my heart. I don't know why.

It comes to me then. The words to this song make me sad for my sister. Lisa isn't with us anymore. Christmas is blue without her.

My sister is missing from our family.

Chapter 8

Lone Wolf & The Patron Saint of Lost Causes

Year: 2018, Mal—44 years old

I stand in the parking lot of Main South's infamous funeral home, Graham Putnam & Mahoney, which has become legendary over the years for taking care of the bodies of many of the guys who'd died after being stabbed or coldcocked. It became a pariah in the state when they took care of the body of Tamerlan Tsarnaev, one of the bombers at the Boston Marathon. Every other funeral home had refused to take him.

My mother is leaning on Greg, toddling toward the steps. I'm standing still, breathing thinly in the early afternoon light. Lisa is already on the landing. There's a dirty diaper on a patch of weedy grass in front of what looks like a cold storage shed, signaling that this isn't your average funeral home. Yet somehow it fits here in Main South. I start walking, keeping my eyes averted down.

I move slowly as I make my way up the steps and meet my family. The building itself is remarkable: an enormous Victorian mansion with ornate cornices, two arched stained-glass windows, and a massive door with about ten layers of peeling, chipped black paint.

Greg looks at me. I smile nervously. He pushes the doorbell. An old-fashioned church bell sound reverberates.

An older gentleman with a hunched back opens the heavy door, slowly. "Hello. Ahm Paul," he says.

He has blue, watery eyes that are profoundly crossed. Still, there is a gentleness about the way he looks at us.

I experience the strange awkwardness that comes when you want to stare at somebody, but shouldn't, so you avoid eye contact altogether.

He guides us over to a seating area and gestures for us to sit down.

Lisa looks up at me, like a child. I nod, letting her know it is okay. I can only imagine what it's doing to her, losing Davey all over again all these years later.

A man with long, grayish hair slicked back into a ponytail and held together with a thin rubber band sits at the desk. He is wearing a navy-blue, canvas zip-up jacket, one step above a Members Only jacket, with the name of the funeral home on it. It's dusty, as if he's just come inside from digging a grave. The poor guy looks as if he hasn't taken a shower in a week. What must be a lifetime cigarette smoking habit seeps through his pores. His teeth are yellow and crooked. His fingers are also stained yellow, like my father's had been. He wears several gold and stone rings on most of them, including his pinkies.

The man stands and shakes hands with my husband and then my mother, and I wonder if I'm imagining how limp and bony his hands look. When he shakes mine, his grip is as cool and noncommittal as you might expect from a guy who spends most of his time dressing up dead bodies.

"Afternoon. My name is Lone Wolf. Lone Wolf Hannigan. It is my uhttermost pleashah to meet yah," he says.

I chuckle. I like this guy. I appreciate his odd sense of humor.

Then I realize he isn't laughing. Neither is anyone else.

He isn't joking. This guy's name is Lone Wolf. The blood rushes to my face and I feel terrible at what a jackass I've been. At the same time, I want to keep laughing. The whole thing is so utterly ridiculous.

I clean up my act and take a seat.

The funeral home is a cavernous place. Even though it's obviously taken care of—the thin carpet vacuumed, the nightmarish silver candlesticks on the mantle well-polished—it has that same odd quality of disuse, of profound displacement, as the rest of the buildings in Main South have. Perhaps it's just the antiquated decorations: faded flowered wallpaper, a heavy lamp with its red shade, the grotesque Jesus statue that likely haven't been altered since the mill owners lived here. Or maybe all funeral homes feel a little estranged.

The place stinks a little, too, mainly of smoke but also a cabbage-y scent I don't want to guess at.

Lone Wolf is talking. He isn't just talking though, he is spinning, launching some kind of cataclysmic sermon like a hurricane, kind of like my mother did when she was on speed—folding socks and scrubbing invisible stains. He has a thick Worcester, New England accent like my father, swallowing *r*s in the middle of words and drawling it into a kind of a hissing, elongated *h* sound at the end.

I take in the beginning of the speech.

"Most folks don't considah the funerah business a highah cawling, but I certainly do. It is what I was put on this earth for. I spent twenty-five yeahs as a pastor, you know. I took on funeruh work ten yeahs ago—in 2008 precisely, because I knew I could help more people heah. We are the funerahl home for people who have no alternative, like the patron saint of lost causes, like St Jude.

"Now I don't have to tell you that things are tough in Wushtah, though of course during tough times there ain't no business more secure than the funerahl business, if you know what I mean. We been around since 1864. That's a long time."

Seemingly astonished by Lone Wolf's near-sermon, my husband stares at the old rug, his eyes snared on a burn hole the size of a thumb. I bend over a little in my chair because my stomach hurts.

"But even so, we have to be careful. We have to try new things. We can't afford to be as fussy as some of those other folks, not to cut cohnahs for ahselves but because we want to provide a decent, affordable service for our neighbahs, because we know how it is. We know what it's like to work hahd, and we know what it is like to struggle, to scrimp and save everything you have just to provide your loved one with a decent burial. We are proud of our work here, but we aren't *proud* if you know what I mean.

"We serve by example and we don't turn anyone away, dead or alive. We believe death is sacred. We ha' buried murderers, serial killers even, gang-stahs—we've buried a lot of gangstahs. We have a reputation for our compassion, because we cahr. We have buried refugees, and immigrants, and drug dealers, as well as good folks that don't cause any trouble like David, like your brothah. When the AIDS epidemic hit and people were afraid they might catch it from corpses, we buried the people who had contracted the AIDS. We bury more poor people than anyone else in the entire state."

"What was that? He's talking too fast. I don't understand," my mother blurts out, turning to me and Greg for advice as if Lone Wolf isn't in the room.

"I say we bury more poor people than anyone else in the entire state," he says.

"Oh, well that's good then, I guess," my mother says.

"Let me explain furthah our, well, our certain peculiarities. Many of our people come from the state of Massachusetts. We have a contract with the state medical examinah's office, the corahnah you know, to take care of all the abandoned or unclaimed bodies. We take on the pauhhpers, you know, anyone who can't afford a burial or cremation like your loved one, the one you are bereaved from.

"We don't do this because we are struggling so much as we believe deeply, in our heart of hearts, we believe that everyone dead or alive has the right to a propah burial. No matter who you are, we are going to take care of you, because that's what God wants—that is what he entrusted us to do, you hear, because we cahe about families."

"Now what was that again? I'm sorry. I can't heah you so well," my mother says.

"What's that? I say God entrusted us to take care of your families."

My emotions are poised on the top of my chest, the place that's been heavy as if somebody has been pressing down on it with four fingers ever since I learned of Davey's death,

Lone Wolf stops speaking, abruptly, like he just noticed we were there.

"How old are you, suh, now?" he asks Greg.

"Excuse me. How old? Fifty-one," Greg says in a slow, sedated voice.

Lone Wolf spins around to my sister then, like he is the host of "Let's Make a Deal."

My mother's face drops, briefly, as if all the breath has gone out of her.

"And how old are you, young lady?" he asks Lisa. He winks at her, one big gray eye winking like a horse.

I close my own eyes for a split second and put my hand on my forehead.

Is this freaking guy really flirting with my baby sister?

He horse-winked at her, I imagine myself telling Greg later.

"I'm forty-three, she says in a cherub-like, child's voice. Her shoulders shrug in a coy way. I wonder if she does it consciously because it is easier to deal with men that way, or if it's her subconscious way of trying to stay perpetually childlike, to erase all the damage wrought on her over the years.

"Forty-three. No, Miss. I cannot believe that. If you are gonna tell me that face is forty-three years old, no Miss, I just wah't believe it."

My sister giggles. She actually giggles. She tosses her hair. I can't tell if it's because she's flattered by the attention, or because she's uncomfortable.

And then my mother is giggling too.

And that does it.

I want to stand from the chair and leave this creepy place, just take a few steps and push that heavy, morbid door, to go out in the lot and breathe in the stench of Worcester and all those dirty diapers. My legs are lead, though. My body has slowed down as if everything—my pulse, my heartbeat itself—has decided to turn counterclockwise.

Greg puts his warm hand over mine on the armrest, instinctively, protectively. It anchors me. I can almost breathe.

"Sir, with all due politeness. Can we cut to the chase? What do you need us to do to take care of David?" my husband asks.

Lone Wolf looks at him. A brief steeliness crosses over his expression and vanishes. Then he looks at my five-foot-tall mother, whose feet are extended in front of her. She's concentrating on watching her legs as she kicks them up and down toward the floor, like she's swimming.

I glance at Lisa. Her expression has changed, briefly. There is deep sadness in her eyes. It is so old, I think, older than even her memories of being a young child.

"David. I know. Of course. As I said previously, your family is our family. And our job is to take the best cah of him as we possibly can. That doesn't just include his body, but his spirit. Yes, family, David is with us. David is a young man who brushed up against tragedy. Do you notice hah I said David 'is' and not David 'was'? There is good reason for that. Good reason. That is because David's spirit is still with us. He is still with us, you undahstand, and I'm going to take care of David because he is my brothah just as he is your brothah, and your son, and just as he is my brothah you are my sistah," he says, looking at me.

"And you ah my sister," he says, smiling and winking at my sister.

"And you ah my brothah," he says to my husband, whose face is flushed and who's holding his temple and the side of his head with his thumb and forefinger as he shakes his head slightly, the way that he does when there's something in the world that makes so little sense it hurts him to hear.

"Excuse me. I don't mean to interrupt. I'm having some trouble digesting so much information. You know. It's just a lot has happened and it's hard. Can you please tell us exactly what you need from us in order to get the medical examiner to release my brother's body?" I say as politely as I can manage.

Lone Wolf stares, stunned. Then his eyes soften, like those of a deer. I am mesmerized by how gray they are, how huge. I guess if you live in Main

South as long as Lone Wolf, if you take care of all the bodies riddled and butchered by gangs and drugs and all manner of things ruled accidental, even your eyes turn into ash.

"Well yes, of course. I undahstand. It is a very sorrahful time. A very trying time. Now let me see heah."

He looks as if he has finally lost his train of thought, as if his brain is that little red lamp and it's just blown a fuse. He stands up slowly and wipes his hands on his dirty pants.

"Please excuse me. I will return," he says almost as an afterthought, without bothering to look at us as he leaves the room. I try to turn to watch him, but my body is leaden. The man is obviously deranged, the house caving in from the weight of so many years of death. I try to remember to breathe.

Somebody giggles nervously. I can't tell if it is my sister or my mother. My husband puts his hand on my leg.

Lone Wolf does a little Clydesdale stomp when he returns to the room and sits back in his chair. He is holding a small white cardboard box.

"You know what I'm going to do?" he asks my mother.

"No, what?" my mother responds.

"Now we normally chahge people good money fah this, but I am going to give this to you."

He opens the box and takes a gold cross from it. He holds it in his hands, up high so we can all see it.

"I want you to hang this up in yah house," he says. He keeps holding up the cross, staring at it like it's some miraculous thing.

"Okay. All right. Thank you very much," my mother says.

He holds the cross between his middle and ring fingers, on its side. The long end is sticking out of the front of his hand.

"I was thinking about this. This just occurred to me the othah day. If you take this cross and you hold it like this, you see what it is?"

Everyone is silent. Somebody mumbles, "No." Someone else giggles.

"This is the key to heaven," he says, twisting the cross like he's turning the key to unlock a door.

He puts the cross in the box and hands it to my mom. I'm stunned by how bizarre this all is. My mind is paused like a record caught in a groove, stuck between laughing and crying.

"Forgive me, but can you tell us what we need to do?" my husband asks.

Lone Wolf looks up, agitated that my husband is stopping his show, but then reaches over the desk and takes out a manila envelope, fumbles in it, and starts flipping through the pages.

Finally, he pulls out a stapled series of papers.

"Now, who is the next of kin? I see right heah this is you, Mrs. Wrenn," he says to my mother. He places the papers in front of her. She receives them like he's handing her some flowers.

She looks at me nervously.

"It's okay, Mom. You just need to sign them."

On the one hand, it feels ridiculous for my mother to be next of kin. At the same time, I feel it's appropriate. In this moment, I can't help but feel that she has some kind of direct responsibility for how things ended up. And even if she can't understand that, or handle that, at least this way some of the burden is on her.

I know she isn't going to take an active role in anything happening, even now.

I remind myself it isn't her fault, really. It isn't that she doesn't care or that she's cold. It's just that she isn't capable. She's disconnected.

"Maybe I can get your phone numbah aftahwards, 'Miss 43,'" he says to my sister.

I close my eyes.

When I open them, my mom is signing the papers in her best grade-school handwriting, like she knows she is still the best handwriter in her class. I wonder if she realizes she's signing the paperwork to get her son's corpse from the freezer in the morgue.

"And then let me just look at something heah. Let's see the grand total. Let's just see how many pennies this is going to cost you."

He looks down at some papers and starts adding line items, first with a piece of paper, then pushing the buttons on the large desk calculator.

"It looks like your grand total is $925," Lone Wolf says.

I wait a heartbeat, two. My mother has her head bent.

My sister's cute voice is muffled.

I pick up my wallet from my lap and unzip it. I pull out my debit card and hand it to crazy Lone Wolf.

"I can take care of it," I say.

"Thank you, Marilyn," my mother says.

Lone Wolf reaches on his desk, pulls out a business card, and hands it to me.

"Now, I'm going to need yuh to call me," he says.

Later that week, Lisa sits in my living room with her tiny legs crossed on my tan couch, her shoulders slumped forward. The house is so quiet. The second hand of the clock ticks loudly.

"I think insomnia maybe runs in our family. Mom has it too," I say.

Lisa doesn't answer right away but shifts in her seat, runs her fingers through her strawberry blonde hair.

"Long few days," I try.

"Ya think?" Lisa responds.

I imagine myself going upstairs and crawling under the thick covers, wrapping Greg's arm around me, and closing my eyes.

I imagine myself cracking open my son's door to peek inside.

Lisa is so tiny. The way she only half looks at me, with her button-like features, reminds me of the way she was as a very young child. I know that happens sometimes, that we imprint on the people we knew long ago and can't see what they really look like now.

It's more than that though. Our whole family is struggling for context.

For the past few days, we've all been driving around on the labyrinthine highway that is our memory. Mostly we just coast, reconnoitering, trying our best to disguise our terror of getting trapped or wrecked every time we lose our bearings. But occasionally we find an off ramp, a rest stop, and breathe long enough to try and figure out not only where we are but how we've gotten here.

"I keep thinking about the last time I spoke with Davey. It was fifteen years ago," I say.

She looks at me.

"He asked me to, begged me, to give him seven hundred dollars. He owed it to a dealer."

"You turned him down?"

"Yeah. I mean. I couldn't be a part of that. I couldn't support that."

My throat is raw and parched.

"Besides, it's not like I just had seven hundred dollars lying around."

She shifts positions on the couch, kneels, and tucks her feet up under her bum.

"It's all just fucked," Lisa finally says.

"Ya think?" I ask.

She laughs.

"Ya know what's even more fucked? Mom narced on him. Because he wouldn't sell her any more of his ADHD pills. How ghetto is that?"

I don't know how to respond to that.

"Did you ever see her cry? Once?" I try.

"No. Is she even capable?"

I remember Lisa sitting in front of Lone Wolf while he was talking about Davey, that fleeting moment when her face crumpled.

"Was it different for you and Davey? Because you're twins?"

"What do you mean? Like if we had a secret twin language we lost? If we would have found out we were both good at crossword puzzles or liked strawberry ice cream or rolled our tongues into flowers if we had reconnected sooner?"

"Maybe. I mean. Not exactly. I just always felt Davey was only like half there, most of the time."

"That's not on me. Davey was half there because he was snorting coke."

"God no. That's not on you. I'm not talking about the drugs. I'm talking about before that, when we were still little kids. I just felt that he missed you on some really deep level, like he really clung to me after you left."

Her chin starts to shake a little, and I know that I've made a mistake.

"You think I left?"

She moves from the couch to the rocking chair. Her short legs don't even touch the ground. She uses the force of her body to make the chair move.

"I don't mean that," I say.

She has one hand near her chest, using the other to pick her fingernails.

"That was crazy. Seeing that house on Illinois Street," I say.

"Yeah, it so was. It looked exactly the same." She twirls her hair on her finger, so hard it looks like she may cut off her circulation.

"It did? You were so little. You must have a really good memory."

"Guess I'm cursed," she says. She releases the curl.

"Do you even remember me being there with you guys?"

"Yeah, Lisa."

"Like when?"

"I mean, my memory sucks these days. But I remembered the park, you know, that day in the park. It came back to me, but only after you mentioned it in the car. I think I brought you guys there to try and look for food."

"I figured that out later on. You were only trying to help."

I nod. I can't remember that much about Lisa as a little kid. She was small but spunky. A spitfire. She was a picky eater. It became clear in their elementary school years that the twins' struggles with learning were attributed to nutritional deficiencies and lead paint poisoning.

"You were a picky eater. Even at the foster family lady's house when the food wasn't weird. What was her name, L? Do you remember her?"

"L. Yeah, that's right. She was nice."

"She called you Skinny Mini. She was always trying to get you to eat. Do you remember we had dinner for breakfast every day, because they were farmers? I thought that was so great."

Lisa's pale face squinches up again, as if she is remembering something.

"Did we ever find out where they went? I mean, they must have told them some kind of story if they let you guys go back to our parents," she asks.

"Maybe. I don't know, really. Afterwards everything was pretty much the same."

She stops the chair abruptly, grips the armrests with her palms.

"Except you weren't there anymore. We missed you."

She's biting her lower lip. Her face is so pale, and her features so small. She looks like she's ready to collapse.

"I always kind of thought you lucked out, you know, getting adopted."

She looks at me like I have just decked her.

"Lucky?"

I stay silent. Wait.

"That's what you thought, lucky?"

I don't move.

"We didn't know what happened. You were adopted. Aunt Marybeth wanted you."

"Do you have any idea what that was like? Knowing my parents threw me away. That they wanted you guys back, but they just let me go?"

My whole life I'd believed Lisa had been somehow cuter and more desirable than us, and that's why she wound up in the fancy house in the suburbs with store-bought clothes and three meals per day, the house she had stayed in and never left.

I'd never once considered she may have felt differently.

"My own parents. Threw me away like a dog," she says. Her chin trembles and tears start to roll from her eyes. She pulls one hand from the chair arm, wipes them off.

I'm stunned.

I should stand up and go over to her, hug her, do something.

Instead, I just sit there, my hands two dead fish in my lap.

Davey and Me

Male Wrens

Male house wrens are characterized by a kind of quiet, senseless, yet almost nonchalant form of violence that ornithologists have never been able to fully understand. Most house wrens winter in warmer climates and return to New England in the springtime—and the male wren is always the first. He scopes out the geography where he can build a few nests to entice the ladies. Most of these nests are used like shell games, "dummy" nests that don't have much substance.

The male wren is extremely territorial in a fierce, almost belligerent way. When he finds other shallow cavity nests in the area, often he will plunge his sharp, blade-like beak into the eggs or murder the fledglings. Sometimes they will then claim their enemies' nests as their own. Sometimes they don't. They don't limit their murder spree to their own species either, or to cavity nests. It's a rare bird that participates in this bizarre form of bloodletting.

The lady birds arrive a few days later, following one of the indiscernible songs the male includes in his repertoire. She's markedly more pragmatic than he is, less swayed by the song as the quality of the nest, which she finishes herself after selecting her mate. The nest is lined with odd scavenged scraps like wool, plastic, snakeskin, feathers, or spider eggs to take care of mites.

To maintain their aggressive reputation, the male wren will often challenge another male whom a lady wren has already chosen as a mate, dueling it out until one is bloody and pitched to the ground. If a male wren is feeling particularly badass, he may even attempt to take over an adversary's lady after they've already begun to breed. In that case, the smug winner may then clear out the lady's nest of her old eggs. Whether they are the aggressor or simply wary of being attacked, male wrens are often described as being shy, even secretive to outside observers.

Their disguise extends to their stash of songs. While mating, the male often croons a low, murmuring, nearly inaudible song, so he isn't detected by his enemy. The female lays between five and eight eggs and incubates them for thirteen days, a short window of time during which she rips the feathers from her belly to keep her eggs warm, and the male wren ceases his habitual pillage and murder. He will stick around and continue to sing intermittently from a distance, perhaps as a protective measure.

Wren babies are hairless, pink, blind, and completely helpless at birth. For the first fourteen days or so after hatching, and before the baby wrens leave the nest, the parents bring the babies grub: stringy grasshoppers with crunchy shells, jellied snails, even spiders. The babies have a distinctly annoying, begging cry that sounds like "peep-peep-peep" mixed with a few ounces of desperation. The calls sound something like the adults make when there's danger nearby, an alarm of sorts, though the baby hatchlings calls are louder and of a more guttural pitch.

Chapter

Grasshoppers & Paddy Wagons

Year: 1983, Mal—9 years old;
Davey—8 years old

I push the Krackle candy bar and the purple one-dollar food stamp onto the sticky counter at the Woodland Superette. The lady cashier squishes her mouth up as she picks up the candy bar and makes the register ring. I look at the numbers, $0.40, and calculate the change. $0.60. We only need $1.00 for the one pack of cigarettes.

You see, the government won't let you buy cigarettes with food stamps, but if you buy a candy bar with your food stamp, you get cash back. So, if Davey and I each buy a candy bar, together we'll have enough change to buy Mom some butts. My mom will let us eat the candy, and we get to keep any extra change if there is any.

Davey stands behind me, tapping me on the back as if to remind me he is still there. He does it partly because he's afraid we'll get into trouble. We've done this a thousand times, but the thought of getting caught makes him nervous.

There's something else, though. Davey is uncomfortable being outside if he's not physically attached to my body in some way, like suckers to a window.

It's okay. I don't mind if Davey attaches to me sometimes because he misses Lisa. The time when we were all in foster care is blurry. Neither of us knows exactly why Lisa was adopted and we were allowed to go back to the house.

"Here you go, honey," the cashier says. I stick out my hand and she puts the change in it. I close my fingers around it and pick up the chocolate bar with the other hand. I move to the end of the register and watch Davey, nodding at him while he pays for his chocolate too.

When we're done, we go to the window and Davey hands me his Krackle bar. I push both candy bars into my pockets. Davey hands me the change and I count it again. We have $1.20. Mom's cigarettes are a buck a pack. That means we'll get two dimes back.

I have all the money in one hand.

"Come on," I say, and Davey grabs my left hand again. It doesn't bother me even though he always smells a little like pee. Nobody told me, but I know it's my job to protect him. That means holding his hand when we cross the street, the same way my best friend Lilac holds her sister's hand when they walk.

We walk up to the high counter where Phil sells the butts.

"Your mom wants her cigarettes, Mal?"

I tip my head up. I'm not quite tall enough to see over the counter, but I can see straight up the rows of candy—pop rocks and Fun Dip and adult breath mints—to the tiny, green plastic cup that holds people's extra pennies.

"Yes."

He throws down my mom's Winston's. I reach up and put the money on the counter. He counts it, making a lot of noise with the change for effect. Then I take the pack of cigarettes and jam it between my jeans and my stomach, digging it in there so that I don't lose it. Phil pushes the keys on his register and makes the ringing sound, then the drawer opens and he makes the change.

"Here you go, sweetie," he says.

I hold my hand up and he reaches down and pushes the change into it, then curls my fingers closed. I jam the two dimes into my pocket.

When we whoosh through the door and get back out to the street we start laughing hysterically, gulping the dusty air. It's fun to know we have gotten away with something, even though we don't know exactly what it is. It's hot and I don't want the candy to melt, so I drag Davey behind me, quick as I can, so we can get to our spot without anyone bothering us, and before the candy melts.

It's late afternoon and the streets are empty. A few steely-eyed people sit on the nearby stoops of some of the three-deckers, but mostly the window shades on the dark houses are pulled down. A long, noisy car cruises down the middle of the street a little too close to us, and I pull Davey to the other side of me so quickly he trips.

"Stop, Maaal," he whines.

"Quiet, hurry up. We don't want the candy to melt."

"Don't wannta candy twa melt," he says.

We pass a street I never turn down anymore. On that street is a fire hydrant. The year before I used to play a game where I tried to balance on it, with one of my feet on each of the side knobs. Once in the middle of the day while I was doing it, some old guy came over to talk to me. He was our neighbor, a Puerto Rican guy who had long, black, curly hair and stringy limbs like my father.

At first he seemed nice. He told me about the blue jay birds, how they were so pretty because that distracted the other birds and he could swoop in and get their food. My mouth had gotten a shrinky feeling, like my throat had been sewed closed with thread from my friend Lilac's mother's sewing needle. I didn't like to talk to adults too much, but I didn't want to be rude.

Then he'd reached up as I was balancing there and he'd grabbed me, kind of karate-kid chopped me between my legs. I lost my balance and fell off the hydrant. I didn't say anything but walked away, feeling his eyes on my back as my shadow lengthened behind me in the sun.

That was a while ago but still, I'm not taking any chances with it, especially when there are so many other perfectly good streets I could go down. I still remember the jiggly way my knees felt when they hit the sidewalk, absorbing the shock of the sudden landing. All I know is that man is like a skunk, like the skunks I remember from my foster home on the farm: you have to be careful not to get too close because he could spray poison on you, and people would know. There's a fat chance we'd be able to get enough tomato juice to soak in to get that junk off.

"I'm tired, Mal. Can we just gawe home now?"

I jerk Davey a little at the elbow, just enough so he knows I'm serious. I'm not really allowed to bring him back home yet. I promised my mom we'd stay out. I don't know why we have to. Maybe it's because around the time of month when the stamps come, the landlords start to knock on the door. Us kids have to make ourselves scarce so we aren't noticed.

It doesn't bother me really. It makes me feel good that my parents take us into their confidence, as if we are adults, too. The landlords' visits were just one of those things that were part of our routine, like going to school or something.

"No, we're going to our spot. To eat the candy. Besides, there's something I want to show you there. A surprise."

I pull Davey and we walk quickly, finally stopping at our spot, a tiny yard space between two metal chain linked fences in front of an abandoned triple-decker. We sit crossed-legged, Davey's knobby knees pressed against mine.

I take the chocolate out of my pocket and begin to unwrap one of the bars, deliberately slow, tearing the corners of the paper and then unfolding the silver foil like it is a gift. It's partly to torture both of us, but also to teach Davey how precious the candy is, and how it will taste better if you make it last. It's the opposite of the way we eat food in the house. I've seen girls at school eat like this, and I know it's better.

I hand him exactly one quarter of the bar and eat one quarter myself. I try to eat slowly, but it tastes so good I can't pull it off. The chocolate and Rice Krispies melt in my mouth. The chocolate drips too fast, soda-like down my throat, and it makes me cough.

"Want to go home?" Davey says.

I can't explain to Davey why we have to stay out. But it's nice being outside. I like the way the sun feels on my shoulder blades. Davey, who is very pale and gets sick a lot, doesn't like it.

"Let's look for grasshoppers," I say.

Davey looks at me skeptically, and then his face lights up.

"How do we lawk for gwasshoppers?" he asks.

"Watch me first. I'll show you," I say.

I deliberately go behind Davey toward the middle of the yard and squat down. I watch a tiny patch of clumped, yellowish dirt.

"You have to be quiet and patient," I say.

Davey's face goes blank, the way that it just does sometimes.

I turn back around. Suddenly I see it, one hopping toward me. I lean over, feeling Davey's eyes on my neck, and scoop it up.

I get it the first time and my heart beats in tune with the vibrating sound the grasshopper makes, "tik tik pzzzzz." I like the way that it sits in my two cupped hands, tickling the fleshy pockets at the bottom of my fingers. I walk over to Davey slowly, and he catches the smile off my face.

"Do you want to peek?"

He nods his head like crazy.

I raise my cupped hands to his face. "Okay, look with your eye first."

I un-cup the top part of my hands quickly so he can see, then close it back up. The grasshopper jumps against the top of my palm, wanting to escape. I close my fingers over it tighter, laughing, as if someone is pressing my stomach.

"Can I try?" Davey asks.

"We have to let him go now or he'll hurt himself," I say, gently putting the grasshopper down on the ground.

"Watch him gaw," Davey says and starts hysterically laughing. The grasshopper bounces through the grass. There's something so funny about watching it, jumping up and down past the dirt patches, the metal cans, and the broken glass until it disappears.

We're almost home when we feel it in our bones—coming up behind us is a roaring police siren. Davey looks at me before it pushes past us through the gluey air. It's not an ordinary police car but a paddy wagon, the kind they pull out when there's some kind of dirt-kicking fight between the drunk men on our block.

"Cops!" Davey says.

The car cuts in front of us.

"Look, Mal. Up ahead."

Sure enough, not too far ahead of us a crowd has gathered, standing in a cluster watching. We start running to see the action before the cops break it up. We run so hard, and so spastically because we're laughing, that I get a cramp in my side.

"Do you think it's Dawd?" Davey screams as we are running, echoing a thought that's already in my mind. I keep running, appreciating how the street slaps the soles on my sneakers—which stay on my feet because I did a good job and tied them so tight.

I can't remember if Dad was home this morning. But even if he was, he's definitely gone now, probably at Moynihan's by the time we left the house.

"Come ahn, Mahl!" Davey says as we round the corner.

We stop at the end of the crowd, which has started to press in tighter together, the way that it always does.

"I can't see, Mahl," Davey says, jumping up and down.

A neighbor looks down at me. In the distance I hear them screaming, the two men's voices entangled like cats. I am not sure if my father is one of them.

"Your fahthah...again," the neighbor says, tapping me on the shoulder.

"And his band of merry hoods," it sounds like another person is saying.

The men's voices rise and fall, like that feeling you get when riding the swings at school. My throat is so dry from the sun and the chocolate. I want a cup of water.

The voices change, thinning out, interrupted by the barking orders of cops. Then the crowd parts and changes angle, and now I can see the three or four men with their hands stuck behind their backs and their heads bent, being pushed from behind by the cops who aren't touching them exactly, but moving them as if by some invisible string.

I look at their bodies, at their thin Fruit of the Loom t-shirts and dirty jeans. They all move as one. As the back of the wagon opens and they're all being loaded onto the van, stepping up like they're getting onto the school bus to go to a game, it's then that I catch a glimpse of my father. I know him by his dark red hair, the light, bleached-out color of his jeans, and the odd, bowlegged way he bends into a seat.

People stand for a while, mumbling and staring. But everything changes once it's all over. Nobody wants to scream for effect anymore; nobody's too keen on making themselves known.

It takes about two minutes after the wagon disappears for the crowd to start moving away. They've been standing on the street for a while now. It's time to take their wagging tongues back inside.

"You thirsty, Davey? Let's go get some water."

As we are walking toward the building I spot the landlord, a bald man with a ribbed undershirt, his hands crossed over his big belly. He stares at us, a mean look screwed on his mouth. I pretend not to see him and hurry Davey back into the house.

There's just so much we do not know. The male wren doesn't just sing because he's randy. A bachelor or widowed wren will still sing, producing a piercing, mouse-like squeak when a female is entering his territory. He will make a "thut, thut thutting" sound for no particular reason. There is also a specific cry they can make to express empathy, as well as a peculiar kind of long alarm sound to warn others of an incoming enemy. Other calls are believed to be some avian form of Morse code.

I tend to think that the wrens sing to announce their own presence, as more colorful birds do through their costumes. Although there are some songs that multiple male wrens tend to share, like one of their Irish drinking songs, most of the rest are distinct to the individual bird.

I don't know if Lisa and Davey had some innate biological connection, some secret bleating language that would have bubbled between them if their connection hadn't been severed so young. It's possible that their losing each other resulted in each of them becoming half of what they might have been while they were children. I don't know if it was the reason they may have learned more slowly, or if their shadow selves were a harbinger of what was to come. I don't know if Davey stopped feeling the loss of Lisa as he was growing when she seemed to be fading away from the fabric of us.

My father and I had a connection that was just as ephemeral, one that I'm unable to articulate or describe. It may have been some kind of sticky, webbed bond that predated our family, the warped way I felt responsible for him—the way I understood him.

Chapter 10

The WWF: Rowdy Roddy Piper & Hulk Hogan

Year: 1984, Mal—10 years old;
Davey—9 years old

At night, when I squeeze my eyes tight, I can see red colors, and sometimes it looks like the static on the television screen just after the National Anthem is played, late at night when there are no more shows on to watch. My stomach makes funny grumbly noises. My bladder hurts like someone is pressing it down with two fingers, but I don't want to have to get out from under the covers.

I open my eyes. I'm on the top bunk. I hook my little pinky finger, gently so that it doesn't fall, on the red sheet we have thumbtacked over the window and look at all the pretty stuff outside. There's a small spindly tree. It's green. My dad calls it a spruce. There's snow lacing the green needles and a big moon shining on white.

We haven't gotten the electric on yet. Seeing shapes outside helps.

"Mal, you awake?" Davey asks from the bottom bunk.

I let go of the curtain and close my eyes.

Davey has gotten annoying.

He's not taking enough baths.

He's started to do this weird thing where he asks to smell my dirty socks.

Also, he keeps grabbing at me, always wanting me to hold his sticky hand. I know it's because he and Lisa were always touching like that, so I try not to be mean and just let him.

"Hey, you there?"

"Where else would I be? No duh?"

"Dad's home," he says.

"So?"

"They're fighting."

"So? Go to sleep. Who cares?" I say.

Honestly, I don't know why Davey is so sensitive. Fighting's just what they do.

"Just because you went to high school, you think your Swedish shit don't stink!" my dad yells.

For a second, Davey and me are quiet. Then we both bust out laughing.

"You could have stayhed awn the jahb longer, David! That's all I'm try-inh to explahn. You could ha wahted tilh you gat the money to fuck up!"

"What the hell do you think makes you any different, huh? You aren't slumming here anymore, you know that, don't you. You have full out fahl-len from grace—flat on your big padded ahss. You think those people give a damn about you anymore? You think anyone cares?"

"Shut up, David! Just shut your trahp. You are acting belligerent again. Belligerent!"

"There she goes with the three thousand-dollar words again. You ought to sell those words on the street cornah. Go on down to Piedmont Street and sell those big words, see what all that bullshit is worth. Sell those words and you'll be doing something useful for once!"

"Go tah sleep, David!"

"You go tah sleep. Why the hell you uhp anyhow?"

"Someone has ta make sure you are okay. The kids were asleep. I cohdn't send them aut to Moynihans, could I?"

"The kids have school. Fuck you! Why would you even think that way in the fahst oplahce?"

"What? You are drunkkkk. Drunnnkkk. Just stop it. Stop aggravating me."

There's a long pause. My stomach clamps. It feels wrong somehow to be listening, even dirty. I squeeze my legs to my chest and then force them down. I push my ear into the pillow, searching for the cool spot.

There's a sound that's someone being slapped—a hand slamming against a hollow cheek, hard. There is a whimper.

Their sounds get more demented. They are locked in some kind of wrestling match. They grunt, they groan. It's like Rowdy Roddy Piper and Hulk Hogan are going at it in the living room.

I imagine myself doing a play-by-play—like Mean Gene over the microphone. *In this corner, standing with one shoe on, we have Daaavid Wrenn, aka Daaad! In this corner, wearing sweatpants and a long black t-shirt, we have Cherrrrylll Wrrennnnnn, aka Mommmmm!*

I don't know what each of my parent's specialties are exactly, but I imagine them locked together, twisting each other's noses with their fists and pulling hair. They may be giving each other snake bites—taking each other's wrists in two hands and turning them hard in opposite directions, like Davey and I sometimes do.

"And they say the kids haveta be quiet on the third floor, so the neighbors don't complain we're dancing on their heads. Ha. If that's true, the parents probably shouldn't be doing pile drivers in the middle of the night, huh, Davey?"

There's a suspended inhaling sound like someone has been pushed, then a crash.

Then it's quiet.

"Is it the middle of the night, Mal?"

I peek out the curtains again. The moon has dropped lower in the sky. My dad told me that means something, that somehow you can tell time that way.

"Yes. And they're finished now. Show's over. You should go to sleep. Just try not to wet the bed again. It's starting to smell rank in here already," I say.

Davey is silent for a long, long time.

It makes me feel bad.

I shouldn't tease him like that. He does that because he's nervous.

"Do you like your class in school?" I ask him.

"It's naht fun anymore," he says.

School doesn't come easy for either of the twins. They're different from me. They can't learn right or something. But Davey has it worse than Lisa did. They even put him in a special classroom.

School must be the loneliest place in the world for him without Lisa.

"Can you make some friends then? Talk to some of the boys?"

"Not really." His words come out garbled, like he's swishing the water in his mouth after brushing his teeth.

I take my pinky and peek out the window again.

In the direction I'm looking, through the lacy trees and out past the moon, it's starting to turn blue. There's so much clean space out there, and it goes on forever.

We are so high up, we are almost a part of the sky.

In the morning, I wake up from a cold, earthworm-like sleep, like I'm under the soil of the dark winter house. I want to stay in my bunk and lie under the warm covers.

I don't want to be late for school, though. I shake off the covers and dig for the science book I took to bed with me. I climb down carefully, quietly, so I don't wake Davey yet.

My clothes are all in a pile in the corner. I go over there and pick some out in the dark. Then I go behind the dresser where Davey can't see me, strip off my PJs, and put some tights and purple parachute pants on, along with a long-sleeved shirt that looks white.

I have to pee. When I get to the bathroom someone is already in there.

I go into the living room, stepping blind-man's style through the mess. I unknowingly kick something with my foot as I make my way toward the end of the wall. I pull at the sheet they have tacked on the window, but accidentally rip it off the wall.

White light floods the room. I can see now that it's been, like, totally demolished. There's a big chair upside down on the floor, and broken glass scattered everywhere. My father's Elvis painting is upside down on the floor too, with a part of its frame half-cocked.

In the kitchen, the sink drips. I close my legs even tighter.

The only thing that was too heavy to fall was the old television, which my parents had set on black milkcrates they got at the Mart. I don't want to give up my shot at the bathroom, so I sit down on the floor and pull my legs in. I press two fingers into that spot in the middle of my chest, between my breastbone.

I'm down low enough that I can smell all the house funk. I am at funk level, the level of funk. All the nastiness surrounds me, tickling my nostrils. The dirty clothes piles. Something rotting near the kitchen. I gag a few times, then make sure I stop so I don't go ahead and throw up.

There's something important I was supposed to remember. I go through topics in my mind. My parents were fighting the night before, but it wasn't that. Davey was lonely at school. No.

Then I have my "eureka" moment. It's my hamster Belotte I'm supposed to remember. He escaped a whole week ago. We'd gone nuts trying to find him, but then everyone stopped.

My mother comes out of the bathroom. I make out her bushy, wavy hair, the funny way that she walks, her face squinting. She sees me on the floor and smiles.

"Hello Marilyn. Did you sleep?" Her voice is extra chipper, the way that it usually gets the day after a fight. It sounds a little like a bird.

She walks slowly, like a zombie, holding her hand on her side. When she comes closer, I see her eye is on wrong. It's puffy and green-gray. She moans a little, too. I feel sorry for her. My dad musta won the match. He really tore her up good.

"Mom. You didn't see Belotte anywhere yet, did you?"

"Belotte? Joe had his skinny behind planted at Moynihan's next to your dad's."

"Not Joe. My hamster, Belotte!" I say.

I named my hamster after Joe Belotte, my dad's best friend, who also has bright red hair and likes to laugh.

"After last night, that holy-roller wife of his is gonna be praying for his Sunday soul. Praise the Lord," my mother mocked, following it up with a "Jesus" drawled out loud and hard.

She shuffles over to the kitchen and turns on the water.

"Not Dad's friend. My hamster. Belotte. Did you see him, Mom?"

"Your hamster. Oh, Mal, that thing has been gone a long time."

"It's not a thing, it's Belotte. Dad says hamsters are good in the dark because they stay awake at night and sleep during the day."

I stand up, realizing I really have to get to the bathroom.

"What does that have to do with anything?"

"So maybe he's just playing a good joke on us, or maybe he's just confused about when to sleep."

My mom stares at the water, then moves her hand, as if remembering to turn it off. She hasn't heard a word I have said.

That day I come home from school and toss my backpack on the chair. The heat is still on, but low, and the air is cool on my cheeks. I've slept off the stomachache in the nurse's office at school and am running around slowly, agitating my parents, who are cocooned in blankets in the living room and have left the sheets we were using as curtains only partially open. It's dim anyhow because my father had already wrapped the window in plastic.

My mother has a flashlight on and is sitting near a card table, organizing the smooth, light brown coupons from the Winston cigarette packs to see if she has enough for a prize. It's kind of ironic, because the print on the coupons is tiny and the last time she redeemed them she got a lamp. But the lamp isn't here. We must've left it behind when we left our last apartment in a hurry after yet another eviction.

"What prize you trying for?" I ask her.

It's my mother's way. When we don't have a "pot to piss in," and it's too long until the beginning of the month when our welfare check arrives, my dad schemes outside, sometimes betting on the dog races, while my mom's random luck always helps us by winning a few bucks here and there with lottery tickets. The furious way she rubs the thin sides of quarters over scratch tickets at the bar is etched in my brain. She also sends out applications for things like the Publishers Clearinghouse Sweepstakes, or pastes stickers from tiny magazines on big pages to score deals for subscriptions we'd probably never get, as we'll be evicted before they ever make it to the mailbox.

My parents are good at hustling; they're also good at letting things go. Mom loves to drive stick shifts, for instance, but she messed that up good because she couldn't pay the vehicle excise tax. Then they took away her license, and then she couldn't deal with all the lines and papers at the DMV, and so she gave up her dream to have a car.

If the heat doesn't turn on, you add another layer of plastic on the windows. If you can't win the lottery, you can get twelve magazine subscriptions for a penny.

"I don't know, Mal. They have some nice ashtrays or some jewelry. Stop running around like that, you're making me nervous."

"There's nothing to do."

My father grumbles, annoyed I'm interrupting his daydream.

"Did you find Belotte?" I ask.

"Damnit, Mal. We would have told you if we found the damn thing, wouldn't we?" Dad says, looking up from his dream.

"Stop running around like that. Relax. Don't worry honey. You'll find it," my mom says, looking up at me. There is a softness now to her face. I think she gets it.

"It's not cute, it's a rat!" Dad says.

"It's cute."

"It's just a stupid hamster.

"It's her pet."

Losing the electricity is such a regular occurrence that we're good at adapting, like taking baths when the dim daylight still shines through the bathroom window and eating different foods, like cornflakes and water, or hot dogs cooked over the cigarette lighter. When there's food, we eat it by the window, and once in a while my parents turn on the camping lantern for us or light candles.

Still, anxiety lingers like gasoline someone doused on the floor. It isn't a question of if we'll lose electricity, but when.

There are little inconveniences then, like when you kick something and stub your toe, or lose your lucky blue rabbit's foot. Other than that, it's not a biggie. We deal with it until somebody gets a voucher or finds a way to hustle some cash and then, magically, the lights turn back on.

I'm sad for Belotte, though. I worry for him. This is my first pet, and I took good care of him, talking to him every night and making sure I fed him pellets and changed his water every week. Now he's lost somewhere and listening for my voice. Maybe he's mad at me for not finding him sooner.

"Well, I want to look again. Where'd the flashlight go?"

"Look on the windowsill. While you are at it look under the sink and get me the duct tape," my dad says. "It's just a stupid hamster. He's probably dead," Dad adds.

"It's her pet. Don't worry, Marilyn, you'll find him," my mom says.

I crawl around on the floor, shining the light under the sink with my head half turned and my stomach steeled for a mouse or a bunch of roaches that may be hiding down there. I shine it around the way my dad had taught me, making a predictable pattern and tracing the edges first.

I look from the basket of nails and dish soap to where there's still a roll of silver electrical tape, but none of the fat duct tape, which can be used for everything from patching holes in jackets to jerry-rigging the lights. Behind it are some trash bags. Then I look to the left and my breath catches.

"Holy crap. Crikey," I yell, though nobody hears.

"I found him!" I say, laughing hysterically. Belotte is asleep on a pile of my mother's knee highs, which he managed to make into a bed on top of a box of SOS brillo pads. I scoop him into my hand and cup the other on top, feeling the familiar tickle of his nose and whiskers on my skin.

"Mal? What are you doing in there?"

"Belotte's alive!" I scream.

Dad seems as though he's had a change of heart—I can hear him cheering "whoohoo." Slowly, I stand up holding Belotte and walk into the living room to show them.

PART 4

Fairytales, Friends, & Fathers

Tehi Tegi. A Gaelic tale.

Once upon a time on the Isle of Man, in the Irish Sea between Ireland and England, there was a beautiful little pixie girl, the real Queen of the Fairies, named Tehi Tegi. Tehi Tegi was so friggin pretty—we're talking something like Alyssa Milano and Marissa Tomei mixed with a hint of Cheryl Tiegs, what my dad would call a real knockout.

As is the case with all really beautiful girls, this Tehi Tegi sometimes got the wrong kind of attention. In that way her beauty was like some kind of a friggin curse, because all the guys on the island perpetually hung around her, trying to get her to notice them. They bought her anything they could think of: glitter eyeshadow, Hello Kitty diaries, bunches of daisies. They offered her trips to the mountains and along the rugged coastline.

Tehi Tegi wasn't the least bit miffed by all the attention. Truth told, she kind of liked it. She was one of those girls who was all sparkly and colorful and bold. She knew all kinds of magic—the kind to draw the boys to her, and the kind to drive them away.

It must have been that none of the boys were worthy of the Queen of the Fairies. They had no pride in themselves, for one. When the men followed her, they let all their crops and families go bad. So, one day she led all those dumb guys who were hanging around her to this shallow ford in a river. The river let Tehi Tegi pass, but then rose up like a beast and sucked all of the guys in.

Most drowned. The few who survived ran after her.

Deep down they probably knew better. You can't cage a magical girl like that. Of course, Tehi Tegi was smarter than them. She transformed herself, just like that, into a wren and escaped.

She was supposed to be banished from the island forever. She wasn't supposed to come back. But fairy queens aren't wimps. They don't listen to people telling them where they belong. And she missed the island. She had loved it, even though all those guys annoyed her so much. Her heart was still there. So, every year, on December 26th, Tehi Tegi returns to the island.

And the people all try to hunt her all over again.

They celebrate her arrival on December 26th, St. Stephen's Day. In the old days, the people murdered a wren in a brutal way, like the way the Kilby Street posse of Main South was thought to eviscerate the owners of the stores they robbed and rival gangs that got in the way. They put the wren on a pole, and wren boys dressed up in crazy costumes—some of the guys even dressing like girls—would go from door to door showing people this gross thing and begging for money. Later they buried it in a graveyard.

But now it's a less violent day. A fake wren is tied to a pole that they decorate with ribbons and flowers. There's all kinds of dancing in circles all around it. There's even a special song.

Chapter

11

Fortune Tellers & The Big Spruce

Year: 1984, Mal—10 years old

If there is anyone who resembles the Queen of the Fairies in Worcester, it's my best friend, Lilac. She has magic powers. It's something I can feel, but can't really describe. She's the kind of girl who doesn't, like, flinch from anything. She's always calm. She says whatever she wants, whenever she wants, and nobody ever asks her to repeat herself because she talked too low or mumbled and they didn't understand. It makes me a little jealous, sometimes, this thing about her that I can't describe. But it's also the reason I love to be her best friend. She sometimes puts words to how I am that make it okay. "Mal's not shy, she's selective," she tells people. And then I don't have to do anything more to explain.

Maybe Lilac is so magical because of her bedroom. It's totally awesome. Her parents let her paint it any color she wanted. Well, except black. Instead, she decided on a crinkly, shiny wallpaper that looks like the helium balloons they fill at the Mart downtown. She has posters of C. Thomas Howell and a full-length one of Ralph Macchio. She has so many things I've never consider asking for, like ten thousand Barbies and jewelry boxes filled with lavender and purple plastic beads and ribbons that she weaves onto barrettes and gives out as presents.

"You ready?" she asks.

I nod. I'm still wearing a headband in my hair to cover the bald spot from the last time she cut my hair and gave me the bleached streak with the Clorox. But Lilac knows things: like how to jerry-rig video games at the pizza place so we can play as much Ms. Pac Man as we want, and the secrets about kissing boys.

"Do it already before I chicken out," I say.

Lilac takes a matchbook out, lights one, and expertly holds it over the needle she's threaded. It looks wicked sharp.

"Blow it out! Your mom's going to smell it," I say.

"I have to make sure its hy—geeeyenic," she says, holding it until the flame is down to her thumb tip before blowing it out. "Besides, she can't hear anything today."

"Why, she lit?"

"Nah."

"She'd be pissed."

"She wouldn't give a shit. Besides, she's not coming out of her room today."

It is quiet down below us.

Lilac's parents are hippies. Her mother, Marie, is beautiful with her long, dark Cher hair and her butterfly-colored clothes. Her dad, Wally, has a long, gray ZZ Top beard—almost as long as his hair, which I mostly see pulled back in a ponytail. Usually, there's some kind of music playing, notes from the records or the acoustic guitar that vibrated through the floorboards. And I haven't smelled any pot yet today.

"Wally still on a road trip on his bike? What's that country he was going to?"

"Not a country, it's a state. For a genius you can be really dumb."

I look at her. No words come.

"I'm just in a bad mood," she says.

My cheeks redden.

"He went up to New Hampshire, but he didn't take the bike. Too cold. It's a state. He went to this place in the mountains. There are rock shops there."

Footsteps creak in the hallway. Lilac stares at the door all cut-eyed. Her shoulders jerk back.

Then the footsteps are gone.

Lilac pulls my hair farther back behind my ears, nodding her head.

Then she gets out the thinnest magic marker, just like they do in the mall. She cocks her head and narrows her eyes, measures a thumb nail on one ear and makes a mark, then does the same with the other.

Lilac jumps off the bed then and stares at my ears from farther away.

"Wally came back last night," she whispers.

"Oh."

"Okay, it's now or never," she says.

She takes the threaded needle with one hand and with the other hand she holds a piece of potato gently behind my ear. The potato is cool, but the other fingers of Lilac's hand are warm and almost adult in the way she rests them on the back of my head.

"Hold your breath," she says in a low but steady voice.

Before I have inhaled, she has done it. The pain sears through my ear as I feel the eyelet in the needle go through, followed by the clean, tickly thread. When I open my eyes again, she has dropped the potato and the needle and is gently pushing the first earring in.

"Take this," she says.

She pushes the earring in and does the back.

"Let go now."

I can hardly bear the thought of doing the second ear, but I don't want to disappoint Lilac and I've got to save face. I close my eyes, brace myself, and pretend to be somewhere else.

It's done and Lilac fixes the second earring back on the post.

"Wha-la! We did it!" she says.

My ears throb.

She stands with her arms crossed and examines them.

"Shit, they're perfect," she says.

Then she turns to her dresser to get the hand mirror so I can see and rubbing alcohol to clean them all out.

A few hours later I'm lying on Lilac's bed. My ears are on fire, but I'm too proud of my new studs to admit it to myself. We're making fortune tellers, folding the paper into squares and coloring the numbers, questions, and colors in each flap. Seven, red, how many children will I have?

The house is quiet. It's strange. We haven't been out of the room all day.

"Does your dad have any cans?"

"Mhmm. Just before he left, he stopped the friggin car on the highway and made me get out and pick some up. Doesn't top the time when he had me pick 'em up while my sister ran track, but it's up there. Why?"

"I don't know. Just thinking maybe you want to see a movie or something."

"No duh, you seen the snow out there. No way we gonna push a shopping cart full of cans all the way to the liquor store. Sides, they're all tamped down with tawps."

"Sorry."

"Stop saying sorry."

"Okay."

She picks up her fortune teller and folds it, holding it by pinching the thumb and pointer finger of each hand into the bottoms of the paper, which looks like a three-dimensional triangle. She moves her fingers outward and then inward, so the triangular ends of the fortune teller pop back and forth.

Someone creaks the hallway, slippers walking on floorboards.

Lilac pauses for a second as if she's thinking hard about something. She looks at the door and rolls her eyes. The creaking stops.

We wait quietly, practically holding our breath.

"I hate it here," Lilac says.

I realize the house is different than usual. The kitchen was dark and there were no gloppy peanut butter and carob chip cookies in the lit oven waiting for us.

"Everything okay? Wally came back last night?"

"Yeah," she says, and blows her breath out of her lips upward so it moves her bangs.

I pull my legs up to my chest, remembering the fight my parents had earlier that week.

"Just because you went to high school, you think your Swedish shit don't stink," and then my mom yelling something squeaky back. I remember my mother's face and feel bad that we laughed.

"You're lucky you don't live on top of anyone. That you aren't in a three decker."

"Luck had nothing to do with it. We got this house on the cheap after somebody tried to burn it down while we were renting. Remember?"

"Sorry," I say.

She looks at me and then shakes her head. Her eyes get all squinty like, like little jewels, the way they get when she is formulating a plan. She stares at the door. Nobody's there anymore. Marie probably just went back to her craft room.

"That's it. It's enough. That's it. We are going to do it," she says.

"Do what?"

"Duh, run away."

I pick up my fortune teller and pop my fingers into it, testing it out. I'm surprised that mine works.

"We already established that, given that we talk about it every week."

"No, but I mean we should do it for good. We have almost everything we need."

She hops off the bed, goes into her closet, and starts throwing things out: a purple suitcase, blankets, clothes. Then she pops back out, opens the suitcase, and begins to fill it. She starts yanking Barbie dolls out of the big wooden trunk that sits in the corner of her room.

"Holy. Where did you of all people get so many friggin dolls from?" I ask. I'm more of a tomboy, in that the boys back up when I get the ball in my hand during dodge ball games and wind back my hand, and after I throw it often it gets them in the nuts and they groan. Lilac makes her own jewelry and barrettes with ribbons and beads and does everyone's hair and has started to pierce all our ears. But she isn't exactly the definition of a girly-girl either.

"I don't know. Same shit. Christmas, birthdays, hand-me-down dolls. People send them. Like they don't know I don't even like friggin Barbies."

"So, Lilac, if you don't like them, why the heck are we bringing them?"

"In case Marie sees us on our way out. We can just tell her that we're going to play Barbies. Then if she asks to see them, we can show her. It's genius, right?"

"Oh. Okay."

I stand up, then flop back down on the bed.

"Totally awesome," I say, still trying to convince myself that we have a good plan.

Lilac and I stop in the middle of a long field of snow, halfway between our two houses. The snow molecules have all spread out and fluffed up into a giant blanket, spread out over the green trees and the ground. It cushions everything in quiet. Even the rumble of cars on Main Street has softened.

"This is genius. There's nobody out," I say.

"Told you."

Beside us are rows of three-deckers. The lights are on in some of the apartments. People are there. Some are cooking, others playing scratch offs or cards or watching TV. It all looks pretend.

Lilac moves closer to me. She nods toward the spot where we've set up our runaway camp. It's a fort in the middle of a field, between a green house and a yellow house that we know for a fact are only half occupied.

There are trees there, full, hulking green trees with long arms. Beneath them there's no snow, just soft, dry circular spots with spruce boughs we fluffed up like pillows, which Lilac knows stay dry and are soft to sleep on. We set a tarp over some trees like a fort. Our stuff is buried there: blankets, hairbrushes, a thermos with water, and decorations.

Simply looking at that spot makes me feel warm inside.

Just as I can't describe the power Lilac has, I can't describe the power of this place, which is what running away is. I only know how it makes me feel to imagine being here. It's as if in my chest somebody has knit an itchy wool scarf, and pulled the stitches so tight that they've made it impossible to breathe. But when I'm in this place, the air is cool and open, and it's as if the stitches of that scarf have been let looser and looser, one by one, until eventually the air rises up to fill my chest and I can breathe again.

Running away is cool wind on my cheeks. It's a magical fairyland where I don't feel responsible for Davey's sadness, or embarrassed for eavesdropping on my parent's fights. It's a place where me and Lilac can just be free, where everything is just, like, normal or something. Running away is a place where clock hands move correctly. It's a place where we return to the source of ourselves, to pure cold snow and squirrels eating acorns, to the way things were always supposed to be.

"Let's go," Lilac says and starts running.

I follow her, laughing. The icy shell of snow crunches as I walk. The more I bear down, the louder it is.

Lilac unlatches the tarp. My feet are wet in a few places from the holes in the bottom of my old shoes. The gross, burpy taste is back in my throat. I try to remember when I last ate.

Secretly I pick up some clean-looking snow in my hand, taste it. It's cool on my tongue. I take a glop and press it into my forehead. Coolness spreads.

I crawl into the tent next to Lilac where we've set blankets over the boughs. I lay down on one, close my eyes. Warmer air caresses my cheeks.

"It's so nice," I say.

It's already getting dark inside.

"Perfect, right?"

"Yep."

Everything outside the tent sounds funny, softer, like it is under the covers. I can pay more attention to it that way: the wind, the sound of a loud bird singing. *Coo....*

Lilac stretches out on the ground next to me. Her hair smells like pot cigarettes, like maybe her parents were smoking around her this morning.

I imagine the kitchen in the morning: her mother with her long skirt, her father with his terrycloth robe all cinched up. I imagine the long sweet laughter, their short swift stories that come out in strange hippie code, the gloppy peanut butter carob cookies baking in the oven.

"Lilac. Can I ask you something?"

"Uh-huh."

"Are you just doing this to be nice? To keep me company?"

"No way. You crazy?"

"Why then?"

"Shhh. I have my reasons," she says and lifts herself up, then goes to the other side of the tent to start setting more things up.

"It's getting late though. We should start moseying to your house soon. We have to get your warm stuff. Your pajamas," she says.

"Why don't we just stay here now? We don't have to go to my house.'

The cover of the tent is dark. The air burns my eyes. I close them.

"I think my parents are home," I say.

"So, we can tell them you are sleeping over my house. They won't call."

I open my eyes.

Lilac raises her hands far above her head and laces her fingers together, then stretches, first to one side, then the other.

"They won't call. We don't have a phone," I say.

I remember the fight from last night. It had lasted longer than usual. Whoever had pretended to be Rowdy Roddy Piper had gotten up on that top rope and body slammed the other into the ground a few times. There had been some pile driving too.

I hope they had the decency to clean up after themselves.

It's likely they didn't. I don't know what we'll find when we get there. Will there be broken plate parts on the ground, a soaked carpet? Will there be blood?

"I don't really need to, though. I think I'll be fine here."

"You won't though, Mal. There aren't enough clothes. It gets colder the later it gets. Even if we burrow the hole deeper, even with all the spruce boughs and blankets. We don't want to have to leave in the middle of the night because you got your butt frostbitten. If we're going to do this, we want to make it last."

I close my eyes lightly, imagining what I would pack. A sock for under my mitten to keep the cold out of the hole. My zipper sweatshirt. Pajamas for under my jeans. The leg warmers.

I sigh, deeply, letting the air fill my belly like a balloon.

"Mal. Earth to Mal. Don't fall asleep yet. It's not your time."

I am not sure what she is saying. Her words are half shells, broken under the weight of waves.

The air feels so thick on my chest. A half-smile spreads my lips.

There are nice scents: spruce needle bows, wool army blanket, and wet snow.

"You aren't making..."

Lilac is still talking. There's something important she's trying to say. The wind is still so strong. Her words are crushed letters, new gravel poured over tar.

I force myself up on my elbows. I open my mouth, then close it again. Lilac's mouth is moving too. I stare at her, at the sun wrapped in clouds. It's as if the nurse at school has taken that big wooden stick and pressed it down on my tongue.

"It's okay. You're right. Let's go get my stuff," I manage.

We stand outside my door, and I hear the neighbors setting their plates and cups down at the dinner table. It's a sound that has always made me feel sad for some reason. I smell garlic and red sauce, and something like fried, chopped meat with onions. The burpy taste rises in my throat.

I put my hand on the knob and twist it hard, then push the door open and stomp in, making more noise than is necessary. "Close the door please," I whisper to Lilac.

The first thing I notice is that the heat is on full blast. My father is sitting on the single chair in the otherwise empty living room, his feet planted on the floor, a laundry pile all the way up to his shoulders. The kitchen is completely dark. Mom and Davey aren't around.

"Hi Dad," I say.

He switches off the television.

I start to turn around and head for my room.

"Hey Mal, hah you doing?" he says.

Lilac takes a step back, kind of by instinct. Then she takes a step forward, as if to let me know she is there.

In addition to the laundry there's an open can of something congealing in the corner, and piles of old newspapers and Publishers Clearing House mailers. There are crushed beer cans, and I can see where one has spilled into a puddle. Dad tried to clean it with an undershirt that's now soaking and twisted and releasing the beer scent all over the room. Thank God my dad is still wearing all the rest of his clothes.

"Good, Dad."

My dad stares at us for a long time, at first as if he doesn't recognize us and then does, but maybe thinks we are somebody different.

"W'are done painting the hawse. They only wahnt the insides blue."

I remember now. My dad had a job, what they called day work. He either got paid or got fired. Either way, the job is done.

"That's what happened? Yesterday?"

"Whata-calanata," he says, and then makes a strange movement in the air like he is a train conductor saying "whoot-whoot."

Lilac taps me. I can feel her smiling. I bite my lip to keep from busting out.

My dad stares. He looks at me as if he just remembered who I am. He closes his eyes and opens them again. He clears his throat.

"Marilyn. Did ya dawe your homework?" he asks, as if the very act of recognizing me is sobering him up.

That's one of the few things that's important to my dad—that we do our homework and keep going to school. Lilac was the one I cut with that day he found me and walked me to the principal's office himself.

"It's the weekend, Dad. But we have a test tomorrow. We're going to study in my room."

He looks past me to Lilac and squints his eyes, as if he's surprised another person is standing in the living room. I push her back slightly without knowing why.

"Do you need anything before I go, Dad? A cup of water?"

"No. Uh-uh. Kidten."

"Dad, do you want me to get you a blanket? Maybe take off your work boots?"

Lilac touches my arm, concerned. I walk past her to go to the room and get the wool blanket. When I come back, something inside me is broken.

Lilac looks at me, wide eyed.

"Put him in the blanket. Make sure his head stays on the chairback. He won't even remember we came in," she whispers.

I walk over to my dad and put the blanket over him. I notice his lip is swollen, but only partway, like it got stuck on something sharp—maybe my mother's ring. I remember how early I'd gone to bed the night before when they fought. I wonder, if I'd stayed up later, whether we could have gotten him from Moynihan's without my mother getting mad.

I start to untie the laces on one of his boots.

Lilac is looking away from me.

"You want help?" she asks.

"I'm okay. Lilac, you go, okay. I have to stay here right now. I have to watch out."

"Are you crazy? I'm not doing this without you!" She's whisper-yelling.

I look up, pulling the first boot over his ankle.

"I know. I'm sorry, okay?"

I feel her staring at me sweetly. She waits until I look at her so she can smile.

Her eyes are clear. She nods, in a gentle way that lets me know she gets it.

"It's okay, Mal. It's all ready now. It was just a dry run. Another time. Another time we will go."

Chapter 12

Fuzzy Trees & Complex Relationships

Year: 1986, Mal—12 years old

The air is heavy, almost suffocating under the porches at Clark University. Lilac pinches the joint she rolled out of the bit of weed we stole from Wally and Marie's stash. I take it cautiously between my thumb and my pointer finger. I pull it to my lips and purse them, taking a slow "drag," careful not to "lip" it and get it all soggy. I take just enough so I don't cough. Then I close my mouth quickly and raise my chest like I am inhaling more, and hand the joint back to Lilac.

She takes it without trying, pulls it to her mouth, and smiles.

She obviously knows what she's doing.

I'm still not sure if I do.

It's like every time we smoke her parent's pot, I don't feel anything very different.

I worry I am doing it wrong.

Or maybe I am just immune to it, because the truth is I don't really want to be stoned, to have the world shift underneath me and my mouth gab without me while I just try to hold on. I don't want to wind up like my dad, passed out naked on the chair with one shoe on, farting while he's sleeping, while us kids run past him and pretend it isn't a thing. I don't want to lose control of my motor functions, thank you very much.

"So, how's Manuel?" she asks, passing me the pot.

I take the pot rolled up cigarette from her, pretend to take a toke, hand it back, wait a few seconds, and blow what I think is an acceptable amount of smoke.

Manuel Martinez is my boyfriend. We're both in the sixth grade. I really like him. He is so cute with his Puerto Rican accent, freckles all over his cheeks, and hair that falls into his eyes. I like the shy way that he smiles, and his plump upper lip that he sometimes uses to kiss me.

"Good," I say.

"Good" she says, then pokes me in the ribs. "Just good?'

"What do you mean?"

"Well, what base have you guys made it to?"

"Almost second."

"Almost?" Lilac's furrowed brow is doing all of the talking.

"Yeah, I mean over the shirt."

"Okay. That's good," Lilac says, her brow relaxing now.

I nod, unsure what she means.

"I mean, I'm not sure I really want to. It's not like I have a handful or anything."

"Oh, that doesn't matter."

"It doesn't?"

"Yeah. They don't care. They just want to be able to say that they touched it."

"Oh."

The grass in front of us is green and perfect, like a carpet they rolled out on the ground. There are some kind of yellow flower bushes that have just started to bloom. A few students are walking by; we can see up to their hips.

"But I might break up with him anyway. It's getting too complex."

I like the way the word complex sounds when it comes out of my mouth. It's a grown-up word. Sophisticated-like. It's fun to talk about a boy that way.

"What you mean? With Carmen Gonzalez?"

Just Lilac mentioning the name makes me feel nauseous. Carmen is a big girl, at least a head taller than me, with broad shoulders. Actually, it's the way she carries herself that feels imposing. Her thick, black, shoulder-length hair and the neatly ironed blouses all the Puerto Rican kids seem to wear make her look bigger to me somehow, as if the clothes show all her outlines.

Carmen has a big-time crush on Manuel. She keeps threatening to kick my ass.

"It's spent," Lilac says and grinds the rest of the joint out on the ground.

"Maybe I mean he's not worth that kind of aggravation. I'm a lover, not a fighter. He's just a boy."

"He's cute."

"That's true."

"But Mal. You know this isn't about Manuel."

"Come again," I say.

"It's not really. It's about Carmen. You are going to have to fight her anyhow, Mal, you know that, don't you?"

"Not really. Not if I choose not to."

"That's not true," Lilac insists.

"Huh?"

"It's like—have you ever been to Whalom Park?"

"Um, no?"

"Well, like, there are rides there. And before you get to ride the ride, you have to meet a certain height requirement. They have the signs right in front of the rides, with a big ruler—you know, with the notches like moms make for how tall you got on the kitchen wall. Well, you're tall enough now, so you're ready to ride."

I start laughing hysterically.

"You are stoned, Lilac! You don't make any kind of sense."

I swallow hard. Am I imagining the trees look a little fuzzy and the yellow flowers have an extra layer of softness to them, like cotton?

"I am, yeah," she says and laughs. I laugh too, for so long the tears start flooding my eyes. I haven't had the nerve to talk about Carmen to anyone, even Lilac.

"Okay, let me put this in simple terms. If you don't fight Carmen for Manuel, she's going to think you are weak. And if you think she is making your life hell now, you just wait. And it's not just going to be her. It's going to be all those bitches she hangs out with, and any other girl who's mad for no good reason whatsoever. You're going to make yourself a target. Like Eddy."

For a second, we are both silent.

Eddy Chappy is someone I feel totally bad for. He's a scrawny kid in our school who regularly gets picked on by some of the bigger guys, especially Mark Jenkins. Mark built some kind of torture ball that looked like it came straight out of *Friday the 13th* or *Nightmare on Elm Street* or something.

It was one of those regular pink rubber balls, except it wasn't. Mark stuck pins all over the outside of it, just for Eddy Chappy. He showed it around the school and told everyone what he was going to do with it.

Then one day when Mark had gathered everyone and was giving Eddy a beating, he wailed on his forehead with this torture ball device. I wasn't there and there are so many different versions of the story, but I do know in addition to Eddy getting his ass whipped publicly, there was blood spurting out of his forehead like a fountain. It's sad because I did see him with a bandage, and he still has scars all over. It's one thing to take a public beating, but to have to live with the evidence of it all the time seems like even more torture than the beating itself.

"I'm not like Eddy, Lilac. I'm not him. I'm not doing anything wrong."

"True. But that doesn't matter because Carmen has decided you are."

"She's wrong."

"So, show her that. You don't fight her soon, you are going to make yourself a target, not to mention you will lose Manuel for no good reason. I've been thinking about it a lot."

"Maybe you are right."

"I am."

"But that sucks."

She taps me on the leg sympathetically.

"You're right. It sucks big time."

PART **5**

Losing Dad

HOUSE WREN HIT LIST: Robins, sparrows, chickadees, bobolinks, blue-birds, warblers, nuthatches, woodpeckers, finches, swallows.

METHODOLOGY: Spearing baby eggs with sharp beak. Knocking baby eggs from the nest. Swoop carrying baby eggs in the nest—flying—dropping it from the sky, snapping fledgling necks. Building double and triple-deckers over the nest.

NICKNAMES BY OTHER BIRDS: Dictator, sociopath, homewrecker, maniac, lunatic fringe.

NICKNAME BY THE WRENS: King of the Birds.

ARCH ENEMIES: Eagles, pygmy owls, hawks, falcons, turkey vultures.

INVISIBLE SHIELD: Protected under the Migratory Bird Act.

Chapter 13

Spaghetti With a Side of Divorce Papers

Year: 1986, Mal—12 years old;
Davey—11 years old

It's an absurdly ordinary night on Hollywood Street. My brother, my father, and I are sitting in the living room while my mother breaks spaghetti noodles into a tiny pot of boiling water. There's laundry on the floor around the table, but she's washed the dishes in her methodical way. Each towel-dried bowl, plate, and glass is neatly stacked, with the cup handles and lines on the plates all facing the exact same way.

My mother is a complicated person that way. There could be dirty dishes on the floor, but she's very careful and excessively neat with her handwriting, organizing things, and even will on occasion iron sheets!

My father is sitting on the chair, nursing a beer and staring blankly at a baseball game that doesn't involve the Red Sox. He's neglected to put on anything but his tighty-whities. Maybe he's distracted by my mother's newfound domesticity, the nice way she brushed her hair, or the way she wiggles as she cooks.

There's a knock at the door, a loud persistent rap. Everyone in the family freezes. The only people who knock are neighbors angry about a noise problem or the landlords coming to collect the rent. My father gets up slowly and looks at my mother. She doesn't turn around. Do I imagine that she is humming?

"Could you get it? I'm cooking," my mother says.

Neither my brother nor I move. Slowly, my father goes to the door, bare footed and bare chested, his knobby knees accentuating his already slightly bowlegged walk.

He peeks through the keyhole and freezes there for a second, just staring.

"What the hell?" he says.

He turns to us kids, squinting his eyes and shaking his head as if considering something.

Then slowly, he walks to the side of the door, undoes the chain, and opens it so that only his chest is exposed.

"What can I do for you, Officer?"

"Sir, can we come in?" a man who speaks extra loudly to cover up the fact that he's probably afraid says. My father steps away from behind the door and opens it. He moves back while the men pass in front of him, then shuts it.

My mind is slow to understand what is happening. I don't yet recognize the blue uniforms of the police officers who step farther into the living room. One scans the room nodding at us, then at my mother in the kitchen with one hand dangerously close to his gun.

"David Andrew Wrenn, Sr.?"

My father nods. I don't know if I've ever heard his full name.

"I have some papers here for you," he says. My father takes them but doesn't look down. Although my father is always the one to sign my report cards, he isn't comfortable around paperwork. He distrusts it.

"What is this?"

My mother half-turns from away from the stove, not fully committed to looking directly at my father. "They're divorce papers, David. I told you, you have to leave. I was serious this time."

"Sir, I have an order of protection here. I'm going to have to ask you to get dressed and leave the house," the officer says, pointing toward the door as he gives my father the up and down.

My father stands there in his underwear, looking around the room like a trapped bird with nowhere to fly. My stomach drops. This is really strange. I haven't heard them fighting for weeks.

I look at the way my mother stands in the kitchen, sweat from the steamy pot flushing her skin, a slightly vengeful half smile on her face. I hate her at that moment.

At the same time, kind of, on some level, I get it. What took her so long?

She may hide away in the bathroom smoking pot, but he drinks away all of our money—when he does have a job, that is. A lot of the reasons we keep getting in trouble are because of him.

But I don't want him to go.

"What the hell is this, Cheryl?" my father screams.

My mother turns back to the pot and continues to pretend to cook.

"No, right now you've got to get some pants and shoes on, throw some clothes in a bag, and you're coming with us. You've got to go," the loud police officer says.

My dad's face is crushed.

"It's a mistake ... tell them it's a mistake, honey...."

My mother doesn't turn around. Her shoulders shrink downward.

"Please don't make this difficult. Just get your things together and leave the premises. I will give you three minutes," the officer says.

To my surprise my father doesn't fight, just puts his hands up in the air like he's surrendered, then snaps them as he goes out of the room to get his stuff. I've never known my dad to back down from a fight.

At that moment, I know how we look to the cop—my half-naked father who had a reputation for drinking and fighting and can barely manage to answer the cop in complete sentences, us kids sitting alone on the couch. I feel so sorry for my dad.

The minutes when my dad is in the bedroom stretch like gum. Nobody speaks. Davey nestles up closer to me, and I keep my hand on his back. In the back room, my father bangs objects around.

A few minutes later he comes back in the room fully dressed in jeans and a t-shirt, hauling a thirty-gallon trash bag full of his stuff. I wonder where he found the trash bag, and how he's gotten packed so quickly. He looks so tiny to me.

He stands in the living room for a second, dumbfounded. He speaks my mother's name. She looks at him but doesn't say anything.

He turns toward us kids. He looks me in the eye, a sad smirk on his face, unsure what to do. He just looks so dejected. I want to run over to him, to tell him how sorry I am, to beg him not to go.

But he just turns and slowly opens the door and walks out.

There's nothing either of us can do.

Chapter

14

Sucker-Punched at Pennywise Market

Year: 1986, Mal—12 years old

For weeks, I just wait. I wait, knowing it is going to happen. Some nights I can't sleep. I wake up in bed in a dry sweat, then pray to God. Sometimes I pray that Carmen Gonzelez lost interest in fighting me. Other nights I pray that God will help me kick Carmen's ass. I really hope I've inherited my father's Irish boxer's spirit, his ability to fake out his enemies by wearing them out and then, when they least expect it, planting them with an unexpected right hook.

I practice punching, with my thumb folded outside my fist so I don't hurt it just like he showed me. I watch WWF, imagine myself doing Rowdy Roddy Piper pile drivers by taking a running dive from the sidewalk, pulling Carmen's hair back so tight she looks like a rag doll, and kicking her in the face.

The thought of the fighting happening hurts me, deep inside. I don't want to kick anyone in the face, I don't want to hurt her. I don't want her to hurt me either.

It's more than that though. I don't really care about my body. It's okay if she breaks it. But it's going to be a spectator sport. It's bad enough to have a teacher yell at me to speak louder in class, but to have everyone gather around cheering as Carmen beats the hell out of me, it's not a humiliation I can survive.

Three mornings in a row before school I get sick in the toilet before I go to school. When I look at the puke before flushing, I swear it's red.

Lilac is right, though. I can't keep avoiding her. It would be suicide to run away.

Maybe there is some long-lost heavyweight ancestor that is looking out for me, because after we have arranged the day and I'm standing in the lot outside the Pennywise Market, I no longer have any fear. My body feels cushiony, warm. I'm almost excited, tasting blood and rust in my mouth, like after my dad tied string around one of my baby teeth and attached it to the doorknob to pull it out.

I am wearing my mother's pale-yellow blouse, not for luck, but because it was the only thing remotely clean in the pile. It has buttons down the front. I didn't know we'd be fighting today. The shirt is kind of silky and soft. It was a mistake.

"*Fight, fight, fight! Kick her ass, Carmen,*" people are screaming as loud as they can. Behind them a car rolls down the street.

"Trash! White trash!" Carmen yells. Her face twisting up into something real ugly.

"Spick!" I hear someone yell in my defense.

My breath is shallow in my chest, hissing, like someone has unscrewed the cap on the tire. Carmen's wavy brown hair is shiny, like it had just been shampooed, and I realize I have an advantage. If I can't punch her, I'll try and grab hold of that hair and pull it, use it to pull her down. I imagine it both ways, if I grab it and it makes a good hook—or if it slips away from my hands.

I don't know what I am waiting for, somebody to ring a friggin' bell.

Before I know what's happening, Carmen has pretty much squashed herself into me, and we're grabbing each other's faces and hair. Then we're on the ground and rolling around. Fighting is strange—it's faster than it looks when you're watching it happen to somebody else. It's so fast I can't process what is happening. I get in a kick to her legs, even a punch, but then she's cupped my chin and has my head backwards so tight I am afraid she'll break my neck. My throat feels boned out, upside down, and I'm going to choke.

I want to tell her that she's doing it wrong, that she has me backward and upside down.

She pushes me, and my spine scrapes the black gravel lot. Before I know what's happening, she's gotten my shirt off. Half my shirt is up over my head and I'm naked here. I hear the kids screeching behind me.

And that does it. I get pissed. With one hand, I pull my shirt down. With the other I slam her forehead hard with the palm of my hand. The move surprises us both but before I know what has happened, we're standing back up. We're standing and the kids are screaming behind us, their voices loud and scattered and then clogged in my ears like strong wind. I'm dizzy and inside me something is screaming. I'm staring at my shirt, trying to make sure it's down.

And then it happens. Carmen decks me, hard—she sucker-punches me straight in the nose. Blood spurts and the pain spikes up my face and spreads into my forehead. My eyes water. I start to cough.

Woah! it sounds like the crowd is saying.

She comes up closer it seems, challenging my very breath, my personal space. A smile is twisting the edges of her mouth. She slaps me hard across the face. Then she's moving backward.

My head is waving on my neck, my shoulders slumped. I'm gazing down. Three of the buttons have popped off my mom's shirt and it's practically wide open. There is blood all over the shirt. It surprises me. How did the blood get there so quickly? My mother is going to have a fit.

I know I should close my shirt better, but my hand is a dead thing at my side. I focus my whole self on staying balanced. The parking lot is spinning slowly. I will not fall.

Wind pounds in my eardrums, undercut by something that screeches.

Then everything is quiet.

In the distance, I see Carmen, studying me as if I am an animal and waiting to see what I'll do. Then her face registers what has happened. She's made a decision. It's over. She's won.

I look behind Carmen. The kids are still gathered in a half circle, and behind them it looks like some tall adults are watching. The expressions on their faces are missing. They look empty.

The crowd all starts going their separate ways, like how ants scatter in their disorganized way when they're looking for a safe place. Too tired to even be embarrassed, I make my way back to the apartment on Hollywood Street. My top priority now is cleaning myself up and getting rid of this shirt before my mother finds out I've destroyed it.

While examining my swollen lip in the bathroom mirror, I unbutton the two remaining buttons and quickly bury the shirt at the bottom of the laundry pile on the kitchen floor. It's a pretty safe bet it won't ever be found down there.

Chapter

Trash Talking & Trash Collecting

Year: 1986, Mal—12 years old

$\mathbf{M}$y dad and I are walking around the edges of Clark University, which is an oddly misplaced and well-kept feature on the edge of our neighborhood, with its giant oak and maple trees that drop their jewel-toned foliage on the perfectly manicured lawns every fall. We're holding a giant trash bag and collecting cans.

"I was just thinking. There should be different pay scales. I mean if you find a two-liter, it should be worth more than that five cents you get for a can of Tab," I say.

My father chuckles but keeps walking, shuffling his feet in the dried leaves on the ground. We push toward the edge of the woods.

"Not the way it wahks," he says

"I know. I was just thinking. And I mean, don't you think there are better spots? Sure, I know we found all those cans near that old bonfire, but that was a fluke. The good cans have to be more toward the courtyard, near the cafeteria and stuff."

"We aaah fine heah. Let's stick to the plan."

I examine my father, with his dark red hair, the way he occasionally pulls the arms of his ratty T-shirt to keep the sweat from staining, the bow-legged way that he walks. He suddenly looks tiny to me, like he isn't in his right place on this fancy campus.

He seemed so much bigger to me when he was still living at home.

He doesn't act like himself either. On this campus, he is cautious, polite. He even speaks softly, coming close to my ear to show me a can or a bottle I should pick up. I know why. He doesn't want anyone to hear his voice or his accent.

I know what it is. My dad has this weird thing about school. He resents the kind of people who can afford to go to college, or even stayed in high school. He talks trash about them when they are out of earshot.

Privately though, he's shy around people like that. Although he doesn't mind having a fist fight on the lawn in front of his neighbors having a bar-beque, or crying into his beer at the bar, he also has a lot of pride. He doesn't like to be shown up.

He also respects some of the rules. Although my mother has the special handwriting everyone loves, he's always the one to sign our report cards. Once when he caught Lilac and me skipping school, he walked us back there and tattled on us to the principal, which got us in detention for a week.

Any other day, he's overly proud and confident, even cocky—like he's always got something to prove. But today, I know he's embarrassed to be here, picking up cans for money. I stick close to him, avoiding the court-yards and fields where all the students might see us.

"We did pretty good. Soon we'll probably have more than we can carry. Why don't we cut uh losses and tuhn em in?" I say.

My dad looks up toward the sky, then at the grass, and picks up another can. He puts it into the bag. Then he nods, as if my idea is brilliant, slings the bag over his shoulders, and we head back to Main Street.

My dad and I sit in the parking lot in front of Pennywise and the liquor store where we turned in the bottles and cans. In the store he gave me my cut—two dollars and thirty-five cents, most of which the store gave me in change.

"We did pretty good, huh," I say.

"Awright," he says.

"What you going to buy with yahs?" I ask.

"A cah," he says, then cracks up royally at his own joke.

He's already more relaxed. I crack up too.

"What are you going to buy, Mal?"

I shrug my shoulders. I already know the money is going straight in my piggy bank.

"Come on, maybe a diamond ring? A bracelet?"

I shake my head.

"An elephant?" he teases.

I bust out laughing.

"What am I, six?" I say.

He starts to chuckle but then he looks confused, as if he isn't sure how serious I am. I try to smile to reassure him, but my face is too tired to do that.

I'm mad at myself for saying that. I didn't mean to hurt his feelings.

For a while we don't speak. I can see by his pale skin, by the way he is grinding his hand in his fist and looking around, that he's ready for another drink.

"I got in a fight. With a girl at school," I say.

He smirks in that toothless way that he has, looks at me like we are co-conspirators. My face heats up but it doesn't matter. My dad knows I don't like people making fun of me when my cheeks turn red.

"In this parking lot, actually," I say.

He kind of fake-punches my arm.

"What girl? Who's her dad?"

I shake my head.

"It doesn't matter."

He looks hurt.

"I mean you wouldn't know him. He's. She's Puerto Rican."

"God damn spick!" he says.

I keep my trahp shut. My dad would kill me if he knew about Manuel.

"Did yah at least win? Did you kick her ass?"

"I held my own. I did awright," I say.

He reaches over and does the thing where he fake punches my arm again. Then he looks toward the edge of the parking lot, half smiling, like someone is telling him a good story.

I think about the yellow shirt, how I buried it at the bottom of the laundry heap. My lip was still a little swollen when my mom came back, but if she noticed she didn't say anything. It was a kid's fight, so there was a slim chance word didn't get around, and if it did it didn't spread as far as my father's rooming house on the very edge of Main South.

"The place you are staying now. That hawse? It's okay?"

My dad flicks at his hair with his hands, without really touching it. His eyes are squinty, maybe because it's daylight. The tips of his fingers are hard and yellow.

"Room's okay. Warm. Too many rules," he says.

I wanted to go to visit my dad in the house that Mom says he shares with a bunch of skeevy old men, but he decided it was better to meet me here. At least this way we could do something productive, so he could buy him some smokes or a 40-ounce before his checks come.

I can tell he's getting agitated. It won't be long before he has to go back.

"Are you going to come visit again soon?" I ask.

"Sure."

"Davey wants to see you, too," I say.

His eyes get happy and he smiles, privately, just for a second.

"Yeah, I'll come back," he says.

PART 6

Losing Mal

Flying the Coop

Male wrens aren't expected to stick around for too long. Like my dad, they fly the coop. Sometimes the male will start his singing escapades from treetops while the female is still incubating the eggs. Often, they slip away into nearby areas inhabited by other male wrens and try to make love to that man's lady wren. They do this in a sneaky, clumsy way, flying close to the earth from shrub to shrub so their adversary doesn't notice them. Once they mate with the female, they can claim them. They offer significantly less protection and support to their second family, though, and the babies often die from starvation.

The wonky male wren's reasons for doing this may be less biological than boredom. It's possible their habit of risky behavior is fueled by their transience. All house wrens migrate south over the winter, but less than half of them survive the winter.

I don't know if my father had other families, but I do know he stuck close to his territory. Though we didn't hear from him often, the boarding houses he drifted in and out of were all in Main South, most of them less than ten blocks away. When he showed up occasionally to take us to McDonald's or to the park, he was no more close or distant. We weren't any more emotionally attached. His shrug-shouldered absence was how it had always been.

It may have been this common acceptance of the transient father that caused me to be more forgiving of my father's transgressions than my mother's; more forgiving of what he had allowed to happen to us. It was more than just forgiveness, though. It was almost as if there had never been any blame. I didn't blame my father, maybe because he was a man and had never physically harmed me. More than that, I hadn't ever really looked toward him to protect us.

Chapter

16

The Limousine & Dorito Dust

Year: 1986, Mal—12 years old

We almost never had a car, either because we couldn't afford it or because of all the times my dad ended up in a paddy wagon. But once we did have a beater car, an old brown car, maybe a Plymouth, and he taught me how to help him to fix it on the street.

My job was mostly to sit in the driver's seat, then reach all the way down with my foot to hit the gas and turn the key until the engine turned over. He also let me come to the front of the car when he popped the hood. He showed me all the parts then: the dipstick, the sparkplugs. Once we got underneath and he showed me the other parts: the engine, the axle. He showed me how every little part mattered, and the way that if one was broken, it disrupted all the others.

I can see now that in our family, our dad was one of those parts, like a rusty axle that keeps the wheel stirring until the day when it finally snaps. Without him, everything is messed up, especially my mother, who is lost, spinning out of control.

I've been thinking about cars a lot because my mother's new boyfriend, Jamie, who she sometimes calls Harold, owns a limousine. He even runs his own limousine company. Don't get me wrong, I'm not complaining. In some ways, it's cool because we don't have to beg for rides anymore. We can go out whenever we want, cruising around Main South in style.

For a family for whom getting a big yellow taxi and taking a trip to the grocery store is a big occasion, the limo is ridiculously fun.

Jamie has let me sit in the front this time. He's cranked some cheesy Barry Manilow and is driving around and around in Main South in circles, allowing us to show off our sudden and false burst of prosperity to the neighbors before we head to his house.

I'm twelve years old. I'm wearing shorts and a tank top, aware of my knees and ankles protruding. I am still flat-chested and have boy hips. My mother's girlfriends always tell me I'm a skinny mini, that they're jealous of me because I can eat whatever I want and not gain an ounce.

I look at my bare knee, which is smudged from something like dirt I didn't notice before. I keep my denim shorts and legs raised slightly to keep from sweating on the clean black leather seats. Jamie is the opposite of every clutterbug that we know. He's squeaky clean and wears new clothes, actual outfits, clothes that look like they go together.

We coast past Main South down toward the highway, headed outside of town to Jamie's house. We might stay there for the night, so I threw a change of clothes in a backpack and convinced my mom to take my hamsters along too. There is a nasty smell coming from the back seat, something like gloppy burning tar. My mom and her new friend, Dawn, are laughing in that low, hissing way that they do, which mixes with the wind whipping though the open window. Dawn's a lot younger than my mom, only nineteen years old, but they spend a lot of time together since Dad left.

I can see myself through the rearview mirror. I'm wearing a yellow tank top Lilac lent me. It's old, but feels new. I can see the new breast buds that are just starting to poke out of my body. I wish I could unsee them.

I snap out of it and look farther back in the rearview mirror and see them. My mother and Dawn in the back seat are sneaking shots of liquor from the individual, fancy crystal bottles in the bar. The hamster cage is on the floor at their feet. We're having a feast: hot dogs and hamburgers and chips and Twinkies.

Something is different about my mom, though. I know she's having a good time, but I'm not gonna lie. I'm a bit worried about her. There's something so, like, I don't know, *intense* about her. She's doing different drugs. She used to drink an occasional White Russian, smoked pot and maybe some hash, but it's different now. Something is angrier about the drugs she's using now.

Of course, I know I should be happy, because Jamie likes me and so she lets me hang out with him and her new friends. He's rich, and my mom says that's important. But there's something weird about the way they treat me, at all the silence that puffs up around me when I answer a question. They laugh at me sometimes, quietly, under their breath.

My legs are pressed together up against the cold air conditioner. I already scarfed down a small bag of Doritos and am licking the fake cheese from my fingers.

"You need to watch those thighs," Jamie says. He looks at me the way adults sometimes do when they want to warn you of something serious. My breath catches. I wipe the Dorito dust from my mouth.

"If you're not careful, you'll have fat thighs," Jamie says.

Everyone in the car seems to shut up at the same time.

I keep waiting for them to laugh.

Chapter

The Cabbage Patch Doll
& A Douche

Year: 1986, Mal—12 years old

Jamie's house is in Rutland, Massachusetts, two towns to the northwest of Worcester. It's a two-story white ranch house with black shutters, on a hill way back from the road. A long driveway leads to a garage in the back yard where the limo gets parked.

Dawn stayed for just a few minutes, which seemed weird seeing that it was such a long drive to get here. After her boyfriend picks her up, Jamie takes us to a room he calls a sunken den. You walk downstairs to get to it. The carpet is shaggy, like a pet. There's a fireplace, and a table that's made only of glass and other furniture he says is called "Fore-My-Kah." Everything is so clean and orderly. There's no dust. It's almost like nobody who lives here ever touches anything.

On my lap I hold a Cabbage Patch doll. I don't usually like dolls, but this one is different. It's a collector's item. Only the richest kids in school have them. It's one of those things I never would admit to liking.

I like the doll, though, even though she doesn't have any hair. The way her knees are stitched together makes them look chubby. She has her own birth certificate inscribed with her name, Heidi, and Xavier Roberts, the doll designer's name, stitched on the butt.

"Thank you for the doll," I say. It's the second time I have said it, but Jamie and my mom aren't paying any kind of attention.

My mom and Jamie are sitting on what is called a love seat in front of a fireplace. It lights up his bushy gray hair. I like to watch the way the fire jumps behind their backs, the way the wood hisses and sings. Jamie says that's because it is damp.

I look at my mom next to Jamie. He's forty-seven, only ten years older than her, but it looks like a lot more than that. Maybe it's because he's so big and my mother, who is pudgy but short, looks like a child around him. Or maybe it's his gray, frizzled hair, or the strange pinched pockets around his eyes. He has a drink, of course, something brown in a fancy glass on a piece of stone called a *coahstah* he put on the table.

They're touching each other, Jamie running his fingers on the back of my mother's arm. She laughs in an odd pitch. Her eyes are lit up at the attention. She's giddy.

"My back still hurts," I say, louder than I spoke about the doll.

Jamie whispers something in my mother's ear.

"Jamie will give you something for that. He knows how to fix it."

"Yeah. Just go wait in the bathroom, honey. I'll be right there."

I leave the doll on the couch and walk through the kitchen, then into the bathroom. It is a nice bathroom, the size of a bedroom. There is a full-sized sink flush against the left-hand wall, a huge clawfoot tub on the right, and the toilet in the middle.

I avoid looking at the mirror, then sit down on the lidded toilet, pressing my bare feet into cold tile.

It smells like chemicals in here, like the school hallway, and a little like lemons.

I wonder if it was a mistake to leave the doll in the sunken den.

The bathroom is cold compared to the living room.

I sit a long time, until the goosebumps push my arm hairs up. I wonder if I heard them wrong, if there's something else I am supposed to be doing.

Eventually I work up the nerve to stand up and go ask them. I walk slowly from the bathroom to the top of the sunken living room.

Then I look down. My breath catches. I shouldn't be in here.

My mother is sitting on the loveseat with her shirt and bra off. Jamie stands in front of her on the floor, bent over and running his clammy hands all over her naked breasts. They bounce as he touches them. Her face is tilted back slightly. There's a weird, childlike smirk on her face.

I want to puke.

I back up slowly, careful not to accidentally stub my toe on the edge of the stairs.

I run back into the bathroom.

I sit on the toilet lid. I wait just like they told me to do. I remember what I just saw, my mom's breasts bouncing in Jamie's cold hands. The picture won't go away. It makes me want to run away.

I concentrate on other things. I count the stripes on the wall. There are twelve on the front wall, and forty-seven on the side. I try to add them up. Twelve plus forty-seven is fifty-nine. There are fifty-nine lines on the wall.

I stand up and press every toe into the cold tile, then sit back down on the toilet.

Being in the bathroom makes me want to pee.

I don't want Jamie to come to the door and hear me peeing.

I don't even know if it's okay to close the door.

They told me to wait.

Jamie has something that will help your back. Go to the bathroom and wait.

I wait and hear tree leaves shaking, the wind howling.

I don't move.

Let's just go home, Mom, I think about telling her. *Let's just, like, leave.*

I wonder if the doll is still propped against the back of the couch like I left her. Is she falling over?

I think about showing her to Lilac.

I really wish I'd taken her in with me.

Jamie knocks on the outside of the door.

I jump. I think to get up.

"Hi Marilyn," he says as he walks in.

His face is flushed. There is something wrong with his smile. It reminds me of the expression on the doll.

He turns and is over at the sink. He bends over and opens a bottom drawer, reaching far into the back.

He pulls out something. It is a long, white rectangular box. There is a picture of a lady on it, her body in profile. She has long brown hair and is wearing a nightgown. There are flowers on it too.

He opens the box on the sink and then walks over to me.

In his hand he holds a long bottle. It looks a little like the spongy thing my mom puts water in and uses to wet the stamps for the Publishers Clear-inghouse Sweepstakes, or for getting all the music tapes for a penny. Only it is longer, much longer and the spongy thing is pointier.

I turn and read the letters on the box.

Masengill

Disposable Douche

Extra mild

None of the words make any sense to me.

"Stand up, Marilyn."

I do what he says.

My knees buckle a little. I worry because I still have to pee.

"This is going to help your back feel better, okay?" he asks. His voice seems weird to me now, trilly.

I nod but I don't know what he means.

I am more shocked than anything else when he unbuttons my pants and pulls them and my underwear down. I want to pull them back up but my body is frozen. I feel only the cold tile on my feet, my overgrown bangs that have fallen over my eyes.

"Now this is what we're going to do. We're going to flush you out so you'll feel better," he says.

His voice is soothing now, the way you might talk to a puppy.

He takes the eraser thing from behind his back. Before I know what is happening, he has shoved it inside me, hard, so my legs almost break. It hurts. Cool liquid explodes inside me. I wonder if I have peed myself.

Then he is done.

I try not to move or look at him.

Jamie is just standing there, rubbing his gray mustache with his fin-ger, staring at me, the doll smile back on his face.

My mother is still in the next room.

I return to the room. My face is hot. I can tell it's red, and I smell funny. My mother is still on the loveseat, in the same spot, only her shirt is back on again. The Cabbage Patch doll is still here. Behind them on the dresser on top of newspaper is my hamster cage with its wood shavings, water bottle, and yellow wheel.

There are two of them in there. Charlie and Lucky, the blind one.

Is it possible nothing has changed?

My mother's face has no expression. She looks at her nails, not at me.

I am standing behind the couch, holding the side of the couch with my two hands. I pulled my clothes back on quickly after Jamie left. Then I wasn't sure they were on perfect, but didn't feel like it was right to fix them. I keep my hand far from them, still, even though I feel like they might be wet.

The bottom half of my body is covered by the couch though.

"Hello ladies," Jamie says. I feel him but don't see him behind me, then he walks past me and the living room and uses the steps to climb up and down into the kitchen.

My mother isn't looking up. She's sitting there, her body all doughy on the loveseat. For a split second I imagine myself going over there and sitting near her.

Let's just go home. Let's leave here, I imagine myself telling her.

But there's something about the way she just sits there, as if nothing has happened.

I push my hands into the couch. My legs are still shaking. My breath is so ragged, in and out.

The longer I stare at my mother, the farther away the couch seems to be.

It's like it has moved when I wasn't looking, like the room is sunk underwater.

I am on one couch. My mom and Jamie are still on the loveseat, my mom lying with half her face and ear smushed in his lap and turned toward the television.

It's on, but the sound is so low I can't hear any of the movie that's playing on there.

The movie has Danny DeVito's wife in it, the small one with the mouth on her that's in the show Cheers. Everyone likes to watch Cheers in Worcester, because the real bar is somewhere in our same state.

Danny DeVito's wife is different in this one. She's wearing a dress with flowers on it. She isn't a wiseass and doesn't crack jokes.

I look toward the door. I'd like to leave here, or at least go outside to sit under the trees in the cold and stare out at the road. I don't like being stuck on this couch with my mother lying in Jamie's lap. I can't stop remembering her pale skin, the way that it looked with her shirt off, that twisted smile on her face.

I don't know why she brought me here with her.

I'm only on the couch because there's nowhere to go.

They haven't told me where I'm supposed to be staying.

"Mom, I'm tired. Are we going home soon?"

My mother acts as if she hasn't heard me. She taps Jamie on the foot as if he is supposed to answer.

"Marilyn. You can sleep here for now," Jamie says without looking at me.

I don't like anyone calling me Marilyn.

Maybe Jamie doesn't know that.

I wait for my mom to say something, but she doesn't.

"I think it would be better for your back if you sleep in my bed, Marilyn. It's the second door on the left. We will be out here for a while."

Chapter 18

A Scary Place & A Safe Place

Year: 1986, Mal—12 years old

Jamie's bed is so high up I had to jump to get onto it, and it's made of heavy wood with another wood headboard that makes me feel so small laying here in the dark, like some kind of dwarf character in a fairytale story that winds up getting taken out by lion or storm.

I can't think. I'm hollow, like the gourds my teacher brought into school. My waist is sewn to the mattress with thread. The air is thin. I keep my lips slightly parted, my head tilted up. I can barely breathe.

My mother is gone. I heard someone pull up in the driveway, heard her leave, the door slamming behind her. I guess she will be back some time later.

"That's good, Marilyn. This is part of the treatment. It will make you feel better."

I'm lying on my side. Jamie's lying behind me, rubbing my back. His hand raises tiny pinpricks over my spine.

The gentler he is, the worse that it hurts.

Please don't touch me, I try. My words are a whisper, a hiss.

He touches my hair, rakes it away from my scalp.

He kisses my neck. My hips clench. I still have to pee.

I stare at the outlines of the dresser, the lamp, the television set.

Everything is oversized in here. Sturdy. Expensive. It's how Jamie tries to be.

His hand reaches around my shoulder, pushes me down on my back.

Please leave me alone, I hiss.

I cannot breathe.

His mouth comes down on mine—his mustache, his breath smothering me.

His hands unbutton my jeans.

I do not move. I cannot move.

Mom, I screech inside. *Where the hell is Mom?*

He takes off my clothes.

A pain shoots through me and gets stuck in my head. It's like a jolt of electricity.

What are you doing, I want to say, but can't.

For a second I feel it, his stomach on mine, his hand on my leg.

His nasty breath hits my face. Somehow he is on me, he is squishing my body; first his fingers are inside me, then the rest of him. He's inside me and the pain sears, and he's stuck on me. Just stuck there. I still can't breathe.

He starts to move on top of me. Something inside of me screams, screams so loud—no words, just a sound nobody can hear that pierces my bones. I scream and scream, and then I split open. I split open in the middle and I am gone.

I am sitting somewhere. Some part of me is left on the bed, but I'm in another place. I'm on the ground. Beneath me are soft brown needles. Surrounding me is deep snow. It's cool, but the cold is sweet. It doesn't hurt. The snow is comfortable—it surrounds me, silencing pain, blanketing everything.

Beside me there's a presence. It's big and old. It's protective. I tilt my head up and can see it: a thick trunk giving way to thick branches, thousands of lacy green leaves. It smells sweet and good here. The air is so clean.

Someone whispers beside me. Before I turn toward her I already know it's Lilac. She's sitting on the ground with her funny haircut. Behind her is our camping gear.

Lilac doesn't say anything. She just looks at me. She's calm and strong; she is the fairy that knows the true source of her power.

Lilac looks at me the way that she always has, like no one in my family ever has.

She knows who I am.
She doesn't believe there's anything wrong with who I am. I'm okay.
I push my palm into the needles. I take a long, slow breath of the air.
I trust her. She lies with me. Waiting. This place is timeless.
I know that she understands.

Chapter 19

School Busses & A Limo

Year: 1986, Mal—12 years old

Jamie isn't driving the limo today. He has a driver instead. The driver pulls up right in front of Rutland Middle School, as if it didn't occur to anyone how embarrassing it is to be seen in a limo. Jamie made a call to register me as a new student. I don't know how long I'll be staying at Jamie's house, but I guess this way I won't miss too much school. I get out of the back of the car, hoist my backpack up over my shoulder, and start walking. My knees shake and my legs are all noodley. I imagine myself tripping before I even reach the steps.

"We'll pick you up right after school here, Marilyn," Jamie screams out of the rolled-down window in the back seat. Kids are making their way from their busses into the school building.

I turn around and nod slightly, hoping he'll go away and won't make me speak. My shoulders and spine are still clenched as if they have been sewn together with twine and pulled backward. I walk up the concrete path, up one step, then another, then another until I'm by the gray metal door.

Another girl opens it and holds it for me. I walk through.

The door closes behind us. I hope the limo has pulled away too.

The hallway is long and less hectic than my school hallway in Worcester. It's a bigger school but there are fewer kids, and they're more subdued. They cluster in the hallway in small groups.

There is something wrong with me. There is something *wrong*, and I know they can sense it. My footsteps echo. The cold floor pushes through the soles of my sneakers, shooting up through the rest of my body like electric jolts. I taste rubber in my mouth and close it. As I walk, I can feel something leaking out of me, like maybe my body is reacting to what happened the night before.

I put one hand on my pants, relieved when I realize I'm wearing my thick cords. They are light though, gray and a little too small. My shirt isn't long enough to cover my behind. I imagine the stuff leaking out of me, staining the back of my pants.

I keep walking, slowly, careful not to step too hard with my toe, stumble, and fall on my face.

The voices of the other kids are behind me, mixed with laughter. They echo, like they're caught in a wind.

The bell rings and I jump a little, as if I've forgotten that was supposed to happen. I head toward the main office to get my class schedule.

The girl's bathroom is a little farther down the hallway. I consider going there first and checking myself. But I don't want to get in trouble.

Chapter

Recess

Year: 1986, Mal—12 years old

I sit on the swing during recess, determined not to give the seat up until the teacher blows the whistle.

Next to me is a girl named Jennifer. She's nice. She became my friend the same way Lilac did, just walked up to me and started talking. I like the way she talks a lot, trusting me with all her secrets, and I never have to worry too long about filling in the quiet.

"I'm also jealous of your shoulders," she says, kicking some of the dirt with her heel. We're almost stopped, just rocking back and forth, gently, on the swings. I didn't see any stains on my pants when I checked in the bathroom, but I'm not taking any chances. On the swings the rubber seat hugs my hips, covering everything up.

"Huh?"

"You have great shoulders. They're small, you know. Curved right."

"Um, okay," I say and laugh a little. Jennifer laughs back.

"Maybe you can come to my house after school," she says.

"I can't. Someone's picking me up."

She starts rocking more, with her bent legs and her feet on the ground, pushing into her shins. I follow what she's doing.

"Want to swing again?" she asks.

"Okay," I say.

We crack up. We're too big for the swings, really.

We both walk backward with the swings, take running starts, and then we push ourselves up and up, pumping our legs in the air to go higher and higher. We're going at the same pace exactly.

There's a game of kickball being played in the field in front of us. We push past it. First, we're level with the see-saws. Then we're up higher than the monkey bars. Then we keep pumping and pumping and before we know it, we're part of the sky.

I can't help it, I start laughing, Jennifer laughs, too, her curly hair bouncing.

We pump our legs and the film that is on me disappears. Nobody can look at me up here.

We pump them some more. We are up high, higher than we could have ever gotten when our bodies were small. I laugh so hard it hurts, like someone has stapled the side of my stomach.

When we are up as high as we can get without flipping over, we relax, the wind cooling our faces as we glide.

Chapter 21

Crosswords & Cross Words

Year: 1986, Mal—12 years old;
Davey—11 years old

I've been staying at Jamie's house for a couple of weeks now. I haven't really seen my mom much except for a few pop-ins and the day that she came by to drop Davey off.

I watch the fireplace—the way it crackles and hisses, the light dancing behind Davey's head and showing the greasiness in his scalp. He's sitting on the floor, trying to trace letters into his black and white composition notebook. His tongue hangs slightly out of his mouth the way that it does when he is concentrating, just like my mom. Seeing it like that makes me angry.

The firewood smells all piney and nice. The smell puffs in the air.

"When is Mom coming back?" Davey asks.

I glance over at Jamie, who is bent over an open newspaper, writing in the crossword puzzle. He's probably smart. He says that's the reason he is so successful with the limousine business and with this fancy house and his perfect clothes, because he knows how to use his brains.

He runs his pointer finger through the fuzzy hair in his mustache and blows air through his nostrils. The sound makes me want to gag a little bit.

"When, Jamie?" Davey asks.

"When what?" Jamie echoes. Then his lip curls up. He makes it no secret that he doesn't really like Davey.

"When is our mom coming back?"

"She's not," he says and looks back down at the paper. He touches his chin with his pointer finger, then fills something in on the crossword puzzle.

Davey is looking at me, his tiny eyes suckered onto my face.

In the fireplace a log falls with a thud. It breaks in two. The fire dies in one part. After a few moments something catches, and the flames start up in another.

"What do you mean, Jamie? Our mom's not coming back?"

"Nope. She left."

"What? Why?"

"She couldn't meet her financial obligations around here and she left."

I watch the fire for a while. Davey has slammed shut his school book. His tongue is still hanging out of his mouth.

I'm sitting cross legged on the floor next to him. The heat from the fire feels good on my side.

"We don't have to stay here," Davey says in the voice of a very small child.

Jamie looks up.

My stomach clenches.

His face is serious. Set in a line.

"You do though. She signed a paper."

"She can't do—" Davey says.

"Saying that I'm watching over you now. Just for the school year. She didn't think it was a good idea for you to have to keep changing schools. And you like Rutland Elementary, don't you, David?"

His voice is friendly, almost sweet, as if it is no big deal.

"Don't you like your new school, son?" he asks.

"I guess."

Jamie nods, satisfied, then looks back down at the paper.

"It's settled then," he says.

I use my hands to lift my bottom and angle myself closer to the fire, feeling more of its heat. Davey has turned wooden like a puppet in a cartoon.

I feel Jamie behind me the way I did last night while I pretended to sleep, his long body casting a shadow over my back.

Chapter

Life Science

Year: 1986, Mal—12 years old;
Davey—11 years old

I sit in the den on the edge of the couch. At first glance, everything is clean, but Jamie never looks at anything just once. The fireplace tools are all arranged facing forward on the right spots on the hooks.

It is nearly one a.m. I put Davey to bed hours ago. He's stopped arguing with me when I do it. It's true he's only one year younger than me, but he has a childish mind and he needs his rest. Besides, he likes to be out of the way when Jamie comes home. Jamie isn't nice to him because Davey's a boy.

In front of me, the solitary hamster is running around on his little wheel. I wonder if he's angry with me. Last month the two hamsters had babies, eleven little mewling, hairless, nasty babies, all with slit eyes and cute noses.

Heat flushes my cheeks when I remember it, and that place in my ribs smarts.

I remember the morning I woke up and saw the bloodbath. The picture of what it looked like is lodged in my head. There were a few dead ones, their bodies bloodied and crunched. One of their heads was on backwards or something. It was so frigging grody.

"The others they must have just gobbled," Jamie said, laughing so hard he'd started to hiccup. His face had looked demented to me right then.

"I can't believe you didn't know they had to be separated. A smart girl like you," he had said, practically choking.

Apparently, I'd started a trend or something. A few weeks later, Jamie's big black and white cat somehow got to one of the adults, decapitating Lucky by the front door.

It's disgusting. I'd like to let the last, lone survivor outside and set him free, but I know that would hurt Davey's feelings.

I stand up, walk toward the kitchen, step up into it, and turn on the bright lights. There's a smudge on the white linoleum floor. I get the sponge from its holder, wring it out, and wipe the floor carefully with the dry part until the smudge comes up. I wring the sponge out again and put it back in its holder.

In the refrigerator is the meal I made for us all: chicken cutlets with potatoes. Davey liked it. I saved Jamie some just in case he is hungry.

I stand there, staring past the U-shaped brown cabinets to the white wallpaper with cutesy little blue flowers on it. It occurs to me that this isn't the wallpaper Jamie would pick out. I wonder who the woman was who picked out that paper. Who was living in this house before me? It bothers me that I don't know who she is.

I leave the kitchen quietly, flicking off the lights behind me. I go back into the living room and sit on the couch. In front of me is my Life Science textbook. I've put two markers in it with index cards. On the blue one is more or less the place I left off at school in Worcester, on the basic structure of a cell. The pink one, which is exactly fifty-seven pages farther in the textbook, is where they are at in Rutland Middle School. If I work hard I can catch up, but it's a lot. I think I'm kind of smart too, like Jamie, but in this place, it's so hard to focus.

My eyes are burning. I extend my bent leg in front of me again, pushing it up in the air. It keeps me awake somehow, doing odd exercises like shoulder shrugs and things like that. Jamie expects me to wait up for him now, because I've been doing it. But it's fine by me. I don't like to be asleep in the bed when he comes home. Besides, I'm worried about him.

I carry a secret inside my bookbag. I got two pamphlets from the school last week. One is called "Alcoholism, getting help." The other is a brochure for a "detoxification and rehabilitation center." Jamie isn't usually mean when he drinks or anything. Mostly he babbles a lot and falls asleep. But he *is* a danger to himself. Last week he took a spill down the basement stairs and wound up knocking his head. If one time that happens and he doesn't get up, we aren't strong enough to lift him.

Also, this is a nice house. He has a good job.

I don't want to mess up a good thing for Davey.

The headlights from the limo roll over the house. It's a slow roll because Jamie lost his license on account of all his drinking and isn't allowed to drive anymore. His driver, Roger, is more even-keeled in his driving than Jamie is.

I make a move to stand up and then think better of it. I open the book like I have been studying it, and it doesn't matter to me that he is home so late.

Still, when the door opens my shoulders clench, and I sit up slightly, on the tip of my spine.

Jamie's suit is unbuttoned. His hair is messy. His face droops, like a flower head that hasn't been watered and has been too long in the sun.

"Hello, Marilyn. I'm glad you are here." He's trying to speak clearly, pronouncing each letter.

"Davey's asleep. There's chicken cutlets in the fridge."

He brushes his gray, bushy hair from his forehead, squinting his eyes as if trying to figure out what I'm saying.

"How was work today, Jamie?" I ask.

His eyes dart around the room. He unbuttons another button on his shirt. He hums.

"Marilyn," he says. He makes his hand into a fist and taps me lightly on the knee with the knuckle of his pointer finger. He's sweating. I can see it under his shirt armpits and on his forehead. His skin is an unnatural color, like yellowish. He smells bad.

"Marilyn," he says again.

"I'm right here. Are you okay, Jamie?"

He shakes his head unsteadily, looks toward the window.

"Not so good, darling. I'm having problems with my heart again."

I close my Life Sciences book.

"I want you to come in the room with me, Marilyn. Sit with me on the bed. Talk to me. Slow my heart down."

I never really look at Jamie's body on those nights when we do things, but we've been sitting here propped up against his headboard for a while. I'm too tired not to look at his bare chest.

He's skinny, and his chest has little nipples like my dad. His skin is pale, and there's a word for the way it looks that we learned in school: sallow.

It's sallow, off color, and kind of clammy looking. There are some brown marks on it, and a line of gray curly hairs going up the middle and near his belly. I don't look at his belly, which is bigger than the rest of him, or past his belly where his pants and belt cut into his waist.

The pillow feels so great on the back of my head. I imagine turning my back on Jamie and curling up on the bed, the cool pillowcase on my ear as I sleep.

"Thank you, Marilyn."

"For what?"

"For being here with me."

My tiredness has reached the point where you're at the edge of sleeping. One more breath and you drift off to nothingness. Sometimes it happens. It is the kind of tiredness that can maybe be compared to when you are so thirsty, every single little cell and nerve inside you is focused only on how much you need water. The only thing that matters at all is falling asleep.

"Tell me something. What did you learn in school today?"

I think about it. School seems a million light years away.

"We did some algebra. I think I aced the test. And I didn't even have to study this time."

"That's great. You're like me. You're too smart for school. You can think those other kids under the table."

"Even the teacher we have isn't so smart. I can tell. He has to look at the book to remember what he's supposed to be teaching, and before he solves the problem on the board, he sometimes has to look up the answers."

My tongue is going without me now. It's keeping me awake.

"I know what you mean, honey. It's like I keep telling Roger. He can try his best to converse with me, but he's never going to be quite as eloquent. We're never going to speak the same language."

As he talks, he takes my hand and puts it palm down on his chest. Sure enough, I can feel his heart beating. It isn't a normal person's heart, I don't think, the spastic way that it flutters. He wasn't lying when he said something was wrong.

"And if he thinks that he can keep up his end of the conversation with me, he's got another thing coming. I may just have to teach that boy a lesson one of these days. I don't want to have to be mean, but I will if I have to."

I do what I can, in my small way, to help, —I push the pressure of my hand down a little more. His heart slows down. I actually hear it slow down.

"What did I tell you, Marilyn? You're an angel. You have the magic touch."

My eyelids flutter, and my neck is falling back on the headboard.

"Thank you, darling," I think he says.

Then I feel him lifting my hand. He puts my arm to my side.

Gently, he takes my body and pulls it down to the side, so I'm no longer propped up against the headboard. I flatten the pillow, turn my back to him, and curl my body into a ball.

"It's okay, girl. Get some sleep, you deserve it."

It's just like I had imagined. The pillow is so cool on my ear. My eyes close.

Jamie's smoothing the back of my head.

It's okay, I tell myself. *It's okay to be here. I've done what I'm supposed to.*

Even when I'm falling asleep, I'm helping.

Chapter

Two Social Workers &
One Troublemaker

Year: 1987, Mal—13 years old;
Davey—12 years old

The social worker lady, Carole, she said I should call her, has light brown hair and eyes that are too close together. Shiftless, my father would call them. It's the combination of those eyes and the high-pitched, unnatural tone of her voice that makes me know not to trust her. It isn't just that she barged through the door without waiting for an answer. That's just who she is.

Jamie wouldn't be happy that these stranger women are in here.

It isn't my fault. It isn't exactly like I offered them a seat in the living room.

They just barged in.

I'll tell him that if he walks in on us.

He won't walk in on us. He's in Atlantic City.

"When did you say Mr. Linden left?"

"I just told you."

"Refresh my memory."

I make an effort to control my face, keeping my expression on neutral. I pronounce my words clearly, with that low voice I learned can soothe old people.

"Well, like I said, he went to Atlantic City with the chauffer Roger about two nights ago. He was only planning to stay overnight. Just, something came up so he was delayed. We're fine here. I always take care of Davey anyhow."

The lady, Carole, seems judgey—the kind of person my dad wouldn't like because she thinks she's better than us. Her expression is controlled, but the way she's quiet so long after I answer her question, I just know she's judging us.

"This is a lovely home."

"Thank you."

"It's very clean and tidy. Very upkept."

Her lips are too thin. If she smiled, I bet they'd disappear.

"Marilyn, who keeps the house so neat and clean?"

I look her in the face, quickly, then my eyes look at the paneling behind her head.

"Can you call me Mal, please?"

"Very well then, Mal. Do you keep the house so nice?"

"Yes. I mean no. Not alone. Me and Jamie do the cleaning and cooking and we take care of Davey."

"Davey, who is that?"

"My little brother, David. The other lady is with him."

"Linda."

"Huh."

"The other lady. Her name is Linda. Don't you remember that I called her that name before?"

Now I know why I don't trust this woman. She doesn't trust me. She's testing me, writing down the notes in her stupid chart, reducing us to paper. Her dumb curlicued words, weighed down on that paper, will decide our fate. How the hell am I supposed to remember her social worker friend's name if she can't even remember my brother Davey's name? It's her job to remember.

I know what to do now. I'll do what Jamie would advise. I'll outwit her. *You can't have a battle of wits with an unarmed opponent*, he always says.

"Linda. Yeah. I remember now." I'm sure to stand up straight and firm with arms crossing my body, my hands clenched in a fist.

"Please remind me, Marilyn. I mean Mal. What is your relationship to Mr. Linden?"

"Like I said, he's my, like my mother's boyfriend. He takes care of us." I tilt my head slightly to the left, feigning interest in what Linda has to say next.

"And your mother left you here with Jamie when again?"

"Like December, I think."

"So, four months ago."

"I guess." I can feel my shoulders round a bit as I hear the facts.

"And she left in December—no, January, beginning of January correct?"

"Yes, that sounds right."

"Excuse me? You're mumbling, Mal. I can't understand you."

"I said January. That's right." I straighten myself in an effort to regain ground and focus.

She makes more scribbles in her paper. She pulls her chin up when she writes, as if that protects what she's writing from me. I can still see the little words.

"And why did she leave you here, Mal?"

"So we could stay in the same school. Here in Rutland." I'm pleading inside to stay though I'm not sure why.

"I see. And Mr. Linden...."

"She signed a paper. She signed a paper that said we should stay here so we can stay in the same school." As if my mother's permission legitimizes things, yet I know it sounds wrong.

"Why do you want to stay in Rutland?"

"Because of Jamie and school, and my mother's apartment isn't so nice." I'm scrambling to come up with as many reasons to be here as possible.

"Well, I can certainly understand that. It is quite a nice place here."

"It's nice where we live."

"What's Jamie like?"

"He's funny, but also really mature and has his life together."

"Does he drink alcohol?"

"Well, he's cutting way down." I find myself struggling to get a lie out and when I do, I can feel red wash over my face. It's a dead giveaway.

"Does he get drunk?"

"I guess. Sometimes."

"What is he like when he is drunk?"

"No, I mean he doesn't get drunk. You're confusing me." She's trying to talk me in circles now and I'm finding it hard to stand my ground. "He just drinks sometimes a little. But just a few beers."

"What happens when he drinks? Does he ever get violent?"

"When Jamie gets drunk, he doesn't get violent. He just sits on the couch and falls asleep."

"How do you feel about his drinking?"

"You know, sometimes I worry a little for him. We brought home applications from an alcohol place, but he doesn't want to go."

She nods, continues writing on the paper. Her chin is turned up and her head is cocked to the left, slanted, just like the way she writes on the line.

"Where do you sleep?"

"In the ... my room." I'm caught between how much I can fib without turning red as a beet, and telling a truth that will get us all in trouble.

"Alone?"

"Yes. No, in the room with my brother." As soon as it comes out of my mouth, I realize sleeping with my brother probably doesn't seem normal either.

"Your brother, David?"

"Yes." It's too late to back out of this lie. I've got to commit!

The woman named Carole puts her pad in her lap and holds her pen dramatically. She stares at me.

"Marilyn, are you angry with me?"

"No."

"You are looking at me like you're very angry."

The truth is, okay, I am angry. I'm ticked off. She should just leave us alone here. We were fine when we were alone. I want to wring her little chicken neck.

"I'm sorry. I just don't know what you want from me."

"I don't want anything from you, Marilyn. We are just here to make sure that you're safe, that an adult is taking care of you."

"Jamie takes care of us."

"I'm sure he does," she says in an almost sarcastic voice. She makes a noise, a small exhale of breath. It's judgey, that breath. I can feel it—her breath *and* her judging.

"Marilyn. Does Mr. Linden treat you well?'

"Yes, very well." I respond quickly and firmly, showing no weakness or uncertainty.

"Does he ever touch you inappropriately?"

"What?"

"Does Mr. Linden ever try to touch you inappropriately?"

"What are you talking about?" I hope my feigned shock will embarrass her into stopping this line of questioning.

"You don't sleep with him? You don't ever sleep in the same bed?"

"I just told you. No."

She cocks her head again, touches her top lip with the side of her index finger.

My face is red, I can feel it. But I won't let myself cry. I won't break down.

I imagine Jamie being here with us. He would put an end to this. *I didn't actually let her in here. She just barged right in,* I would tell him.

In this case, under these circumstances, I know that he would take my side.

"Marilyn,"

"Mal."

"Sorry, Mal. I can see that this house is quite lovely, clean, and that you appear to be in good health and well cared for. I understand that your mother has given permission for Mr. Linden to look after you so you can stay in school, correct?"

"Yes."

"And why did she have to leave in—December, did you say?"

"January."

"My mistake. January. Beginning of January."

"I don't know exactly. Jamie said she wasn't meeting her financial obligation."

"I see," she says and starts writing again.

Then she looks up, but as usual she doesn't look at me. She's staring at a point on my forehead with her beady little eyes. She's probably practiced doing that on people. Somebody showed her how to do it.

"So, all that seems okay, but the problem, Marilyn, what I am most concerned about is that Mr. Linden left you two children alone...."

"I'm not a child. I'm thirteen now."

"And that unfortunately isn't old enough to be left on your own without adult care."

"Like I said, Jamie didn't mean to be gone so long. It was an accident."

"I see," she says, and marks something down.

I don't know how long this goes on. The lady named Carole blathers, grilling me like I'm on the witness stand in one of those shows Jamie likes to watch. Thank goodness I'm tired, because everything in the room is all cottony and far away. I'm not angry or embarrassed anymore. I don't care what that mouse-haired, beady eyed, skinny woman thinks.

But I really do want her to leave.

In my head I pray quietly, *Please just let her go away. Please just make them leave.*

Deep down, I know that isn't going to happen. They can't leave us here. They aren't going to let me off the hook so easily.

They're going to keep asking me.

Somehow, they're going to know.

I look up and see the social worker Linda has returned with Davey. Davey looks a little shaken up, but he also looks happy, relieved. I know he has probably done something stupid, like tattled on Jamie for drinking or being an unfit parent.

She signed you away. Guess you two are stuck with me for a while.

The two ladies, Carole and Linda, exchange adult stares.

"Hi Marilyn," Linda says. Her voice is gentler, kinder than Carole's. Her eyes are big and brown.

"Hi."

"She likes to be called Mal," Carole says.

"It's okay," I say.

"It's okay?" Carole asks.

I bend my head down slightly, brush my bangs off my face.

"It doesn't matter."

"Speak clearly, Mal," Carole instructs.

I look up at her. I've made a decision. I am not going to open my mouth unless there is no alternative.

"Mal. Davey tells me that you sleep in Mr. Linden's room at night, in his bed. Is that correct?"

I deliberately don't look at him but out of the corner of my eye I can see his pale skin, his pouty heart shaped lips. *I'm sorry,* I think to him in my head.

"No. Davey is lying."

"So, you don't wait up for Mr. Linden?"

"Sometimes. I stay up late anyhow. I just like to make sure he's home."

"And do you maybe sometimes stay with him in his bed? It's not your fault, honey. Nobody is blaming you," Linda says.

She has a soft, caring voice. I have to lift my ribcage, grip the edge of the couch with my hands.

Please just make them go away. Make them go away.

"You're a very pretty girl," Carole says. "Do you sometimes sleep in his bed?" she continues.

"No."

"Just tell them, Mal," Davey says. I look at him, there is something so sad and pleading in his eyes. It's as if he picks the sadness and guilt up off of his little face and places it directly on my shoulders. I can't help but cave.

"Yeah. Okay."

"You sleep in Mr. Linden's bed with Mr. Linden."

"But nothing happens. I mean, he doesn't do anything to me. I just sleep there with him sometimes."

They look at each other and exchange one of those looks.

"You have never had sex with Mr. Linden?" Linda says. I can't tell if she's asking or telling now.

"No. Gross. God. No. Can you stop asking that please?"

"We're just trying to make sure you are safe, Mal," Carole says, like they are some kind of co-conspirators or something.

"I'm safe, okay?"

"David said Mr. Linden can be physically abusive, sometimes, when he drinks."

"Not to me."

"But to Davey."

I don't respond.

"You know he is, Mal. You remember the day he was mad at me because I didn't do my homework, and he picked me up by the hair and threw me up against the wall. He hurt my rib, Mal! You saw that, Mal. You know that."

I don't answer. I shift back in my seat, brush at my bangs with my hand.

I'm mad at him for spilling his guts to these ladies, as if it never occurred to him that they may not exactly have his "best interests at heart." I mean, what does he think they can do for him anyway? If they make us leave Jamie, where the heck does he think we're going to go?

I did see what happened to Davey. Jamie did hurt him. I saw that.

But he should know better.

You little troublemaker, I hiss under my breath.

"I am sorry, but you two children are going to have to pack a bag. You can't stay here any longer. It's an unfit environment. At least right now," Carole says.

I can't breathe. I can't believe this is happening. I hate Davey for turning us in.

"Wait. You can't. Where are we going to go?"

They look at each other, these two women who have somehow made themselves Lord and Master of our house, who have somehow forced their way through the door and taken over as boss of us. I don't understand how this could have happened.

"We called your mother. We haven't heard back from her yet. We're going to drive you back there, see if we can find her."

Once upon a time there was a lady named Miss Althea Rosina Sherman. She was a lady in Iowa during those years it stunk a little to be a lady because you had to wear terrible clothes with sucky names like *crinoline* and *pinafores*, lace collars that scratched your neck, and even corsets like the kind they used to make at the Royal Worcester Corset factory in Main South.

Those corsets were torture chambers; you had to lace up tight enough that they wrenched your spine and forced your body to stick out like Betty Boop, or those barmaids my father's old-man friends spoke about in the old country with all the sad rain and the green, rolling hills. My dad once told me that ladies sometimes pretended to faint from wearing those corsets, because somehow that made them look weak and men liked that and caught them in the air. Women in those years got the short end of the wishbone, I guess.

Miss Althea Rosina Sherman wasn't that kind of boring, fainting lady, even if she did live during those crazy times. She didn't waste all her time fainting for men, cleaning the house, cooking the dinner, and wringing out all the laundry.

Instead, she paid attention to what she loved. And what she loved most were birds. She was an artist and used to sketch them, like all their pretty feathers and their talons clinging to a branch and their intricate tails. She was an ornithologist, which means a smart person in college who studies birds. She studied the birds and wrote stories about them that got published in college places, books and stuff.

Well, Miss Althea Rosina Sherman had her act together, but she did one thing wrong. She built some bird houses, and when she noticed some of those unremarkable midget birds related to my family starting to take over those boxes, because she didn't know any better, she was happy to have them as visitors. She watched and watched, and when she drew them—even though they were plain—she gave them some umph, like little wood sprites or fairies.

She romanticized the wrens just like other bird watchers did, writing about some of their better qualities: their talent for singing for one, and the way both of the parents seemed to take care of the babies when they hatched. She wrote their love stories, their street brawls, and the way they raised the babies. She was charmed by them because, like my parents, the wrens were pretty good at being charming. They had some lovable qualities too. They had spunk.

If Miss Althea Rosina Sherman really knew anything about wrens, she may have predicted the bloodbath they would make of her yard, and how they would make a horror movie-freak show of some of the nests of the other birds she loved so much that lived in there too. She had ten wren families on her property at one time, which would basically be like putting a whole block of Irish and Puerto Ricans in Main South in one or two triple-deckers; not such a good move. Before long, those darn wrens had catapulted eggs out of the nest of a Phoebe bird, pierced their sword beaks into the shells of Black-billed Cukoos, and who knows what other kind of slaughter went down.

It must have been something freaking serious though, because Miss Althea Rosina Sherman's opinion of the spunky little wrens changed pretty dramatically. She no longer enjoyed their antics. She didn't write about them anymore or draw their pictures. She did what the landlords all over Main South did to us time and time again. She tried her best to boot them. And just like the hapless landlords in Main South, she was infuriated to find it took a lot more effort than evicting any other kind of bird. The wrens were stubborn and scrappy, especially when someone told them they had to go.

Miss Althea Rosina got mad. She didn't just get mad, though. She went completely friggin' ballistic on the wren name; she wrote all kinds of articles about them, calling them out as the degenerates she believed they were. She called them all kinds of weird names: demons, devils, criminals, and felons.

She took it even further than that though. It was like after that time I had the fight with Carmen Gonzalez, that one night she and her friend jumped me and I threw a house phone I'd borrowed at their heads. Miss Althea Rosina Sherman wrote those wrens into her will. She made sure that after she died, the wrens would be bounced from her backyard and not be allowed to breed there ever again.

I can't say I would blame Miss Althea Rosina Sherman if I'd met her. Maybe she'd been like those polite but clueless social workers who came to Main South and called all my relatives and neighbors out as they saw them. I mean, let's face it, Main South was lame. It could be bad for your health. Everyone knew that, even the people who lived there themselves.

But I can't help but feel a little annoyed with Miss Althea too. I mean, if you bring a bunch of plain jane birds into your yard and watch them long enough to see the good in them, watch them long enough to see the charm in their weird romances and their throw-downs ... how can you turn on them afterward? Wrens aren't really evil. Sure, they get belligerent, but that's mostly when they're fighting for space. They don't know any other way.

Even when I was gone at Jamie's long enough to get away from Main South, to breathe away from all the rot, there was always a part of me that was homesick. Main South was where I came from. I didn't *get* it, exactly, but I knew what it was. I didn't always know why people acted like fools there, but I knew who we were.

That is the reason Miss Althea Rosina Sherman didn't have anyone to blame for those wrens' behavior but herself. She was the one who invited them into her yard.

And it wasn't their fault she hadn't been able to see them in the first place.

Chapter

Big Butt Barflies

Year: 1987, Mal—13 years old;
Davey—12 years old

I'm tired. It's not just like I'm tired because I haven't slept, but like all the life I've ever had in me is draining through the seat. We've been driving around forever—to the apartment on Hollywood Street, to all of my mother's scummy boyfriends—and all we get when we knock and knock and knock is no answer. The stupid social workers should have known better than to make us pack all our stuff up before they took us on this wild-goose chase across the world. What, are they going to take us home with them or something?

"Is this the bar, kids? M-ulk-ayes?" Carole asks, pronouncing each letter funny.

"Is it, Mal?" Davey deferring to me.

"Yep," I say.

While Moynihan's was Dad's home away from home, Mully's is my mom's hole of choice with her newly found, post-Dad freedom.

We have pulled into the side street off Park Avenue in front of the bar.

Linda turns off the car. She and Carole pick up their purses and get out of the car, then open the doors so we can get out, too.

Mully's is that kind of place that operates 'round the clock, that smells like dirty old ashtrays and stale beer, where they only kick folks out at five a.m. so they can hose the place down and abide by the state regulations, then let them back in when the sun comes up. Names have been carved into the barstools with keys, and old important folks' photos and signed dollar bills hang along the long, Windex-streaked mirror over the bar. There's a plastic clip caddy with stale chips and a clear jug of pickled eggs on the countertop.

I want to laugh as we walk together, these two proper-looking social workers entering Mully's with me and Davey. What are they expecting to find here? At best, it'll be my mother sitting her big butt on a bar stool, laughing and talking trash with the other barflies.

At the same time, something has crawled up inside my stomach and died. I want to see my mother again, but I seriously don't think I can handle it if she doesn't want to see us back.

We walk through the doors. The sunlight is gone. The bar is familiar, as I remembered it: dusty light, the jukebox playing old beating down music, the jar of pickled eggs, a bunch of people's big butts pressing against the chairs at the bar. Other than that, it's quiet.

"She's there, right there," Davey says.

It takes me a second to look up and notice my mom, the bubbly-boggle hourglass shape of her, her straw-colored, barely picked hair. She's laughing, I think. I can't tell, but her body is shaking.

The social workers take our hands, like we are suddenly somehow connected, and walk us toward her. Honestly, there's something nice about Carole's warm hand in mine. But I push the sensation down abruptly and take my own hand back. Everything inside me is crumbly.

"Mrs. Wrenn," the social worker says, poking my mother in the back.

She spins around as expected. That should be part of social worker training. Don't ever sneak up on somebody at a bar. No duh.

"Yeah," my mom says. Her face is wider than I remembered it, but her expression just as blank. It takes her a while to register what is happening.

"Marilyn. David. Well. Hi kids! What are you doing here?"

"Mrs. Wrenn. Could we possibly have a moment alone?"

She looks at the social workers, then at us, maybe trying to count the number of people surrounding her. My mother's mind is deep, but really slow. She knows exactly what she's doing, but it takes her a while to process things.

"I'm Cheryl. I'm not Mrs. Wrenn. You look good, Mal, Davey," she says.

"Pardon me. Cheryl. Can we have a moment of your time?"

"Okay," my mom says in her sweet little kid voice and jumps off the stool.

Davey moves in closer to me. I let him. I don't understand any of this either.

Chapter

House Call

Year: 1987, Mal—13 years old;
Davey—12 years old

We're back where we started. I didn't realize this bit of information before we lived in Jamie's spic and span place, but the apartment where we live back with our mom is a pigsty. The laundry piles have moved into the living room. I notice among the dirty, gnarled up socks and jeans and T-shirts is an old pair of Davey's pajama bottoms, the ones with the blue-birds on them.

Jamie wouldn't approve of this place. No wonder he never came up to our apartment. It's disgusting here.

"Excuse the mess," I say, the way that Lilac's mom sometimes says when there's too much stuff in one room of her house.

The social worker ladies have returned—they're putting their noses where they don't belong. They're sniffing the air, like dogs looking for a place to pee who then realize there *is* no spot that it's good enough for them to pee in.

Carole's mousy chin points up a little. She looks at the other one, the nicer one, Linda—the one I keep imagining talked to me first instead of

Davey. Carole's skinny lips seem to be turning up slightly, like she wants to laugh. I don't like her.

There's a lot of noise coming from Davey's room. He's desperately trying to clean up. As if that's going to make some kind of big diff.

Of course, they don't ask if they can sit down. There's only one armchair and it's got dirty clothes all over it. Next to the chair, a butter knife with peanut butter on it is on the floor.

"Where is your mother?"

I shrug my shoulders as I bend down to pick up the dirty knife. When we called Jamie, he told me not to give them any more information than necessary. Otherwise, they may take us away.

"I'm babysitting."

Again, they look at each other *that* way.

Carole takes a deep breath, then sighs.

"Marilyn, I hope this doesn't make you uncomfortable, but we have to ask you some questions. Would that be okay?"

I shrug again and steel my body up tightly. They're taller than me, these women. The top of their stockinged legs reach to my stomach.

"We need to know what goes on when you sleep with Mr. Linden, Marilyn."

I take a step back, move my shoulders back. I don't breathe.

"Nothing," I say. I hear my own voice. It quivered.

Stay tough, Mal. You don't have to answer anything you don't want to.

I wish my voice was stronger.

"You aren't in trouble, Mal. You didn't do anything wrong," Linda says.

There's something about the soft way that she looks at me that makes it hard to not be on her side.

I walk to the other side of the armchair and peer over at them.

"It's not that," I manage.

The women look at me, waiting.

"He has heart problems. If he works too hard or gets upset his heart hurts."

Linda narrows her eyes slightly.

"So, when that happens, I go to his room with him and sit on the bed and talk to him, just talk to him until he calms down. I help him."

"Does he see a doctor for this heart condition?"

"He doesn't like doctors."

"I see."

"Once he was in Holden Hospital and then they transferred him to St. Vincent's, but that was the only time," I say.

Carole closes her eyes for so long I wonder if she's about to fall down. Then she opens them up, wide, and looks at me like she is mad.

"He doesn't touch you? Did he ever ask you to take off your clothes?"

I step back, decide that I am done.

I brush the junk off the armchair and sit on it. I know it's rude to leave the social worker ladies facing my back. But if I don't do that I'm going to start blubbering, breaking the promise I made to myself to stay calm.

"Just let her be," I hear Linda whisper.

"I'm sorry, honey. We didn't mean to upset you."

"Heaiahh," Davey's small voice pops up behind me.

"Hello, David. It was nice of you to clean your room for us," Carole says kindly.

Linda responds sharply, "You children must know. You aren't allowed to go back to that man's house again. You cannot visit him. You cannot live there."

"Tawh late," Davey says.

"Excuse me."

"Mom is letting us go back. We're supposed to go back to Jamie tonight."

"No, you absolutely cannot," Carole says.

"No way," Linda says.

I turn around and look at Davey, who looks even smaller and thinner from this distance. I narrow my eyes at him. He sees I'm angry and turns back to the women.

The two women are gabbing behind us. It sounds like they are arguing a bit, even though it's in a whisper.

Linda pulls out a white pad. She leans it on an empty cardboard box, bends over, and starts writing something. Carole stands behind her, watching.

When she's finished, she stands up and rips the paper from the pad. Carole takes it and reads it. She frowns, then nods and folds the paper up in two squares.

"Marilyn, I want you to make sure your mother gets this. It is a note that says your mother must keep you at home. You are absolutely not allowed to go live with that man. There may be no contact. Do you understand me?"

My hands are shaking when I take the paper.

"Okay," I manage.

When they leave us and Davey closes the door to the hallway behind them, I stand there, unfolding it in my hands.

A Daydream & A Promise

Year: 1987, Mal—13 years old;
Davey—12 years old

The feeling I used to get when I woke up as a kid and couldn't figure out where I was is happening again, but it's worse. It's so much worse. I don't know exactly what happened since the day the nutty social workers appeared in our doorstep.

I'd returned to Jamie's house without Davey. He'd picked me up. I remember that much. I'd gone back to school in Rutland even, passing notes to Jennifer. At first, I was relieved to be back there—in the better school and the pretty house where I could be there for Jamie so he wasn't alone.

But it was like I was stuck in a daydream, a daydream that slung out like one of those old black and white movies he watched on television with the sound so low I couldn't make out what the actors were saying. I was sleeping in the big bed and it was like I had a fever, all the blood draining out of my body. I sat on that couch in the living room looking at the last living hamster, whose behind was no longer plump, and watched the way he walked around the cage and then frantically clawed around the bottom of the cage, scratching the glass and sending all the wood shavings up in a volcano.

"Nobody's blaming you, honey. It's not your fault," Linda had said. Her gray eyes were sad.

I remembered the relieved, hopeful expression on Davey's tiny face after I admitted I'd slept in Jamie's bed.

What felt worse wasn't any of that—it wasn't even the critical stick-up-her-bum way that Carole had told me I had to speak up. It was how she complimented the way that I cleaned.

I never wanted to be the girl who cleaned up a house.

"I think I have to go, Jamie. They called again. They said they are going to come back to the house. It's going to get us in trouble, me being here. You said it yourself."

And then we're back in the limo, Jamie and I sharing the backseat. He's pushed his legs in very close to mine. He keeps taking his fingertip, tracing tiny shapes on my knee.

"I'm sorry," I repeat.

He doesn't say anything but stops his fingertip on my leg. He pinches my thigh, hard. Then he eases up and starts drawing those shapes again.

"Are you going to be okay?" I ask.

"I'm fine, Marilyn. I'm just a little disappointed, that's all."

He stops drawing imaginary shapes on my leg and turns and looks out the car window. His face has gray stubble all over it today; somehow it drags his face down, making it look long.

"I'll deal with it," he mumbles.

The car is pulling into Worcester now. Places start to look familiar to me. We roll under the white concrete freeway and stop at the crossroads where the Miss Worcester Diner is. It's one of those that looks like an old train car. I see people's blue jeans in there at the booths, diners with dirty hands holding up mugs to sip their coffee.

Something in my chest relaxes. We used to eat in that diner. The whole family went for breakfast there one time.

Jamie turns to me.

"You know, darling. I'm just concerned you're going to grow up and find another boyfriend and not be with me anymore. Promise me that you'll never have another boyfriend."

We make our way up the hill, cruise over the barrier over the railroad tracks. The pocket of streets we turn over is familiar.

"I promise, Jamie."

Returning to Hollywood Street is like listening to one of my parent's old records on 45 speed when it really was meant to be played on 78 speed. At first, I'm a little agitated. Some off kind of sound is stuck in my body. I'm agitated with myself because I've disappointed Jamie leaving him all alone. The tone of my mom's voice scratches inside me, especially when she's with all her friends in the living room.

It's like that record was always playing on that 45 speed, though. It doesn't ever sound exactly right or feel natural, but it becomes so distracting I get used to it. After it plays long enough I don't have it in me to try and remember what it sounded like when it was on the right speed anymore. It doesn't even matter. It's just how it sounds.

The sky lightens outside the window of the top bunk, and I'm still awake. I've spent the whole night with my spine pressed into the bed, waiting for the occasional sound of the ceiling creaking as some fool upstairs stumbles to the bathroom. It's so empty in my room. Even though Davey and I haven't slept in the same room for some time, being in that room alone makes me miss him.

When the sun has tipped over the horizon I force myself out of bed, and later, into the living room.

My mom is sitting on the couch. The television is on, low, but it's more like she's having a staring contest with some spot of the air. It takes a sec for her to even acknowledge my existence, and then when she does, she turns slowly toward me and her eyes actually look kind of addled.

"Hi Mom," I say in my gentle voice, like the kind you use on stray dogs you don't want to spook. Her lips move slowly, like they have glue on them.

"Mal. What time is it?"

"I don't know. Early."

She frowns.

"A few more hours until school probably," I say.

I walk quietly into the kitchen. The floor is disgusting; there's something crumbly and sharp sticking to the bottom of my feet. I open the fridge. One jar of mustard and a Styrofoam container. I open it. French fry crumbs. I consider licking my finger and eating them but decide against it. I put it back in the fridge and slam the door shut. I notice a funny thing then—the countertops are sparkling white. They smell different too, like the hallways at school.

I climb up on the counter and balance on my knees to reach the top cabinet. I close my eyes and feel around and all the way in the back, there's a box. I claw at it until it topples down. Potential score. It's an old box of Pop Tarts. I jump down quickly from the counter and land on the floor.

"You want a Pop Tart?" I ask my mom.

She turns toward me. I hold up the box. It's like her face is coming awake.

"Sure. Okay."

I unwrap the crinkly silver package and smell the Pop Tarts, then plug in the toaster and wait to see if it gets hot. It doesn't get red, but I can't remember if this one does. A few minutes later I put my hands on the outside of it. Stone cold.

I take the Pop Tarts over to the couch and hand one to my mom. She takes it. Her face is better now.

I take a bite. It isn't terrible really, but the cherry filling is too hard and there's a weird aftertaste. I watch my mom stare at hers, then take a tiny bite only from the corner. It takes her a really long time to chew.

I remember breakfasts at Jamie's house, the fluffy scrambled eggs he taught me to cook by just barely keeping the flame on, the extra crisp bacon with the grease that was dried with the paper towels, a slight waxy haze hanging in the kitchen. I remember the scent of fresh coffee and Jamie in his boxers, standing between the kitchen and den.

Davey sits in the den on the couch, playing with his memory cards, his back shaking slightly and his eyes slit because he's trying too hard not to look up at Jamie. I remember the hamsters dead in their cage.

"I didn't sleep so well," I say to my mom.

My mother keeps staring at the food like it is something she doesn't understand.

"That's too bad," she says in her strange sing-song voice.

"I think it's because I miss having Davey in there."

She takes another bite, chews and chews and chews. The sound of a car with a bad belt screeches outside. There are sparrows in the spindly tree next to the window, singing their raucous song.

"Davey went to the foster home right after coming back from Jamie's house?"

"I already told you Mal. Yes."

The car starts up again. A hood pops. There are two loud voices, someone trying to help jumpstart the bad engine. It reminds me of when my dad taught me how to do that to that beater car we once had.

"He wanted to go?"

She shrugs her shoulders and moves her hand like a big bird trying to get up off the couch. Crumbs fall out of the corner of her mouth.

"I told you. I just couldn't handle him anymore."

I sit, eating in silence. I like the way the new sun pouring through the window presses on the back of my head. The dust floating in air somehow makes everything feel peaceful.

My mom clears her throat and then smiles at me playfully.

"It's just us girls now, Mal. Us girls gotta stick together."

PART 7

Losing Mom

Nobody knows why male wrens build so many dummy nests, those flat, loosely constructed mounds. These are all pretty much slapped together and are missing the essential egg cups, which the lady wren eventually fills in with fur, grass, or some poor kid's hair they snatch up. The males may make so many funny nests because they are bored and anxious waiting for the ladies to land. They may feel kind of funny over the way their pointy tails poke up, or about their puny drab chests. Perhaps the nests are a way they overcompensate for their shortcomings, a way they try and wow the ladies with their ingenuity.

They may do it to expand their territory, like carpenters that build Tyvek houses trying to take over a neighborhood but never finish them entirely. Other birds aren't all as deft as the wren and can't take out sticks and twigs like the wrens can. So, they don't exactly need to finish the job to keep them out.

The nests may be decoys; a street shell game to keep predators from honing in on their families. Or perhaps they build this haphazard, loose network of potential egg laying nests as kind of a ploy, like the Irish mob marking their turf. Over the years, the wrens' rep has no doubt been recognized by birds ranging from cardinals to towhees, birds who have had their babies stabbed by wren beaks and snatched up in mouths and flown away to be splattered all over the ground. No doubt there have been phoebes and robins and bluebirds and sparrows who have been forced to abandon their fledglings after a wren built double and triple-deckers over their nests like greedy landlords, turning their old homes into graveyards.

Any classier bird not prone to massacring their neighbors might steer clear of a wren's turf if they had any sense.

Chapter

Barflies & Fleas

Year: 1987, Mal—13 years old

I'm sitting at Mully's at the bowling game secretly nursing a White Russian with ice, which I hide on a stool on my left side, away from the door. My hair has grown out from the latest unfortunate cut Lilac gave me. I teased it two inches high with a giant can of Aqua Net hairspray. I am wearing long, dangly, purple feather earrings in the holes we pierced, and Jordache jeans my mother picked up from the thrift store. I keep looking at my own reflection in the dark in a bar.

I can vaguely make out the reflections of the barflies behind me, including my mother. They're at that point in the drinking where they're starting to roll with laughter. I recognize the pitch of my mother, who like me is probably nursing her drink. My mother can have fun in a paper bag, but she was never a big drinker.

There's a tinted window in front of me that looks onto the street where the occasional haggard-looking person walks by, but doesn't stop in the bar. I've taken my coat off and draped it over my bar stool. My mother's friends, who have been slipping me the drinks, showed me how to keep the drinks down low, stressing the importance of not letting anyone see me.

Every now and then, someone's sneakers pound on the sticky floor as they walk to the jukebox next to me and play a tune. The band Boston's "Amanda" comes on.

The people at the bar have gotten quiet. I turn around, looking at them in the long mirror behind the bartender. They're sipping their drinks, their heads and necks bent slightly down. My mother is taking a long pull of her Winston and a guy is rubbing her shoulders. I turn back around, slightly embarrassed but also a little buzzed.

Without thinking about it, I reach down and scratch my ankles. There are no bites there now, but there were. Since our Hollywood Street eviction, we've bounced from friend's house to friend's house, from one couch to the next. The latest of my mom's friend's houses we're staying at is named Kathy, and her apartment has fleas. So many fleas that you can see them jump up off the wall-to-wall carpet as I walk across the living room. I spray bug junk all over my body and the couch they have me sleeping on every night. Still I can't sleep, imagining them biting all my skin off.

I stand up, conscious of my body in the new/used jeans, pull some more quarters out of my pocket, and dump them in the stand-up bowling machine. The white mini-sized pins get reset. I grab the silver puck and let it fly.

"Hi."

Somebody is behind me. I manage to grab the puck as it ricochets back to me. I could smell him coming first. He's wearing Drakkar, which is an expensive cologne some of the kids at school have managed to get a hold of. I look up at him. He is a tall, good-looking guy with sandy blond hair speckled with gray he's feathered back and strong arms and shoulders. He has scruff on his cheeks and the voice of a man. He's about twenty-five, I guess.

"Hi," I say and glance back toward my mother, who's sharing some kind of joke with another woman, laughing in that hiccup way that she has when she's really on a roll.

"I'm Carl. I'm your mom's friend."

"Hey. I'm Mal."

He stares at my hips. My stomach drops. He looks into my eyes.

I feel stronger than I have before with the boys at school.

We play two-player bowling. He stands next to me. He's so tall that my hip only reaches his thigh.

Goosebumps rise on my arm. He brushes it lightly with his own arm.

As I lean over the little bowling puck, he touches this spot at the bottom of my spine. His touch is gentle, protective. He's old but he feels like a cousin or a friend. Somehow, it's less lonely with him here.

We play for a long time. I sip my drink carefully but can't tell if I'm dizzy from the booze or from him. I feel tickly inside. It's an uncomfortable feeling, but there is something about it I like.

We play. We play until the drunks' breaths have turned with the clock, until the pitch of their voices becomes unnaturally loud and someone starts bitching, then another person makes a joke and calms him down.

I know from experience with my father and my father's friends that by the time the clock hands reach the six or possibly the twelve again, somebody will be passed out and somebody else will have gotten angry or broken down in tears.

Just before that happens, Carl asks me if I want to go back to his house.

"I don't know. I have to ask my mom."

"Okay, sure."

He takes my empty glass and walks over with me to the bar to go talk to my mom. We reach her stool. He puts his hand on that spot on my spine.

"Hey Mom."

She turns around. She has that look on her face like she'd been laughing for hours, like the laughter has cleared her out.

"You know Carl," I say.

She looks way up at him and nods, happy to see him.

"Hi," she says.

"Hey Cheryl. Mal and I were just playing some bowling."

"Great," she says. She looks at me then. Do I imagine something like worry or agitation passes over her face? Is it worry that I'm with this guy, or that she remembers I'm here and might dampen her fun?

"I'm thinking of going back to Carl's house to hang out."

"Okay."

She's still staring toward us.

"See you later," she says.

She turns back to the bar as we leave. I'd expected but don't feel anyone watching or hear anyone gossiping as Carl and I button our coats. No stares, no gossiping from the bar flies, but I can't help but feel that if I were leaving school or Lilac's house with Carl, people would look at us cockeyed. Somehow at Mully's, this is all okay. I mean, I feel like I'm mature enough for Carl though.

We hop in Carl's Volkswagen Rabbit and make our way to Carl's house. He lives in a nice section of Worcester, in a single-family house. Nobody lives upstairs, nobody lives downstairs, which means you don't have to walk so delicately, no constant worry about pissing someone off for walking around too hard. This house belongs to Carl's parents, I guess he lives

154 MAL WRENN CORBIN

here with them. We stumble upon them in the kitchen. They almost match in their almost elderly appearance, both quiet, and sweet. Carl and I stand there holding hands, he introduces me.

"Ma, Dad, this is Mel...."

"Hi, I'm Mal," I say somewhat quietly so as to correct him, but also not be obvious that I'm correcting him.

They look at us, their eyes, all four of them, large and stunned. They have a quiet sweetness about them still, but I'm feeling judged, embarrassed.

Carl grabs a quick snack, then we leave and head over to Kathy's house. Nobody's home right now, so it's quiet, except for the jumping fleas. After pretending to watch a bit of the movie, *Gremlins*, we make out, awkwardly finding our way around each other. Carl is really large, not in a chubby kind of way, but in a way that reminds me of a big statue, solid, taller in a weird way that seems more like a man than Jamie.

We have sex on the living room sofa, our clothes half on and half off. We hustle to get the rest of our clothes back on when one of Kathy's other roommates shows up suddenly in the kitchen. The roommate opens the fridge door, pretending to not notice us, but I get the sense he saw what we were doing. Carl throws on his corduroy jacket, walks past the roommate with me close behind, and we hop back in Carl's car. We drive around for a while, making small talk, before Carl needs to head back home. He drops me back off at Kathy's for the night. It looks like Mom is still out.

I didn't see Carl much after that. He did pick me up in his Rabbit again the next day so we could go for another drive, but this time it was to let me know he made up with his ex-girlfriend, so he'd have to end things with me. Funny thing is that same song, Amanda, by Boston, is playing on the radio again.

Chapter

Pennies, Dimes, Nickels, & Skittles

Year: 1988, Mal—14 years old

My mother's boyfriend when we're on Chelsea Street is Paul, a goofy twenty-five-year-old knucklehead with a haircut caught somewhere between John Bon Jovi and MacGyver with way too much gel in it. He is super skinny, and when he's inside he wears muscle shirts that show off his tattoo and skinny arms.

Something about my mom dating Paul doesn't make sense. She is pretty, okay, but she's also like thirty-eight years old. I guess that them being together has something to do with Kilby Street, with all of the drugs.

"Tricks for Trade. That's what happens on Kilby Street," Lilac said.

I didn't ask her what she'd meant. I didn't want to know anything about it.

We've been here in our Chelsea Street apartment for seven months.

Paul is bent over and stubbing his cigarette into the sawn-off coke can. The smoke lingers everywhere but it doesn't cover up what they'd been doing before I came home—that junk they smoke that leaves the air smelling gross.

Once, at school, a girl was trying to make a torch by spraying some Aqua Net through a lighter. She messed up and burnt half her hair. The unnatural scent that her hair made after they put the flames out, mixed with the scent of freshly laid tar on the street, is the closest I can come to describe it. But it isn't really either of those things.

The drugs aren't the only reason I don't like Paul.

He half looks at me, his eyes like smudged windows. Not in a pervy way, but in a somewhat dazed, paranoid way, I guess. Normally, I don't stay anywhere remotely near them after school. I try to make myself scarce.

It doesn't matter where I am though. When I lay in my room, I'm, like, hyper-aware of them through the door. In between the pauses and laughter, they occasionally say my name.

Paul stands up. I examine his pockets, looking for a bulge, listening for any tinkling of change. Yesterday it happened. I went into my room and found they had raided my frigging piggy bank. I'd looked at the piggy bank, a free-standing, see-through bank in the shape of an oversized beer bottle that came up to my thigh. Before they robbed me, the coins had run up to my calf. Now there's nothing left except a few coins that barely reach the tip of my big toe.

So far I've wimped out of saying anything. Part of me thinks I should just let it go. But since it happened, I can't sleep right. It's partly the principal of the thing. Some of the coins I've had for years, from turning in bottles and cans with my dad or from the occasional visit to my Nana's apartment on the Swedish side of town. It's more than that, though. I need that money. I don't know what I was saving it for exactly, but I know it was something important.

"Mom. I don't even want to have to bring it up. I'm not mad. It's just upsetting. Do you think you can get him to give it back?" I'd rehearsed saying to her over and over as I sat in the classroom staring out at all the snow, cold ice cracking on the windows.

My mother stands at the counter hoarding handfuls of Skittles. Paul has slipped up behind her and put his arm around her thick middle. He's whispering something in her ear.

A low, dull scream echoes in my body, its undercurrent like radio static nobody but me can sense.

My life no longer has any rhythm. I don't just go to school, hang out and play, then come home at night, done. No way. My mother bounces from one boyfriend to the next, each of them doing their best to push me out.

The worst thing in the world is being where I'm not wanted.

My mother is feeding Skittles to Paul one at a time. She doesn't look at him but toward the living room. Her face is squishing in laughter as he eats each piece of candy. The dye has leaked on her fingers.

It makes my heart ache to see her like that. My mother needs my help.

"Mal, Paul is going to leave now."

"Okay."

Paul whispers something in her ear.

I pretend to be concentrating on my cuticles, on digging the dirt out of my nails.

He deliberately stamps in front of me, then sighs loudly like a big baby as he moves through the room. The door opens, then slams.

A few seconds later, his giant motorcycle revs up and peels off down the street.

My mother is staring at me in her odd way, indirectly, as if she's looking at something just to the side of me instead of at my face. Her skin is very pale and her cheeks are flabbier than before, as if someone has started to pull them down.

"Mal, you were rude." She spits the words out like a bunch of candy she'd been holding in her mouth, sticky and clumped up but has since lost its sweet taste.

"What?"

My voice is shaking.

"To Paul. You're so rude to him. It hurts his feelings. Why don't you like him?"

She comes around the kitchen into the living room and sits on the sofa. She tucks both her legs up under one of her butt cheeks.

"I like him. He's fine. It's just.... Okay. Mom, there's something I wanted to tell you."

"Okay," she says in her girliest voice. She's still chomping down on the Skittles.

"Mom. I don't even want to have to bring it up."

"That's okay, Marilyn."

Her voice is like a teeter-totter.

"It's just Paul took my money."

"What?"

"From my piggy bank. In my room. He took all my change. I'd been saving it up for so long. Now it's gone."

158 MAL WRENN CORBIN

My mother bounces on her butt, readjusting herself. Then she stands up and walks over to the laundry pile. She does a crazy thing. She picks up a T-shirt, shakes it out, and starts folding it.

"I'm not mad. It's just that money is important. Do you think you can get him to bring it back?"

I watch her fold. There's a slight smile on her face. She takes the shirt she's folding and walks over to the TV stand, dusts it with the shirt. She won't even look up.

When I rehearsed my speech in my bed, I'd imagined having to convince her that Paul took the money.

Now I think maybe she knew about it.

Worse than that, she may have helped him.

I imagine them ignoring the *Do Not Enter* sign on my door and opening it. They touched my clothes, picked up the piggy bank. They sat on the bed to empty it and counted it out right there.

I bet they were laughing. To them it was all a big joke.

My cheeks get red.

"There was maybe thirty dollars in there. I was saving it for such a long time."

What did they need so bad that thirty bucks could have bought them anyhow?

"He's my friend, Mal. He wouldn't do that. He likes you. He wants to get to know you, but I tell him you're shy."

"I'm not shy, I'm selective."

She goes back to the pile of laundry and starts folding, as if she just remembered that it was important.

"Okay, Marilyn?"

I walk over to the kitchen, pull my hand up and swoop it down toward the floor, snapping it at the wrist like a towel. I turn the faucet on and off. I make as much movement as I can.

"Not really."

"I don't understand what you want me to do. Tell me," she says.

I look into the sink, at the water droplets that are dripping toward the drain. I grab the Skittles bag she slapped on the counter, open it, shake out two leftover pieces of candy, and pop them into my mouth. I break their hard shells and chew them slowly, then swallow.

"I want you to stop doing the drugs," I say in an astonishingly calm voice.

Her chin is tilted upward slightly, her mouth puckered.

"At least in the house. I just can't watch it anymore. It's so bad for you. It can make you sick."

She takes the other half of the shirt at the arms and folded a second crease. She smooths it down, sharp, like the creases the Puerto Rican girls wear at school.

"I don't take too much."

"Please Mom, can you just stop doing it? Can you just do this one thing for me?" I say.

She pouts. "Oh, okay," she says in a voice so flat it's almost dead. "Okay Mal. I promise then, I'll stop."

Chapter 29

Shakespeare & Meaningless Words

Year: 1988, Mal—14 years old

I slam through the door in that ferocious way that I only can manage at home, propelled by the copious amounts of Fanta that Lilac and I had downed after school in the parking lot in front of the Mini Mart, as well as the weight she sheared off my hair with the lousy haircut I've got now. This time I've even got a rat tail that she dunked in a dixie cup of bleach.

I'm relieved that the room is dark and that my mom and her friends aren't around to make me self-conscious.

I throw down my book bag, then flick on the light and sit down in the living room. I run my hand along the pilled, scratchy surface of the rented couch. In the crevice at the back are barbeque potato chips. For a brief second I consider fishing them out and eating them, then almost puke in my throat.

Oh my God it was friggin disgusting, I imagine myself telling Lilac in school the next day.

I laugh now because I won't laugh later. In my mind, when I am imagining my own conversations, I'm funny as hell. When I'm thinking about what I would say in the future or rewinding the past and focusing on what I *would* have said if I was paying better attention, I'm freaking hilarious.

In real life, even around Lilac, I'm never that smooth.

The shades, which are the color of a nicotine-stained cigarette filter, are shut, muffling even the voices of the kids screaming on the porch upstairs. The light from the bathroom trickles into the room and reminds me that the power hasn't gotten shut off in a while. *But soft, what light through yonder window breaks? It is the east, and Juliet is the Sun,* I recite from Romeo and Juliet in my mind, in a strong triumphant voice that would make my teacher Mrs. Eressy proud.

I think about kids during Shakespearean days. Mrs. Eressy explained how they had short lifespans back then, and that's why they went ahead and got married and popped out babies so young. I wonder if short lifespans turned people into sappy fools too.

I think about my new boyfriend Steve, who lives upstairs from us. Steve is cute with his shiny black hair and olive skin. He has veiny biceps and long legs that make me feel even tinier when he pulls me on his lap— but the boy never even graduated from high school. Plus, he isn't exactly the chocolates and Valentine's type. Steve is nineteen years old. He would have been considered practically geriatric in Shakespeare's time.

I'm starving, but I know better than to get up. It's too late in the month for the food pantry. If there had been anything left in the fridge, my mother's friends already got it. I look at the potato chips in the couch.

Then my eyes fall to the table next to me and my stomach clenches, like somebody has stapled it shut. On the table is a mirror. On the mirror is a razor with residue of white powder on it.

I slam my fist down on the couch, practically bruising it—the cushion is just a slab of thin foam.

The scent of the drugs returns to me—the burning hair, the tar. Even though Mom leaves the windows open, that smell is always there, just a little, traces.

"Disrespectful." The word forms unbidden in my mind. Her vacant face returns to me, the way she looked when she had promised me she wouldn't do any more drugs in the house. I see it again: her slack mouth, her pale blue eyes.

Really? Does she think I'm stupid? I think, trying the words out in a pretend conversation with Lilac.

And it occurs to me.

Maybe she *is* stupid.

I notice it the same way as when I'd looked at her one day and suddenly realized how short she is, how lines have formed around her eyes. She's different than how I imagined her.

I think of her doing her puzzles in the kitchen, or making notes on the back of the envelopes of bills that come in the mail. I think of when she's figuring out some scheme for the numbers, or for her to rent the furniture or pay just enough of the rent. I think of the eloquent way that she speaks around official people—so unlike my dad with his sixth-grade education and clumsy tongue.

My mother isn't stupid, actually. Maybe she just doesn't care? Do my words mean nothing to her? Did she promise she wouldn't bring the drugs into the house to make me shut up? Did my *feelings* mean nothing to her?

Us girls gotta stick together, I remember she'd told me after she sent Davey away. I'd been such a sucker to believe her.

Davey's face comes back to me, just the edges of him, the way that he looked that day when he chased the man away from the park when we were secretly hunting for food. Then I remember how broken-hearted he looked when I lied to the social workers about sleeping in Jamie's bed. Or all those times I yelled at Davey for following me around, for clinging to me with his dirty little hands. Davey could be annoying, but he was a good kid.

I hear from people around Main South that Davey's over at Gates School now, which is somewhere far down on Main Street. I wonder if he thinks about me—if he thinks that me staying with my mom means I'm two-faced or that I betrayed him.

Chapter 30

Babies

Year: 1988, Mal—14 years old

The baby has stopped crying. I make a nest for her out of pillows in the living room and stick her in there. I put the ratty blanket her mother left over her, tucking it as tight as I can on the sides.

"I'm sorry baby girl. I don't know what the heck I'm doing."

The baby isn't looking at me. Her eyes are big and brown and they're focused on her toes, as if she's already learned how important it is to tune out what's happening. Her skin is pale but has red blotches on it. Was her skin blotchy when they dumped her with me, or did it get that way because she was crying so long? I watch her chest rise and fall because a part of me is afraid that she'll cut off her oxygen with all that wailing. How long can a baby cry and not hyperventilate?

Thank you, God, I repeat, because at least I remembered the bottle and how her mother told me how to warm it up.

Her name is Yasmine. I don't know exactly how old she is, but thankfully she's the age where she can hold her own head up and it doesn't flap around like a chicken. I don't know anything about babies, but Lilac once explained it to me—how there's a soft spot on their heads where the bones haven't grown in and if you drop them or touch 'em funny they could die. Thank God she doesn't have the death spot. Still, she isn't old enough to stand on her own or even to crawl or do anything for herself except stare at her toes and drool.

For the first hour or so I was so mad at them, mad at my mother and her friend, Maria, for insisting on leaving me alone with an infant while they know I don't know the first thing about taking care of one. I thought of them running around on Kilby Street, the place where people go to buy their drugs and do who knows what else in some drug house where they lounge around smoking stuff that smells vaguely like burnt hair until their eyes glazed and their mouths hung open wide. I pictured them falling asleep, or worse than that, croaking, and me left alone with this poor kid.

But the baby's angry crying seems to drain that impulse out of me. She stares at her toes. I stare at her: at the peach fuzz on her head, at the way the soft skin puckers at her tiny elbows, at the fascination with which she is now staring at those amazing little feet. She's pudgy, even kind of cute, and so helpless. If they're leaving her when she's an infant, what kind of shot does she have for the rest of her life? I feel so sorry for her that it hurts.

In my life I've had many endless nights, many nights I spent coaxing my body to stay awake so I could make sure the adults don't do any more damage. But this night with the baby is the worst. She's so tiny, so fragile, and if I do anything wrong, if I turn away for one second, she could crash to the ground and that would break her.

My anger keeps me going. I am not mad at them for my sake, but for the baby. I've been gnawing on this anger, like raw rice in the dark, and by the time I hear my mother and Maria cackling and fumbling around with the keys in the door, I am so tired I want to throw up.

I stare at the door, waiting for it to open, waiting for them to appear.

They finally do, smashing their clumsy bodies through the open door. They're amped up, laughing.

"Mal!" my mother screams, raising her hands like the character on that cartoon where the people go over Niagara Falls.

There are so many things lumped in the back of my throat.

Maria barely glances at the baby. I imagine myself grabbing her by the shirt, forcing her down to the couch to look at her. But I'm too tired and maybe too chicken.

"How did it go?" she says, her voice garbled like she's slipped under water.

"Fine," I say, my voice flatlined.

"Did she cry?" my mother asked.

"Of course she cried. She missed her mom," I say.

They both laugh as if this is the most hilarious thing in the world.

"Got good lungs, that one," Maria says, her words round without any edges.

I glance back down at Yasmine, at her tiny fists balled at her hands, at her cute little puckered face. *We made it, kid,* I whisper in my mind. I want to reach down and touch her, to kiss her on the peach fuzz of her head. But I don't want them to believe I enjoyed it.

My knees creak as I start toward my room.

As I move, they talk, the pitch of their voices rising and falling unnaturally in confusion. I take another step. They pause. I can feel their eyes glued to my back.

"Hey, Mal," Maria says.

I stop, breathe, turn around slowly.

"Thanks for looking after her," she says.

Something about the word "her" sounds strange to me.

"No problem," I respond. "She's a really sweet girl."

Then they are silent. Their skin is pale. Their expressions are vacant.

"Mal, if you want to go to sleep now, you can," my mom said.

I stare at my mom, unsure how to respond. Is she seriously treating me like a little kid with a bedtime after I spent the whole night playing nurse to her friend's baby?

They have settled onto the couch.

I look at Yasmine and kiss my fingers, then place them on her forehead.

Then I turn and silently walk out of the room.

Chapter # 31

Yellow Eyes & Green Privates

Year: 1988, Mal—14 years old

The next day, I wake up and am relieved to see Yasmine is still there on the couch. I guess I was a little worried for her. But more than that, I like her. It opened up something in me, being around her, taking care of her. I've always been good around kids and I've missed them, especially with Davey and Lisa gone.

I walk toward the kitchen where my mother's cold coffee sits, with a glossy milk film that has been floating on the top now for days. There's waterlogged bread in the sink, and cigarette butts that have been stamped out and smeared all over the counters.

"Mal, could you come in here?" my mother screams. She has since made her way from her bedroom to the living room.

Maria is there now, too, Yasmine hoisted over her shoulder so that I can't see her face. I want to go back to the kitchen. It freaks me out some-how, being in the same room with them. It's hard to tell if the smell of musty wool and junk sickness is coming from them or from our Salvation Army couch. In either case, it reeks of dank stitches popping out of the knitted air.

RAISING WRENNS, A MEMOIR **167**

"Hi, Mal," my mother says.

"What's up?" I say. I brush back the jet-black wing that is perpetually falling over my eye and making me blind.

"I have some good news," she says.

Maria laughs behind her, a trilling dizzy laugh. The baby looks too fat being held up by her rear end like that. She hasn't moved.

I wait, unwilling to give them the satisfaction of asking about what I am sure is earth-shattering news.

"We're gonna move in with Maria!"

You can't be serious, I want to say, but don't.

"What?"

"Won't that be fun?"

I don't respond.

"We can't stay here anymore," she says.

I take a deep breath. It's not like I didn't expect we'd get kicked out anyway. And it's not like I really cared. It felt less like my own house than the others because my dad wasn't there, or my brother. I'm the only one left.

Still, we've been on Chelsea for several months.

I look at the baby, notice her small brown hand clasping a lock of Maria's hair. I remember how empty I'd felt staring at her, trying to make a space for her to sleep on the sofa. *Who will take care of the baby?* I think. The question hurts. I know I'll be stuck with the baby. Her care will be on me.

"Wait a second. Where is Maria's house again?" I ask.

"It's on Piedmont," Maria says.

Piedmont Street is hell on earth. It's the street where all the hookers go to sleep with their men. There are giant billboards at the bottom of the street with yellow-eyed people warning of VD. I don't know exactly what VD is, but I think it's something that makes your privates green, something that makes you poison to other people. The last thing in the world I'm going to do is get trapped there while my mom and Maria do whatever it is that they do while I'm stuck babysitting that poor child. I wouldn't be caught dead living on Piedmont Street.

If I live on Piedmont Street, I am pretty sure I *will* be caught dead.

It will always be two against one.

"I'm not moving to Piedmont Street."

"Mal, we don't have a choice," my mother says.

I look from the light peeking out under the window shades, to the dust collecting in the dim light, to the table with its smushed metal cans and balled-up toilet paper. We've used up this apartment.

"Where else are you going to go?" Her face has absolutely no expression on it as she asks.

"I'll go move upstairs with Steven," I say, using his full name as if I had said it before.

My mother looks at me, then at Maria.

"Okay," she says in a fake resigned tone, as if she has no choice but to let me go.

Sometimes, lying in bed listening to Steve snore, I think about Tehi Tegi. Well, I don't think about Tehi Tegi as much as the guys who were attracted to her.

I have learned that you don't really have to be a total babe to attract guys to you, because I don't consider myself pretty but I obviously don't have much problem in this department. I don't exactly like the attention, but something inside me relaxes when I get it. I guess it means I'm not a total dog.

I can also see how it's kind of annoying when guys want you like that, how those fools had gotten on Tehi Tegi's last nerve and she had wanted to dump all of them in the river. I don't have that power.

The part of Tehi Tegi's story that bothers me is what happened to the guys in the first place. I mean, had they always kind of been dorks, or had she done something to them? Was there something in Tehi Tegi that caused those guys to lose their pride, to turn their backs on their crops and their families? Instead of drowning them all, was there something she could have done to make them be better? Was it her fault that they drowned?

Because that's what I always think about when I stay with any of them: with Carl and Steve and especially with Jamie, when I put my hand on his chest and felt the weighty yet hollow thump of his heart. There was something wrong with him. Things withered around him like those hamsters that died. I know it wasn't entirely my fault he was like he was. But still, he'd always made me feel responsible for his feelings, that there was something I could do that could fix him. Sometimes I managed to help, so I knew that I at least had the ability.

There is something about all of them that isn't quite right: that edginess and frustration, that dark, heavy weight in their bodies they always look to girls to relieve. After a while they all seem so empty, like something is missing inside them. I imagine the villages in Tehi Tegi's land—the houses abandoned, the windows wide open letting in cold. I imagine the corn on the cob in the fields rotting, that it turned into the dry, Thanksgiving kind of corn that rich people hang on their doors.

I wonder if those foreign men had a hollow place in their hearts too. Were all guys like that or did they only turn after you denied them your touch?

Sometimes I picture Jamie lying in the dark on the huge bed, alone. I wonder if he blames me for his loneliness.

Chapter 32

Jailbait

Year: 1988, Mal—14 years old

I'm standing in the kitchen cooking a no-name box of Mac and Cheese. The guys are all behind me sitting at the kitchen table: Steve and his thirty-year-old brother, Martin, and Martin's friend, Jim. The kitchen smells like an old ash tray and the smoke is so thick in the air it burns my eyes. They're swilling beer and laughing like little girls. I'm preparing to tell them that— if one of them makes a comment about my ass or my cooking, I'm going to say that they're a gaggle of little girls and God knows how they made it this long living like this. It's the ammo I have been storing up every night that I have lived here. I've fantasized about what I would do if somebody says something rank to me about being homeless or the daughter of a whore who lives on Piedmont Street and doesn't want her.

But I know the guys are probably not that perceptive. None of them know exactly why I am here, but I don't think they are smart enough to try and *imagine* why. Though we still sleep in the same bed, Steve is no longer really interested in me. That means it's only a matter of time before they kick me out.

Of course, I won't let that happen. I won't stay long where I'm not wanted.

That's why I'm in this kitchen staring at a friggin' pot of murky water watching tiny bubbles that refuse to start rolling. That's why I'm trying not to stare in the sink that's stopped up with old food and a gummy napkin, at the cigarette that has been put out on the counter, or the over-spilling ashtray. Yeah, I'm cooking, but that doesn't mean they have any kind of control over me or that they've won. It just means I'm hungry....

"I'm starving, Mal. What the hell's taking so long?" Steve says.

And besides, it takes time to make a good plan.

"You don't like to wait, cook your own food," I stammer. I wanted so badly to yell, but the words barely come out of my mouth.

Behind me, the guys laugh, almost cackle.

"You better talk to your woman," Martin says to Steve.

"She ain't no woman, she's a girl" Jim says.

"Pretty girl though," Martin says while donning a weird sideways smirk.

"Just a girl," Jim repeats.

"Leave her alone guys. She's just trying to help." Steve's making his best effort as kid brother to stand up to Martin.

"She's not doing jack. She can barely cook the freaking macaroni."

"She's trying."

"What's the big deal?" Jim chimes in. "Have a little heart. She's not hurting no one. Besides, she's Stevie's girl."

"That's another thing. Stevie shouldn't be sleeping with no fourteen-year-old jailbait. Stevie shouldn't be sleeping with jailbait. That's bad for us all." Martin's furrowed brow was on full display across his square forehead.

"I'm not sleeping with her. She's a good girl. She's a friend. Cut the crap, okay. Have a little class. New topic."

"We ain't got no class, Stevie. You should know better than that."

"First true thing he said," I mutter, but not really loud enough for anyone to hear me.

"So, how's it going at the garage, Marty?"

I listen to them talk as if I'm not there, steeling my body. My eyes are slits holding back tears. I look out the window at the moon that is spilling onto the porch illuminating all the crap out there: rusty oil cans, rubber boots, a crate with an old fishing rod, a shit ton of old magazines.

When I am sure the conversation behind me has picked up, that it has veered away from me, I turn the flame all the way up to distract them, turn, and tear past them out of the room.

I'm balancing on the ledge outside the bank of windows of our triple-decker on Chelsea Street. I am up as high as the trees, and imagine myself jumping off the ledge onto one of the branches. The air is warm up here.

Jim stands down below. Even though he's a close friend of Martin's, he's a nice guy with a brown almost-mullet. He is broad shouldered but small—he even wears work boots to give him a few extra inches. He is smoking a Newport, the kind of cigarette I once tried smoking. Lilac said the mint flavor would disguise the scent on our breath.

"What are you doing up there, girl?" he asks.

I don't really want to talk to him. He's old, something like thirty, and I don't like the way he looks at me. He's not pervie or anything. It's something about the tone of his voice and the way his upper lip snarls slightly. And while he's a "nice" guy, it's as if he knows he's attractive. The guy's pretty full of himself.

"Nothing. Just climbing," I say.

"Nothing, just climbing," he mimics.

"What are you, twelve?" I ask.

He laughs.

"What are you, fourteen?" he asks as if it's an afterthought. It would have been a good joke, but his delivery sucks. I almost feel bad for him.

A small red bird jumps from one branch to another until it disappears below some leaves. It occurs to me that I've never seen a bird that color before.

I pop the gum I have in my mouth, a grape Bubbalicious that has lost its flavor and turned into wax.

"What's that shirt you're wearing, girl? What's that shirt say?" he asks.

I pull the strings on my sweatshirt and turn my body slightly away from him. It's a gray sweatshirt and it says Harvard Law in maroon lettering.

"What's that sweatshirt say. Harvard Law?" he mocks.

"So what?"

"You want to go to Harvard Law, huh?"

"Steve's not here. Leave me alone," I say.

"Steve's not here because he's out flirting with Celia," he says.

I don't respond. I don't really care who Steve flirts with. He's my boyfriend but I'm losing interest in him even faster than he's losing interest in me. I've lost interest in all of it. I've heard them bitching about how I don't pull my weight around here—how the least I could do is cook something every once in a while. Yeah, I can pull off a basic Mac n' Cheese here and there, but I'm no domestic goddess. In fact, nothing pisses me off more than when people assume I'm going to do domestic shit just because I'm a girl. And there's no way in hell I'm going to stay somewhere I'm not wanted.

"Girl. There ain't no way you going to college. You know that, don't you?"

I look down at him, staring with what my brother used to call my Jedi death stare. It works and his pale blue eyes pull away.

"Who says that? If I want to go to college, then I can go to college," I say. The words are at once a threat and a promise.

He laughs, a loud, uncomfortable, murky laugh.

"Girl, get some sense. There ain't no way."

Just like that something steels inside me, some resolve I didn't know that I had. I liked the sweatshirt because it was thick and warm and because, okay, maybe it felt a little rich and special to wear. But I wasn't wearing it because I wanted to go there. I hadn't even thought about it before.

I am my father's daughter. That's one thing about me. If you ever want to get me to do something, the best thing you can do is to tell me that it's impossible.

Chapter 33

Hey, Laaadddddddyyyyyyyyyy!

Year: 1988, Mal—14 years old

Walking down the street in Webster Square wearing my crappy Papa Gino's Pizzeria uniform always makes me feel like Hester Prynne, with all the cars zipping past me on Main Street, some of them slowing to take a closer look along the way. I don't mind working, but there's something about that outfit, the dweeby collar, button sleeves and the red ankle-length wrap around skirt. It makes me feel the way the guys do when they sit on their butts and assume I'll clean up their messes: the cigarette ground into the mac and cheese I'd made; the napkins submerged in their glasses.

"She has to start pulling her weight," Steve's brother said.

"Jailbait." Martin's words echo in my head.

I wouldn't care really except deep down I know that he's right, though we have different reasons. There's no way I'm going to ever work enough hours screaming "Bon Giorno! Papa Gino's!" into the phone in that cheesy, cheery tone and restocking giant cans of marinara at $3.65 an hour to contribute anything toward their rent.

It's the worst feeling, being a mooch. Steve is being kind, but he's starting to sleep with grown women. I won't last there.

"Where are you going to go?" my mother had asked as if I was officially my problem now.

It doesn't matter that I'm only fourteen.

"She has to start pulling her weight around here."

I don't want to be there anymore. But as hard as I wrack my mind, I can't figure it out. There is absolutely, unequivocally, nowhere to go.

I don't belong.

I stomp down the street. Another car lays down on the horn, and a man screams out the window as if I was living on Piedmont Street after all. Enough horns have honked while I'm daydreaming—pretending the sound of traffic on the highway was the waves in the ocean—and scared the crap out of me unexpectedly. It baffles me that guys do this. There is absolutely no logic to it. What's the purpose? Is it to humiliate me? Is it some kind of caveman battle cry?

I think about telling Lilac about it. I'm no longer sure she'd understand. It's been so long since we've hung out. So much has happened since moving to Jamie's house and switching schools. We've somehow lost touch and I can't see her still having respect for me anymore.

In the distance I see the shopping plaza, the red-painted building where I work. It's comforting to approach this part of Park Avenue, where the light is and the traffic starts to slow and then still.

The job sucks, but there's something about it I like too. It's the organized nature of it: the clear start and end of the shift, a free slice of pizza, the hours that turn into money. It's something my parents rarely did. That's part of the reason I keep it up.

I'm hiking my backpack up when another one rolls by. It's different somehow—the car is slow, the voice distinct.

"Heyyyyy laaadddddddyyyyyy! Your ass is hangin out!" a man screams.

The car rolls slowly past me and lingers. Something about the way he said it sticks, and I close my eyes, feeling as if a two-by-four has kicked back and knocked the wind out of me.

Please no. Please, I beg in my mind.

Slowly, I put my hands on my back and half turn. Sure enough, the wrap-around skirt has become unraveled and half my ass is hanging out.

The Bridge

Year: 1988, Mal—14 years old

I'm walking over the little concrete bridge on the way to school from Steve's apartment. I've finally perfected my wardrobe for the cold. I wear a single pair of tights under jeans with wool socks, a turtle-neck, and a flannel under the thin coat my mother was able to score from her friend, Dawn, two years ago.

The coat is tight with all the clothes underneath, but I was able to snap it. My wool hat keeps my head warm, though my cheeks redden in the wind.

I stop in the middle of the bridge. The metal railing has a slightly greenish, powdery tint, and is rusted in areas. I look below to the old railroad tracks where the Providence-Worcester line sometimes runs, the giant engine vibrating the bridge, before the train whizzes past this hell hole toward other worlds.

The cold is painful. My body is heavy. It takes me so long just to get to the bottom of the hill to get to school. The boys' apartment is only a half mile behind me, but I cannot bring myself to turn around.

She's not a woman, she's a girl.

Has to start pulling her weight.

Their words return to me. I remember how it felt to stand in front of the stove waiting for the friggin' bubbles to roll with their eyes on my ass and my back. The sound of Steve snoring returns, the sour way he looks at me when he awakes. His room is sweat socks and cigarette butts. It's a boy's room. It's his. I don't belong.

It's enough. It's enough.

This bridge is like a little private fairyland, removed from the rest of the traffic whizzing by on the street. I slow down, the faint sun on my neck, my shoes crunching frosty leaves.

I try to remember what brought me to this place: my father's absence, the fireplace at Jamie's house, the seven long months where my mother's friends pushed me out of my own room.

That old dull thud screams in my body.

It dissolves in the cold.

Somewhere deep in my stomach I feel it.

I have to change my life.

Once I think it something lifts from my body. I can physically feel it leaving my shoulders. A warmth settles all around me, faint, like the sun.

I stop in the middle of the bridge. I look at the empty train tracks and the crushed pink gravel underneath them. I imagine myself pulling off my layers in the warm classroom, sitting at the desk in the brightly lit room. My ribs relax.

I hang over the bridge, my hands bracing the green oxidized railing, my shoulders and head pitched slightly over to take a closer look at the tracks below. The traffic moves in fits and starts, as if the bleak sky has thickened around the highway down there. Beyond the road I notice how sad the rows of triple-deckers look, with their dim lights and cracked windows, almost like animals who have been overhunted and don't belong.

I suddenly want a cigarette, an impulse I've never had before. I think of the kids in the smoking section at school—the way they reapply their frosty lipstick in the bathroom, how the smoke clings to their sweatshirts and hair.

You're not going to college, Steve's brother's friend had said.

The feeling that bit down on me when he said it returns.

There was a certain freedom that went along with everything going to shit, with losing my home the way I have so many times before.

I think about the way it was when I first went to the school in Rutland, the way the kids looked at me at first like I was a stranger. It had occurred to me then that I could be anyone that I wanted to be. I could reinvent myself.

It occurs to me that it's also possible now.

I don't have to go back to the boys' apartment.

I can keep walking. I imagine the path I will take over the bridge, past the traffic, how I can walk so fast my heart will pound, how walking up the steep hill will feel tugging my calves.

The two office ladies stand behind a plate glass window, the kind that they had in the check cashing place and the Chinese restaurant. I give the glass a knock. One of the office ladies has her head slightly bent, her poofy gray curly hair sticking up at least two inches over her head. She's looking at some papers.

I'm standing right here. I'm standing right here, but it's like I am invisible.

My knuckles have started to defrost and I knock on the glass a second time. My ears are clogged and I hear my heartbeat in them. I knock a third time.

She finally looks up, a bit befuddled to see me standing there. She takes her time opening the small window and clearing her throat.

"Can I help you, young lady?" she asks as if she is almost annoyed to see a student here.

"I think I need a foster home." I say.

She looks at me oddly, then mumbles something to the other woman, who comes over to stand near her.

They stare at me.

Excuse me?" the woman says.

"I think I need a foster home."

They stare at each other. One has a slight smile on her face. They look confused, as if they're trying to figure out whether I'm pulling some kind of prank.

I guess I have no choice but to continue.

"It's just like, okay, my mom left. I've been living with my boyfriend, but I have to get out of there. It's not, like, comfortable. I don't know, it's just not a good place for me anymore," I say.

The woman who's standing to the side moves in closer.

"What's your name, honey?"

"It's Mal. Um, Marilyn. Wrenn, I'm sorry I just didn't know...."

The rest of the words don't come out of my mouth right, but it's okay. I can tell the women's attitudes toward me have changed. They look concerned, even sad. They get it, sort of. At least they're now on my side.

The day passes by in a fog, with me sitting in the guidance counselor's office mumbling at the social worker who says the right words but stares at me like I'm a space cadet, like it's annoying him to have to be organizing my escape from Steve's.

That's how I come to think of it, as an escape, when we head back down the steps of the apartment with all my stuff shoved into two cardboard boxes. We pass down the stairs. I pause at the door of the apartment where my mom and I had once lived. It feels strange standing there. There are no noises and no lights. I imagine it's still a trash heap, with that coating of crunchy dirt on the floor that always stuck to bare feet. I don't think anyone new has even moved in.

I get in the passenger seat of my social worker's Dodge Aspen while he puts my two boxes in the trunk. I don't look at the house or the neighborhood, don't want to imagine who's watching the show. The social worker obviously doesn't belong here, and it isn't just because he isn't related to anyone. He's tall and lanky with a bald head and glasses, and wears a dweeby sweater vest and gray suit pants with creases. He's obviously official.

It isn't like people aren't used to DYS moving in and taking kids away. Heck, some people even make a game of it, tattling or lobbing lies about their neighbors, then sitting at their windows with Jiffy Pop or something while they watch them being hauled into the cars. Even if it's for a real reason, it's always a little humiliating to be taken away.

I don't look up as the social worker gets in the car, stretches his long body back in the seat, and starts her up.

"You okay?" he asks without pulling out.

I nod slightly.

"Are you alright, Marilyn?"

"Yes," I say, hoping he will take a hint and start driving.

When we pull away from Chelsea Street, I start to think I made a mistake. I don't know exactly what it *is*. I just think my parents wouldn't approve. In our family, we book from the authorities. We don't call them in. Who does that?

I imagine my mother's face again: her wild hair, her slack mouth, that way she stared slanted with her pretty blue eyes. She thinks I'm at Steve's house. What if she needs me? What if she tries to find me and I am not there?

We cruise around for a while: past the Mart and the Boy's Club, past more rows of houses, then the Church and the Mustard Seed Soup Kitchen. I keep catching glimpses of myself in the rearview, the road rolling out behind my teased-up hair.

When I look up again, I realize we're on Kilby Street. Rangy young guys stand on the street corners taking long drags of their cigarettes and making their bodies as still and inconspicuous as possible. A cop car cruises slowly near a basketball court and the people playing veer to the other side. Those standing around duck their heads down.

The streets we had been living on in Main South were filled with scrappy, poor Puerto Rican and Irish folks like my parents who moped from house to house, got in bar fights, and lived on government cheese. But Kilby Street is where all the gangsters defend their territory and push their drugs. I had only been here once, in the car, when my mother went to buy.

When the social worker parks the car in front of the blue house at the end of the street, my stomach swishes.

Nobody deliberately goes to Kilby Street.

I feel like an idiot.

It just isn't the way we do things.

I made a mistake. I know that I made a mistake, but it's too late to fix it.

The social worker has gone to the trouble of going all the way to Steve's to pick up my stuff, to make the arrangements. He only did all those things because I was whining about being in trouble.

I pull the silver button on the door to unlock it. I lift the door handle. Then I get out and stand on the sidewalk, trying not to look toward the place I'll be living.

A giant woman comes to the door in a tattered housedress, her short black hair greasy and unkempt. Her jiggly arms reach across the screen to push the door open and the smell of body odor greets us before she can. The social worker and the woman chat like I'm not there until we reach the dim room.

It's hot, at least. I can hear steam hissing from the radiators. A bowl of fake fruit sits on a plastic pink tablecloth. In the living area a small child lays on his stomach watching a television on so low I'm not sure there is any sound.

"I'll go get her boxes," the social worker says.

I keep my head bent slightly. I try to breathe right. I try not to jump when the door slams behind him.

The woman is staring at me, her face all screwed up and a little pouty.

She was like a big cow. A big angry cow. Moo, I imagine myself telling Lilac when I finally get out of there. I realize how long it has been since I've seen Lilac, that she's a part of that life that has vanished.

"Read these," the woman says, shoving a laminated list of rules into my hand.

There are thirteen rules.

I look at the list, quickly, and scan down until I see one that disturbs me.

No Toll Phone Calls.

"Excuse me. It says no phone calls. Does that mean I can't call my mom?"

She looks at me, unsmiling. Her eyes are dog droopy. Even her chin is puckered.

"Is it a toll call?" she asks.

"I don't know. I think so," I reply.

"No, you can't call her."

Well, alrighty then, I think.

Chapter 35

Insta-Family

Year: 1988, Mal—14 years old

I lie in the bedroom. It's the foster kid's room, which is different from the room where the woman's two real kids sleep. Although there are no other actual kids in the room, I'm only allowed to keep as much of my stuff that fit in two tiny drawers. I had to carry the boxes with the rest of my stuff in them down to the basement for storage.

It's dark but the light shines through the window, illuminating the four empty bunk beds around me. Above them, other kids who had once been here drew all over the wall in pencil.

Jimmy was here
KZ Heart JM
Damnit

Kilby Street is dark, but not quiet. Through the closed windows drugged people shout nonsense and heavy feet shuffle by. From the other room, a staticky television blares.

I don't know what I'd expected from a foster home—some kind of insta-family? Just add water and suddenly you get beautiful, perfect little children that also looked like my brother and sister? Everyone would get along and be happy, sitting around a table eating a well-balanced meal?

I'd been totally delusional. This place is a rat's nest, and the foster mother is cold hearted, the kind of person you flinch from.

My stomach feels empty. Again, I imagine my mother's face, her pale blue eyes. She doesn't know where I am. If something bad happened on Piedmont, if something bad happens to me while I am here, she wouldn't know. At least at Steve's house I was locatable.

Compared to the Ice Queen in the living room, the woman eating stale Doritos she bought with blood money from her revolving kingdom of foster kids, my mother's as warm as a puppy.

Headlights from a car pass through the lacey curtains and over my stiff body pressed into the bed metal. Emptiness winds through me, making it hard to breathe right. I've done something permanent here, severed my last connection to my family.

I run all their faces through my mind: the twins, my dad, my mom, and try and figure what has changed. The Wrenns are different, okay? We aren't real sentimental like Lilac's family is, kissing and hugging each other and saying I love you and strange stuff like that. We don't take care of each other. But when we lived together, it was all cool. The rhythm of life was measured. We may have been in our own worlds, but we joked with each other. We weren't alone. In that way, there was always someone looking out.

No, you can't call her.

There's one thing I like about myself. Once I know something, I know.

Something is wrong with this place. I've made up my mind. I won't get too comfortable here. When the cloudy light breaks through the window tomorrow, I won't stay.

Warmth, Wind, & Quiet

Year: 1988, Mal—14 years old

I don't know how I come to be facing Mrs. Eressy in the hallway, or how the tears are slipping down my face. I am amazed by them, the way they tickle my cheeks and seem to be falling from some odd, emotionless place that isn't really connected to me at all. It's as if they aren't really my tears. They just fall.

"Sweetheart, what's going on?" Mrs. Eressy asks.

Her voice is gentle, there is no sense of urgency or panic in it.

Her green, kind eyes focus on me.

Tell me, those eyes say. *Whatever it is, it's okay.*

I stand one foot crossed in front of the other. It's one of those times when my body feels wrong, the bones of my hips and knees too severe, and I'm not quite sure how to hold it all up. I run my hand along the peach fuzz growing in on the shaved sides of my head.

"Tell me," she says.

"I don't have anywhere left to go."

She looks at me, unhurried. Students are already smushed in their next classes; quiet, expectant, settling down.

"Do you mean to live?" she asked.

I nod. My chin trembles, my jaw clenched.

She is waiting for words.

"I was staying with my boyfriend. But that didn't work out. I went to a foster home yesterday. It isn't a good place. I just can't go back there. I don't know where to go after school gets out."

My bangs are heavy on my eyes. I brush them off, then jam my hand in my pocket to stop it from shaking.

"Where are your parents?"

My face turns red and I shake my head. I can't tell her where my mother is living.

Mrs. Eressy just looks at me in that serious yet nondramatic way that she has, soaking in the situation. She squints, the same way she does when she's trying to remember the line of a poem in class. I notice how beautiful her blonde hair is, how clean. I didn't take a shower at the foster home the previous night. I'd slept in my clothes.

"It's already last period. It's late," she says simply, quietly. "You need to rest. Tonight, you can stay at our house. We can figure out a longer-term plan after that."

I lie on the couch in Mrs. Eressy's living room with the knitted afghan she gave me covering my body. I lie very still, as if any motion I make may disturb the fragile peace of the family's home. But she's left the curtains open, and I can cock my head and look out the frosty window at the quiet street and all of the stars.

Mrs. Eressy doesn't live in Main South. There's a difference I can feel. The most obvious thing is, of course, that the curtains are open but it's still warm inside—warm enough that my jacket is hanging up on a hook and I don't miss it. There are no screeching fan belts or people. Only wind cries along the wide streets.

I think I could make a poem about it, about the warmth and the wind and the quiet. I've never written a poem in my life; but being at Mrs. Eressy's makes me believe such things are possible. The calmness of the place matches the calmness of her.

In the other room, Mrs. Eressy and her husband are still talking. It makes me cringe hearing their muffled voices, imagining they are talking about me. It's so nice being here, but I also know I don't belong. And I'm getting sick of this feeling.

Their toddler stirs in the other room. She makes gurgling kid sounds.

Mrs. Eressy and her husband get quiet, listen. The toddler cries. Mrs. Eressy stands up, opens the door, and walks into her room. I listen to her cooing until the toddler settles down.

I jolt up when she comes back through the living room, then goes into the kitchen and fills a glass of water. She brings it over and puts it on the coffee table next to me.

"In case you get thirsty," she says.

"I didn't wake her, did I?"

"The baby? No Mal, stop worrying honey. Let yourself rest. You are safe here. You aren't bothering anyone."

Reflections Over Cheese Doodles & Root Beer

Year: 1988, Mal—14 years old

The next night I prepare to sleep at Cherie Levasseur's house. Cherie is a friend of mine, but she's different than Lilac. Cherie is a good girl who follows the rules. Except for tonight. Tonight, we're hiding me. We're hiding me because her parents don't like me. Her mother started giving me the hairy eyeball around the time I got the new haircut, but frankly, she's always had a problem with me. I guess it's due to my family's illustrious reputation as a bunch of bar-scrapping drunks and druggies or whatever they believe about us.

I can't really blame them. Cherie's mom is perfect, with her blonde hair and perfectly painted nails. She goes to PTA meetings. She's one of those women who has always colored inside the lines. It makes sense that she is worried if Cherie hangs out with me, the girl with the rough edges and vagabond parents, the girl who doesn't even have a home.

It occurs to me that I haven't had a home in what feels like a long time. For some reason it's even crazier now, because I'm homeless without my parents. When I was with them we were part of a unit, and they knew how to do it. They may have been scrappy, but they always knew how to make us a place, a nest.

I'm no good at it, though. I'm only freeloading in other people's spaces, spaces where I don't belong. I wish I knew the secret.

"I can't believe we are doing this. Are you sure you don't mind the closet?" Cherie says.

"This is the best closet I ever stayed in," I say and we both laugh hysterically.

"I'm sorry about this," she says when we start to breathe normally again. "My mother is just kind of nervous. She means well, but she's got these, I don't know what you'd call them, hang-ups or something?"

"I don't care really. It doesn't bother me. It's nice in here. Cozy."

We both bust out again.

I like Cherie. I doubt her motivations for hanging out with me because, despite being a good girl, she's cool. Cherie is everything I wanted to be—with her acid-washed Jordache jeans, the neon bangle bracelets on her arm, and her perfectly winged hair. She's a nice person who comes from the kind of stable background I don't always trust. Her one act of rebellion seems to be sneaking me into the closet. For that reason, it's kind of hilarious.

Don't get me wrong. It's a nice closet, definitely big enough. She jerry-rigged a lamp that swings in from the open door and helps me see the layout of my new digs. There's literally a whole foot or two between the nest we made for me out of blankets and pillows and the entrance to the door. Cherie has lots of clothes: five pairs of jeans, and carefully ironed blouses and sweatshirts with the collar cut off like Jon Bon Jovi. It all hangs over my head. There are shelves with plastic boxes of wool things that could be hats or gloves or leg warmers. She's also placed her five whole pairs of shoes on the shelves so they don't poke me in the back.

"I'm flunking geometry," I confess.

"That sucks. Geometry sucks," she says.

We break down laughing again. I don't know why I told her. Under normal circumstances, flunking geometry tortures me. I've always been a good student. School is orderly, the only place I go where things make sense. There's no reason I should be flunking geometry. It's just so hard to focus on studying lately.

Cherie's bedroom is right next to the kitchen. That makes it easy for her to sneak me the giant tub of Cheese Doodles and 2-liter bottle of A&W root beer, but it's hard to feast quietly enough. When Cherie has to leave her room, it gets a little lonely. I close my eyes and listen to the sound of her mother setting the table with the cups and plates and silverware. I think about the would-be poem I was starting in Mrs. Eressy's house—something about the wind. I remember Mrs. Eressy's kind, steady stare.

When Cherie's family sits down to dinner, I'm surprised by how quiet they are, how unagitated. Their voices are low, lulling; rising and falling as they laugh and tell jokes. I suck on a cheese doodle until it is soft enough to be quiet and then mash it in my teeth until I can swallow. I take a swig of the root beer and gargle it around in my mouth. The scent of real homemade food, gravy and some kind of roast and potatoes, is torture. I hope Cherie is able to bring me some, even cold.

I have another swig of soda in my mouth when I hear something that almost blows my cover.

"Where the hell is the root beer?" Cherie's mother cries.

I laugh so hard but so quietly my stomach seems to be stapled shut, and the root beer goes up my nose.

Chapter 38

A Boarding House By Any Other Name

Year: 1988, Mal—14 years old

I'm sitting in the bathtub at my friend Robyn's house, up to my shoulders in warm water. It's peaceful in here, but somehow a little sad. I don't want to get out.

For the first few days at Robyn's I woke up in the morning and thought I was back on Chelsea Street with my mother in the kitchen and the scent of her coffee brewing. Once, I woke up and couldn't remember where I was. But I've been here a few weeks now, long enough for my body to digest where I am. For some reason that makes it worse. Although Robyn's parents haven't said anything remotely negative to me, I know they're confused. I can see it in their eyes, in the way they are overly attentive to me, always asking if I have enough food or am warm enough.

Of course, I can't help but feel that I *am* imposing.

I'm not supposed to be here.

I rub the soap on my whole body, even the crux of my elbow. I rub hard, as if the motion will make my mind work and help me to figure out my next move.

I think about my father, about that tired boarding house he was living in when I last saw him, all the scruffy old men sitting on straight chairs in the hallway. I wonder if he's still there.

It's been cold out, one of those brutally quiet winters where the whole wide world seems hermetically sealed. I have to wear most of my clothes all at once to have any chance of not getting my skin sheared off in that glass wind.

I pull my knees to my chest, scream without making a sound.

I know I can't keep this up for much longer.

At the same time, I can't see another way out.

Chapter 39

The Rez

Year: 1988, Mal—14 years old

The plastic-scented smoke from the bonfire the boys built in the woods is making my eyes burn. I keep my head down. Around the circle, they've already started to form drunken clusters.

My eyes are tearing. The clumpy *wet n wild* mascara will run soon.

The party isn't exactly the usual Main South kind of crowd. It's a lot of jocks and preppies. I've been kind of between groups since I returned to Worcester. It's like something has shifted in me, like everyone I used to hang with can sense I'm not one of them anymore. At the same time, the middle-class kids don't really get me either.

Lilac's face returns to me. We hang with different crowds now. I can't say I expected us to pick up where we left off when I returned here, but I don't exactly know how we drifted apart either. Don't get me wrong, when we see each other we say hi and stuff. But sometimes I miss her, especially the way she laughs and helped me to feel okay with being shy, with the way that I was. Now is definitely one of those times.

I pick up the cozied PBR can and lift it to my lips, pretending to take a tiny sip. I put it back in the dirt and squeeze my gloved hands over it.

Dan Bryk is sitting near the beer case with a couple of his friends, all big guys with cloned red and white Varsity jackets. He keeps staring at me, but I don't know why.

It annoys me so I finally meet his eyes. They're sexy, at least given the circumstances: gray-green and watery from the beer. I drag my eyes from him like a fishing hook and stare instead at the heavy snow on bare oaks.

"Go Jimmy," somebody says as two of the imbecile guys start fake wrestling in the woods. Despite it not being her usual crowd, Lilac happens to be here, but she still has not acknowledged me. Two kids have set up a smushed cardboard beer case and are playing quarters, bouncing them off the ground into an empty can.

"Damn, it's friggin' cold," one of the girls squeals.

"I'll warm you up baby," one of the guys says.

"In your dreams, Pete!"

"Yeah, his wet dreams."

Everyone laughs. Pete goes back to doing this thing where he has clasped his hands together and rolling his arms around like they are a snake.

They're loud, the way I've noticed people can get when they reach that point drinking, where they somehow believe it's important to scream in order for people to hear them.

My father did that sometimes. Even if he came home missing a shoe or with a black eye after somebody cold clocked him and started off trying to whisper, he'd always wind up shouting at my mom or the TV or at ghosts.

"In your wet dreams!" Pete yells.

People laugh.

"Not for nothing Pete, but that happened like ten minutes ago."

"A little late du—

"A little slow on the uptake."

"Fuck you."

"No, Dad, what about you," Lilac says, and everyone laughs.

I look in the direction we came from in town. We are far back in the woods, at least a mile from school. We are cushioned all the way back here. The snow seems to absorb not just our sound, but our bodies somehow. We are a secret back here. Safe.

Suddenly I'm nostalgic.

I have made a decision.

Okay, it's not exactly like I have an actual home or anything here. But I still belong.

I'm sitting cross-legged but pull my legs in a bit and raise myself a little higher. I put the beer can in the dirt and punch my thigh. I imagine myself ripping off my glove and smashing the beer can with a bare hand.

Dan Bryk is staring at me again. I finally manage to look back. He smiles, in a cute way where his lip curls. Beard stubble shadows his face. He stands up. I look back down at my knees, which look fuzzy in the fire-light. I don't breathe.

I feel him behind me. Before I know what is happening, he kneels down, then struggles to arrange his giant body next to me.

"Yak Sie Masz," he says quietly, then stares at another boy, challenging him with his eyes to mess with him, carving out space.

"What?"

"It means how's it hanging. In Polish," he says.

"Oh—kkaaay."

"I'm Dan."

"Hi."

"You're Mal, right?"

"Yeah."

I push my legs down with my hands, force my ass to sit on the ground. My breath turns inward, stabbing me.

"Nas-dro-y-ya," he says and holds up his beer, then nudges his chin toward mine. I pick up mine, and we clink them together. I take a sip, forcing the liquid down.

"Guess that means cheers?"

"You catch on quick," he says.

I look toward him, unsure if I should come up with something smart-alecky in return, but then just laugh. He's too goofy to be mad at.

"You've spent nearly an hour nursing that beer," he says.

"So?"

"So."

I stare into his face. He mimics the way I raise my eyebrows. I would get mad, but there's a gentleness in his face. He's joking with me like we're already friends.

"What, you don't like beer?"

"Not really."

"You don't like the taste?"

"Nah, the taste is okay."

"So why not?"

"Why do you care?"

"No reason. Just curious. Making conversation. Give a guy a break here Mal, toss me a bone."

I laugh.

I like the way my name sounds in his mouth.

At least he's taking the pressure off me, sitting alone.

"It's just like, I just don't like, you know, what it does to people, you know. I don't like being drunk," I say.

"What it does to people? You mean like when they start shooting fire-crackers out of their assholes?" He pokes me in the thigh playfully.

"You're not right," I say, tapping my head with my finger.

"Newsflash. I mean, tell me something I don't already know. But, nah, I do know what you mean about drunk people. They do weird stuff, start playing with their own hands like that fool over there," he says and we both look at Pete.

"He's been at that a while," I say.

"Right?"

"Right."

He moves a little closer, just enough so that his thigh is kind of touching my knee.

I pick up the beer can, take a small sip.

I feel his breath on my cheek.

"What?"

"Nothing. It's just you're pretty," he says.

"Thanks."

"Isn't your neck cold?"

I laugh. My hair still hasn't grown out and the coat I have always rides down to my shoulders.

"My neck is fine."

"Yes, it is."

"Seriously." I grin like an idiot, amazed at the words that have come out of my mouth.

He taps my leg playfully with his bare fist and laughs.

"I know, right?"

Something shakes the trees behind the circle and snow dumps to the ground. The drunk chatter has softened. Shapes are forming in the fire ash.

"You know, Mal, I've been watching you."

"I noticed," I say and force myself to look at him again. Then my eyes fall to the ground. I put the beer can down, pick up a rock, and start digging it into the ground.

"Not just here. At school too. Were you on the field hockey team?"

I put the beer can on the ground, push my glove into a rock.

"Are you really only a freshman?"

"Yep."

"But you don't seem like one. You are like more mature, or more serious or something."

"And you're not that serious at all," I say.

I gather the courage to really look at him. When I do that, something happens. His eyes soften, relax. I can't let go.

"It's true. I'm not always so serious. I like to have fun when I can. I mean, life is kind of serious enough, no need to make it worse, you know?"

He pushes his thigh closer to me. He's so solid. So large.

"You get it, right?"

"I don't know, maybe."

"But you know, I'm serious when it's necessary. You know, like at work."

"Where do you work?"

"Wonder Bread, Hostess ... you know, the factory. With my dad. So, you have to be, you know, *on the ball* for that."

I pick up the beer can and take a sip.

Two of the girls are standing near the fire, doing some kind of spinning dance.

I take another sip.

"But I'm not going to be there forever you know. The factory. Just to be clear. After school. I'm going where there's opportunity. I'm not going to stick around Worcester forever."

I nod. He pushes his hand closer to my knee, knocks on it playfully. I smile.

He reaches over and grabs my gloved hand, covers it with his own.

I turn toward the fire. Someone has thrown more wood on the fire. One boy is standing behind a girl with his big arms wrapped over her chest. I like how relaxed she looks as she stands there, leaning back, warming herself with his body.

Some versions of Tegi Tehi say that she wasn't a fairy but a sneaky witch, that the beauty that made the men's tongues hang out of their mouths could also stop birdsong from raining out of the sky.

In this version of the story it was her fault then that the men were lazy slobs, that they didn't fix the houses with busted water pipes and roaches squirming around all the baseboards even when they lay down the Borax. It was her fault the clothes stiffened on laundry lines. She was responsible for the tiny weed-choked yards soaked by factory chemicals for so long that nobody knew any other tomato besides the mealy kind slid between the fake meat and the soggy McDonald's hamburger bun. It was her fault that the only time they picked the thorn flowers were for funerals, and that the fireplace chimneys hadn't been cleaned or the firewood aged.

She had sent the nasty skunks out to replace the cows, made the men split their lips on crushed beer cans, and set them to feed only pebbles to their children and kick at their dogs. *She* laughed maniacally when she saw what her beauty had done. *Her* black heart was responsible for them losing their pride.

The further I circle away from Main South and then Worcester, the more familiar this version of the story sounds. It's just like the litany of complaints that came from the men who blamed their wives for making them drink or spending their food stamps on the kids, just before socking those wives in the mouth. It reminded me of the way Steve's brother called me jailbait, as if I'd carried into their apartment some kind of poison between the pages of my schoolbooks. It was this unnamed thing that made me feel ashamed, this film I couldn't scrub off no matter how long I stayed in the shower.

I carried this witch dust with me, from place to place and guy to guy.

Until the spell was broken.

I think it was Dan who first helped me to understand that I was no witch, that like Tegi Tehi there was nothing shameful or evil about me. I wasn't responsible for cleaning the dirt out of their nasty houses, or for lying to the social workers about Jamie's drinking, or why he couldn't drive his car or keep his job.

A person couldn't make another person be shiftless.

The Uncomfortable Good

Year: 1989, Mal—15 years old

I sit with Dan on the bleachers behind the football field. He's holding my hand on his thigh, and I have let my head fall on his shoulder. The football field is unlit, and the cold is starting to seep into the bleachers under my butt.

It occurs to me again how large he is. I feel so small next to him.

He slinks his hand around my waist and squeezes.

"You're so cute," he says.

I am not quite sure what to make of the word cute. We've been together about a month, but I still have no idea why Dan picked me. I'm not exactly the fashion queen of South High. He could have had any girl he wants, any other girl he would have called hot.

"I don't like that word," I joke.

He comes closer to me and I jokingly push him away. Things are different with Dan than anyone else, because this is supposedly normal. The feeling of being with him is so good it's kind of uncomfortable. I still can't figure out whether I like it or not.

He pulls me close again, his giant hand resting around my waist. This is one of the best things about Dan. He is respectful, even shy.

"Damnit, I don't want to go to work, now."

I nod. I don't know much about what Dan does at the Hostess Cupcake/ Wonderbread factory where he works with his father, the job he goes to every night after football practice, except that he works his ass off and steals me boxes of cupcakes. I don't know much about the other work he hustles at which allows him to help his parents send money to their relatives in Poland and to pay for the gas and insurance for his gray-blue Mustang GT.

I know he's not exactly operating on the up and up, as my dad would call it. But around school everyone respects him as solid, a real stand-up guy. And unlike my family, he works, however he has to. He gets stuff done. It makes me trust him more somehow.

You know darling. I'm just concerned you're going to grow up and find another boyfriend and not be with me anymore.

Jamie's words have come back to me lately, as soon as things started getting serious with Dan. I remember the feel of his wiry mustache on my cheek, his chapped lips, his old-man breath.

They revolt me. I realize now how messed up that whole year was. I imagine myself seeing Jamie again, telling him what a pig he is to his face.

It's not your fault, the social worker Carole had said. I remember the concern in her eyes that day. It was there.

Theoretically, I know that is true.

I was twelve years old. He was forty-seven.

But some days I have to remind myself.

"Hey. Everything okay with you, Mal?" Dan says.

"Yeah. Why?

"I don't know. I guess I don't know, you seem far away."

"I've been thinking," I say.

"Uh-oh. Now we are in trouble. Alert the authorities! Mal Wrenn has been thinking!"

"Don't call me that," I say, hitting him in the arm.

He tickles me and I laugh, then elbow him in the stomach.

"Quit it," I whine.

He laughs and tickles me one last time, then relaxes his hand on my knee.

"Thinking about...."

"Geography."

"You have a test?"

He squeezes my waist again.

"My aunt, her name's Marybeth, and my sister, Lisa. They said I can live with them."

"Really?"

"Yeah. I called to talk to my sister on my birthday and when they heard I was kinda on the lam, my Aunt Marybeth said I should come stay with them.

"Where?"

"Auburn."

He whistles, a thin sound carrying out over the empty field.

"And you don't want to?"

"No. I don't know. I mean I'd probably rather not friggin' leave Worcester. But like, you know, my options are kind of running out. It's not like I can stay at Robyn's house forever."

"Haven't heard from your mom yet?"

"Nah."

"That sucks."

"I'm getting tired of this, though. I mean I don't like being in the way, or you know, always imposing, always going where I don't belong. I just want to, you know, be somewhere. I just want to be."

"Do you think you'll be more at home at your aunt's? I mean, it's family."

The word family means something to Dan. To him, family is a father whose double-shifts at the factory have twisted barnacles into his hands, and a mother whose thick accent makes people stare at her like Daryll Hannah in the broken TV scene in *Splash*—who actually gather together for meals. It is easy jokes, real conversation, and thick envelopes filled with money postmarked for relatives in Poland. The way Dan believes in that word just fascinates me.

"I don't know really. Maybe. I mean, my sister is there. But then if they don't really want me there, I'll be trapped."

He traces his hand over my arm for a while, making little patterns, and I am again surprised how his giant paw can be so delicate.

He is thinking, slowly, the way that he does. Then he stops and knocks my knee with one finger.

"Well look at what's in it for you. You're smart. Auburn's a better school. You could actually learn something there, have a good shot at college."

"Yeah, but you're at South High and you'll go to college."

"Yeah, probably because of football."

"You want me to go to Auburn. You want to get rid of me?"

"Girl, are you crazy? Look at me," he says, takes my chin with his thumb, and guides my face around.

"I like you, okay. I got wheels. Auburn is, like, right there. You can spit at it. You're not getting rid of me so easy," he says.

PART **8**

Guardianship

Scientists haven't been able to crack the code to determine why wrens do most of the quirky things that they do. Their science doesn't get results that seem remotely like the hypothesis, like we practiced at school. They're more like hunches: gut feelings that turn into boxes checked at the stinky smoke storefronts of Off-Track Betting; conclusions gleaned from the way my mother sometimes closed her eyes before using a penny to reveal the losing numbers on scratch-offs.

The scientists know the puzzle of wren behavior will always be missing a few of the key pieces. It isn't only the big questions they pose either—ones like why wrens commit infanticide, snatching robins' eggs and flying them out over the forest before they drop them from the air and crash them, splat, on a rock.

Scientists are also baffled by the way wrens accomplish the things that they do. They don't know why wrens add spider egg sacs to the nests that they build. Lab experiments have found the spiders eat the mites that sometimes cause parasites in wrens. In the wild, however, the spiders do no such thing. It's possible the spider eggs make the lady wrens swoon, or the dumb male wrens just think that they do. Or maybe they like having the spiders around because they're cold blooded, just like the wrens.

Scientists have also tried to decode the wren's songs, but failed, miserably.

They don't know how these homely birds that weigh no more than two quarters can use their syrinx, the bird voice box with thin membranes that pull out all the lungs' air, to belt out staccato rhythms that would rival the best jazzman's improv—to hone those tunes to a pitch so high and frenzied it can make adult humans dizzy. They don't have a clue on how to decode them. I suspect that the songs my father sings are somehow engrained in his DNA, and course through his blood. Though he probably could never speak in words their true meaning, he could feel it—that these sounds he uttered were a washed-out version of the dirges his ancestors sang, and somewhere in the world their true meaning is inscribed on the walls of a cave.

A Jellyfish on Top of the Sea

Year: 1989, Mal—15 years old

It's a strange feeling being reunited with my sister. That seems funny to say. I mean, she's my sister, and I've seen her here and there since she was adopted, but we haven't lived together in nine years. She and Davey were five years old and I was six when we went our separate ways after leaving that foster home on the farm. And yet, somehow, it feels like we're just picking up where we left off. Like we haven't skipped a beat.

Lisa is sitting with her legs criss-crossed on the floor and Marybeth is behind her, brushing her hair. There's something so natural about the way she does it, pulling the brush through one section of Lisa's strawberry blonde hair at a time. The routine is obviously familiar to them.

I can't remember my mother ever brushing my hair.

"Why don't you ask her, Mal?" Lisa says.

I ignore her, noticing again how dwarfed she looks next to my aunt. It isn't just her body, which is as diminutive as my father's, or her little pointy nose and pale skin and freckles, which also comes from his side of the family.

It's the fact that although she is fourteen, my aunt treats her like a baby. She isn't allowed to do anything: to date boys or go out after school or even to work. It pisses me off that it doesn't seem like she's ever fought the rules in the house.

I've spent my whole childhood doing whatever the heck I want. Lisa knows this, and her comment is meant to bring me down to the same obedient level she's on.

"Mom, Mal has a question," Lisa says.

"Well, don't keep me in suspense," Marybeth says.

"There's nothing to ask, really. I mean, Dan still wants to take me to his prom."

"I'm sorry, Mal. I told you I can't afford a prom dress now for some boy's prom. When it comes time for your own prom, we can talk about it," she says.

"I know but it's okay. Dan, he's working, you know. He said he'll buy me the dress himself. You don't have to worry about it."

Marybeth scrunches up her face, the way she sometimes does when she's angry. Later tonight I'm sure I'll hear her having a hissy fit in the kitchen, slamming the cabinets.

"No Mal, I don't think that's appropriate," she says.

I pick up my bookbag and put it in my lap. I open the metal clasp on the front, loosen the strings, tighten them, and flip the clasp back again.

I don't think that's appropriate. The words cut me, though I don't exactly know why. Is she implying I am doing what the women over on Piedmont Street do, that I'm dating Dan for money?

"I don't understand what you mean. It's normal. We aren't doing anything wrong,"

"Watch your tone, young lady."

"You aren't being reasonable."

Some days the prospect of Marybeth officially applying for guardianship of me comforts me. I feel like I can adapt to this normal life in a colonial house in the suburbs, like one of those fish we read about in biology class who adapt to the leeched-out colors the deeper they travel in the ocean. Other days the prospect of her adopting me sits on the top of my heart like a jellyfish on the top of the sea.

It has something to do with the righteous way she acts, and moments like this when she shows her iridescent stingers in the sun—the way she will obviously always favor Lisa over me. And how could she not? She's been Lisa's mom for nine years now, and I've been a mere "extended family" member.

"Look, I'm sorry, Marybeth."

I've tried to follow Lisa's example, to manufacture the way that she not only obeys Marybeth, but seems to believe in the reason behind that obedience.

There's a reason she guards Lisa so ferociously, something that maybe Marybeth's afraid of out there.

I try to imagine the place my father and Marybeth were raised in but can't.

"Marybeth. It's just, you know. I want to be normal. I just want to graduate school and go to the prom just like the other kids do."

"Being normal is overrated," Lisa says, her voice high pitched and wound up like the energizer bunny on a television commercial.

I cut my eyes at her, and then immediately feel terrible. I've noticed my sister and I share a tendency to always want to be good, to be people-pleasers. But I can tell there's a part deep down inside her that wants to rebel.

Chapter 42

A Daydream
Year: 1989, Mal—15 years old

A few weeks after I started Auburn High as a sophomore, I'm walking down the hallways and catch a glimpse of myself in the trophy case glass. Most of the black ends of my hair have grown out, and my longish, shiny locks are coiled around the back of my head in a nub. I am wearing a preppy green argyle sweater and carrying my orderly textbooks with their brown, grocery-shopping-bag covers held together by a thick blue rubber band.

My friend Kelly Rae walks beside me. She's one of those smart, bubbly people who is steady and has a talent of attracting people to her. It's something about how non-pretentious she is compared to some of the other kids in school, and let's face it, she sought me out as a friend when I needed it. She's pretty too, with her shoulder-length, curly blonde hair.

It's one of those daydream, deja-vu moments. Everything about it is: the suburb, the modern-style colonial on the wide piece of land, the closet where I hang my clothes, my aunt who irons her shirts and goes to an office every day, an actual sister. I have a boyfriend. I have a best friend. It's all still strange.

At the same time, I almost believe for the first time, after all those years of dreaming about it, I've almost done it. I've successfully reinvented myself. I am me, Mal, but I'm also better somehow, closer to the person I always believed I was meant to be.

The things I left behind remain, though, in the deepest, most secret recesses of my body, cramped up like a kidney stone or something that one day will pass. Jamie, Carl, Steve, and all the other men who ran their hands over my body, who did things to me I didn't completely understand, and who ultimately rejected me are still there, of course. But they aren't relevant most of the time. While I'm living my ordinary life: wearing a ruffled, royal blue satin dress to prom, suiting up for the field hockey team, hanging with Kelly and laughing about boys ... when I am walking down the brightly lit hallways, they may exist, but they don't actually matter. They're kind of irrelevant.

"So is Dan coming to pick you up after school today?" Kelly asks as we veer through the doorway to Miss Papikyan's Spanish class.

"Yeah," I say, keeping my head bent slightly over my book. I imagine myself walking up to Dan where he stands in front of his car showing off, the way that he cups the back of my head when he holds me and pulls me into his chest.

We sit in the classroom, putting our bookbags on the floor beside the tiny desks with their long metal legs. Miss Papikyan stands in front of the classroom. She's a plump, sweet, tiny woman no more than five feet tall, with a shiny black bowl haircut, big brown eyes, and a syrupy, disarming way of speaking. I love her because she's so innocent, but also worry about her. It's only a matter of time before the students take advantage of her.

"Okay, my loves, pop quiz time, I'm sorry," she says, slapping her hands together like she's doing something between clapping flour in the air and directing a marching band.

The students in the room let out a collective groan. Not me, though. I love Spanish. It's one of my favorite subjects and I don't have to study much.

Once the tests are down on our desks I start filling out the first section: you have to match the Spanish words of the food to the photos: *papas fritas, hamburgesa, lechuga, tomate.* I hear Kelly groan next to me, feel the way that she stretches out on her chair nervously. She doesn't know anything for this class. She doesn't like to study. I worry about her, because although she's the goofiest friend I've ever had, she takes her studies seriously. She has big plans to go to college and become an accountant.

I'm pretty sure she doesn't guess, cannot sense, how much her friendship means to me, how indebted I am to her for not only making it so I can get by with the popular crowd, but for making me laugh. Kelly has lived in Auburn her whole life; she's been part of this world of normal families and decency. There's no way she could possibly understand where I come from, who I am. She doesn't know how being friends with her makes me feel normal, or how important that is.

She taps me on the shoulder.

"You understand this," she whispers in that way we do. She barely opens her mouth, but I understand her completely.

Slowly, I push the test to the side of my desk. I look at the clock on the wall, its giant gray hands moving so slowly they are practically moving backwards.

I wait, counting in my head—three, two, while Kelly copies my paper. One.

"MARIELENA!" Miss Papikyan says, harshly, and I almost jump out of my seat.

Heat rushes my face, making it barely impossible for me to breathe. It's like all those years of history have caught up with me, like I'm still me, Mal, and not the good one. I'm the girl who lived in Main South, who fled with the parents who didn't work or pay rent to fifteen apartments before I was fifteen, who slept with Jamie, a forty-seven-year-old man. I was this girl who had done things, shameful things, and who would always be afraid.

She walks closer to my desk. I feel her round yet small body shuffling closer—her plump arms, her tiny legs. She is my favorite teacher.

She picks up my paper and walks to the front of the room, then stares at me. Her disappointment pierces. There is mumbling, eyes of other students on my back. I bend my head slightly, turtle-like toward the desk. The moment strips me, slowly, layers of my new self peeled to bone. I am no longer the girl on the field hockey team, with a boyfriend and a sister and a sparkly friend with ringlets in her hair.

What's left of me is something distorted, deformed, raw. It's the essence of the girl who was a surrogate to my mother's boyfriend, who snatched the potato chip crumbs from inside the couch, who wore the decomposing, no-name sneakers.

The teacher stands in front of the classroom and holds my paper in her hand. I can't bear the disappointed way she looks at me. School is my last refuge. There's nothing worse to me than being in trouble.

Beat-beat-beat. The wren's little wings beat. The shifty wren flies through the quiet night, catching wind drifts, coasting occasionally, and determined for some unknown reason to make it to his winter roosting grounds thousands of miles away. How does he have the guts to do it knowing that there's a good chance he will die on the way, that even the strongest and lithest among them will not live to be older than nine?

How does the wren fly so high or, despite his belligerence, manage to slow down and balance deftly on blade-sharp branches no wider than twigs? How does the wren get the nerve to keep moving, to ride the heavy currents of air?

As I got older, I regarded my father differently. I watched how his hands shook before he'd had enough booze to still them, or the nervous way he looked around my aunt's house because it wasn't a place he'd ever belong. I'd somehow grown almost as tall as him. His biceps were stringy and his wrists thin. I saw how he chattered in order to make a question he didn't like or understand disappear, the way his forehead sometimes crinkled like he was watching TV static after the shows. It was his fragility that I saw, this tough old bird who had survived the long journey but had spent his whole life nervously flitting precariously from branch to branch, knowing he could never stay in one spot for too long—that a bird with his nature was incapable of landing.

Chapter 43

Another Haircut

Year: 1990, Mal—16 years old

My father sits at the dining room table across from both Lisa and me. It's only been a year since I've seen him. He's dressed like always in his Fruit of the Loom undershirt and faded jeans. But he looks rougher to me, with patchy, red skin and greasy hair. Or maybe it isn't that he is different, but that he appears different in this regular room.

He's having a hard time slicing into the chicken and potatoes my aunt has cooked. His hands shake.

"Here's your mail," my aunt says, putting a pile in front of him.

He puts the fork down and flips through the envelopes until he gets to one he likes. It's one of the long white ones with the cellophane window on it. I remember the envelope. It's a check from the State.

He opens it carefully and then peeks inside, pulling only the top of the long green watermarked check out so he can study the amount. Leaving the envelope on, he flips it over on top of the others, like it's some really big secret.

"Eat," my aunt says.

My father dutifully picks up his fork.

"How's Worcester, Dad?" I ask.

He scrunches up his nose like he's smelling something weird, like he can't figure out why I would ask such a question.

"Eh.... It's awright, I guess."

I'll admit it's a dumb question. I just didn't know what else to ask him.

When I learned my father was coming, I'd spent nearly an hour preparing for his visit, wetting and gelling the new short hairstyle I had recently gotten that had won both Dan's approval and the approval of the girls at school. They'd been impressed by the boldness of the change: a style I had gotten from a magazine and brought to the haircutter. It's something like Joan Jett mixed with Sally Jessie Raphael, and I am deeply proud of it, of this move I made to reinvent myself.

So far, my father has not noticed my hair. This lack of acknowledgement on his part is making me unreasonably angry.

"Hey, I have some news!"

"What is it, Mal?"

"My guidance counselor, Mr. Stoyanoff, he told me he sent out a recommendation for me for a scholarship. It would pay all of tuition and room and board for four years at a Massachusetts public school."

"You are already in school. What's wrong with Auburn High?" Lisa says.

"No, I mean for college."

There's a long, strained silence.

It's odd because at Auburn High, unlike at South, for the first time it's cool to be smart. I don't have to downplay doing well in school in order to try and fit in with the popular crowd. I'm a student athlete with a boyfriend, a girl who gets good grades and may have a shot at going to college—an odd caricature of a person living a life I'd only seen on TV on the *Cosby Show*.

"I don't understand. You're only a sophomore," my aunt says, resentment clipping the edges of her voice.

Lisa has a learning disability. Marybeth is deeply protective of her.

Somehow, the way school comes easy to me is insulting to Marybeth.

"She can go to the Wuhstah State," my father says.

The discussion makes me nervous. I have love for both of these people, but I don't want either of them responsible for planning my future, and going to college is my absolute dream. I feel as if a college education would rescue me from the past, from who I really am deep down inside.

"What about you, Dave? You working on getting out of that home?"

"Come on, Marybeth. It's no home. It's a boahding house, and yes, as a mattah of fact, I have some wheels in motion."

"Suit yourself," she says.

Marybeth normally has no tolerance for broken people. She calls them losers. She always badmouths my mother after the rare occasions when she calls. She loves my father, though. She scowls at him to his face, but she once told me how she respected my father because at least he would give a stranger the shirt off his back.

And it's true. He would. I've watched him do things like that.

"Oh no, uh," my aunt screams.

We all turn and look where the expression of horror on her face is focused.

Lisa has taken the bowl and capped each one of the fingers of her right hand with an olive. She sticks her hand out and waves each finger like it is a fan.

There is a pause, then my father busts out in laughter. His face is crinkled up the way that it was during the good days while his body heaves and contorts.

Chapter 44

Three of Hearts

Year: 1990, Mal—16 years old

The sound of the playing cards slapping down on the table between Lisa and me reminds me of how quiet it is in this house, how silence just seems to travel through the large empty rooms.

"Rummy," Lisa says and slams the cards down.

"Good job, Li!" I say.

She shoves down her cards, fanning them out, then staring at the patterns.

"You don't have to do that."

"Do what?"

"Talk down to me like I'm a little kid. "

I love my sister Lisa dearly, but in some ways, she's a stranger to me. I know she'd rather it be Davey who lived here with her—her twin, her other half.

They were fraternal, with their looks seeming to be split between our two parents. Lisa with her strawberry blonde hair and freckles and tiny cherub body was the spitting image of Dad, while Davey had the light brown hair, distant eyes, and slow reactions of my mother. I had snatched features from both my parents and so never really felt right taking sides.

She scoops all the cards up, collects them, then starts to shuffle. Her face is intently concentrated. Carefully, she shuffles the cards into a bridge, raising it up and then down.

"Dad show you how to do that?"

"Yeah," she says, smiling until her chin is dimpled.

My mother sometimes recited the story of the twin's birth, as if it was a fairytale that had been told to her when she herself was a child on her own birthday, how somebody had explained giving birth was something special she'd done. For this reason, I knew that they had been too small, each being diagnosed with something called "failure to thrive," which had something to do with them not getting enough food and was part of the reason they'd both had trouble learning in school. They also had a problem that my father had said was caused by lead poisoning, from paint they may have eaten in one of the apartments.

She deals the cards slowly, ten each. The automatic heat kicks in, rushing the vent. I still find that strange—not only the mechanics of it, how the heat can travel through pipes inside a wall, but also how it can make a house lukewarm. In Worcester there were only two temperatures: scorching hot when the landlord cranked the radiator, and drafty, which was most every other time.

We pick up our hands. I don't think the cards were mixed well. I have the four, five, six, and seven of spades in my hand.

"You go first," she says.

I pick up a card, a four of hearts that doesn't match any of the cards that I have. I put it in my hand and throw down the five of spades.

"Marybeth wants you here, you know. She wants to adopt you."

I nod while Lisa picks up a card and puts another one down. I don't really understand why Marybeth keeps mentioning filing to be my guardian. If she does want to adopt me, it's more to prove she can do it—that she knows how to fill out the right paperwork—than because she actually wants me. I know this for a fact.

Sometimes she dangles that adoption in front of me like it's some kind of prize, at others like it's an offer she's going to rescind.

"Look, Lisa, don't take this the wrong way. I love being here with you. You're my baby sister. But Marybeth and I don't always see things the same."

"So, you don't have to see things the same. But you don't always have to make her so mad."

I push my spine back in the chair and hold onto the edges. The blinds are open, exposing a bird landing on a Christmas waxberry bush, the bluing sky.

"I'm not trying to, Lee, I swear. It's just kind of strange for me. You know I'm already kind of grown up. I'm not used to all these rules."

My sister's chin is doing that shaking thing that it does when she's upset.

"Cheryl didn't have rules?" she asks.

The way she pronounced "Cheryl" sounded just like Marybeth.

I vaguely remember being with them both in foster care for a year, before Aunt Marybeth adopted Lisa, and Davey and I were eventually sent back to our mom and dad. I'd always considered her lucky—believed that Aunt Marybeth took her and not us because she was smaller and prettier and because she looks like our father.

I pick up a red three of hearts, put it next to the four, and throw the four of spades.

"Your turn, Lisa," I say.

"You know what, I'm sorry, I don't want to play anymore."

She throws the cards down, then makes a show of spreading them in a big mess on the table. Then she starts collecting them, turning them over so she can see what they are, arranging them in tiny neat piles on the table before marching off.

With the shuffling and slapping of playing cards quieted, I make my way to the fridge for a glass of milk where I pass the daily mail pile on the kitchen counter. I don't typically get mail, but something makes me glance at the pile today and, sure enough, I see an envelope peeking out from the pile as if it's asking for someone to take notice and open it. It looks important and official. It's addressed to me and the sender reads:

THE COMMONWEALTH OF MASSACHUSETTS
MASSACHUSETTS DEPARTMENT OF HIGHER EDUCATION
OFFICE OF STUDENT FINANCIAL ASSISTANCE

I look up and quickly glance around to make sure I'm alone, then gently open the envelope seal, careful to not tear it as if I might get in trouble for opening my own mail. There's a simple letter inside with a fancy gold seal in the upper left-hand corner with words in Latin on it. The letter begins:

Dear Marilyn,

On behalf of the Massachusetts Department of Higher Education, I am pleased to inform you that you have been selected as a recipient of the Christian A. Herter Memorial Scholarship. The Herter Scholarship was created by the Massachusetts Legislature to enable disadvantaged high school students in the 10th or 11th grades who display strong academic promise but whose socioeconomic background and environmental conditions may inhibit their ability to attain a post-secondary education and degree.

The letter goes on to outline all of the official details, but I can't get past those first two sentences. I read them over and over and over again. Tears race down my face so quickly, as if they can't get out of the way fast enough for the tears barreling behind them. I'm slowly processing what this means. I've always been adamant that I'd go to college but was never really sure how I'd make it happen. This thin yet fancy piece of paper means I actually have a true shot at going to college!

Chapter *45*

Ward of the State

Year: 1991, Mal—17 years old

I'm sitting my room, covertly eating a chocolate cream-filled cupcake from the stash under my bed. Outside the room, Marybeth is slamming cabinets. It's her thing, it's what she does—she slams cabinets when she's angry. I imagine she's still on the phone, pacing back and forth and twisting the cord.

There is a timid knock on the door, four or five raps. It's Lisa's MO. I swallow the cupcake and take a sip of the Dixie cup of warm water next to me. Then I clear my throat.

"Come in!" I scream. It's impossible to raise my voice loudly enough for Lisa to hear it but not my aunt. Fuck her, I think, hoping she's preoccupied enough with her adult tantrum not to listen anyhow.

My stomach seizes. As things have gotten progressively worse, the room has become not only my sanctuary, but also my jail. It's the place where I gorge on cupcakes that Dan scored from the Hostess factory and crank Bon Jovi up on my Walkman to avoid having to listen to them laughing and eating their open-faced, roast beef and gravy sandwiches.

218 MAL WRENN CORBIN

She's sulking, my aunt said one time when I pulled them off my ears and tried to listen to their dinner conversation.

I dig my fingernails into my forearm. She's the one who was sulking over some imaginary thing I had done to offend her.

I'd tried a few times to trace it back. I can't really. It was no one thing. It's like she resents me for getting good grades, for getting the big college scholarship, for having a boyfriend, for being everything that doesn't come easily for Lisa or, more likely, what she was afraid Lisa would become.

But this time, Marybeth is pissed because I've asked for permission to spend the rest of the summer with another aunt ... Aunt Laney and her family.

"Hey," I say. Lisa walks in timidly in her slightly bow-legged way, red splotches on her face. She gets rashes when she's nervous.

She sits down at the end of my bed, her legs hanging over the edge.

"What's going on out there?" I ask.

"She's pissed."

I laugh.

"Yeah, I figured that one out. Want a cupcake?"

"No, thanks."

"What's she pissed about? I mean in particular this time."

"Why do you want to go, Mal?"

The tone of her voice makes me sad.

She jumps off the bed and stares out the window.

"Can you still see it in the lawn?" I ask.

She nods and smiles.

"I can still see a bit of the F. And the C," she says.

"That was so fun, the day that we did that," I say.

She doesn't respond. It had been fun. Lisa had loved to ride the lawn-mower around and sometimes took me on the back with her. She'd had a wild-haired idea that we should write F.U.C.K. in the grass with the mower. We'd spent hours tracing the letters. It had worked, somewhat, but the letters were so big they weren't immediately recognizable.

"It isn't you, Lisa. It's great spending time with you. I love having my little sister around."

"You think you're too good for us?"

"What? That's insane. Did Marybeth tell you I thought I was too good for you? That doesn't even make any sense."

"She said you're just like Cheryl. You think you're too good for us. You can't be bothered."

Something inside me slows down.

I struggle again to remember those early years, what had caused us to wind up in the foster home in the first place. Even back then, Lisa with her tiny body, red-blonde hair, and clingy babylike nature had always felt to me like the one who had been cared for, wanted. My aunt had chosen her. She was wanted.

"It's got nothing to do with that, Lisa. It's hard to explain."

"Well try. You could at least do me that courtesy."

"I just don't like to be, I can't be, where I'm not wanted."

"She wants you here."

"She sure has a sick way of showing it. All she does is criticize me, put me down. She treats me like I'm some kind of a slut," I say, spitting the words out like the boys do chew at school.

"She's just worried about you."

No, I think. *She's worried about you, Lisa.*

"Why else would she be on the phone with Aunt Laney telling her not to come."

While Aunt Marybeth is my father's sister, Aunt Laney is my mother's sister. All that my mother doesn't seem capable of being, her sister Laney is. She's polished, sophisticated, has her act together, a warm, loving family, a kind and gentle husband, and she, too, has three children. It's almost as if Laney sucked up all the good genes so there was nothing left when my mother came around.

After learning of the tension between Marybeth and myself, Aunt Laney and my Uncle Ron made the generous offer for me to come spend the summer at their summer home out in the country. Yes, they have a summer home! It would give Marybeth and me a chance to take a break, to reset.

That suggestion didn't go over so well.

I shoot up out of the bed, my body moving without my mind's permission, and yank open the door.

In the kitchen I find Marybeth, pacing around the linoleum like a maniac in a cage. One of the cabinets is still partially opened—the dishes and cups in there are probably still rattled.

"Over my dead body," Marybeth says, her face contorting and turning red.

"I don't understand you. I thought you'd be happy. You said if I couldn't follow the rules, I should leave."

"You think it will be easier there. You think they're going to give you a free ride."

I just barely make out Marybeth's words between the clashing of pots and pans being shoved into cabinets.

"No, I don't. I just think it may be good for us all to have a little break, take a breather, you know, even if it's just for the summer. At least they don't hate me."

"Don't be so dramatic. Nobody hates you!" Saliva spattering onto one of the cabinet doors. You just have to learn how to behave."

"I'm going." I'm looking plainly at her now, my arms down by my side. I have resolve, and I've made up my mind. This moment feels just like that day on the bridge when I made the decision to change my life.

"Over my dead body."

"I'm going."

"I already told Laney if she even thinks to show up here, like she says she's doing, I'm going to call the police," Marybeth says.

"You can't do that. There's no paperwork."

I don't know why I never fully agreed to allow Marybeth to push the paperwork through sooner. Officially I'm what's called a "Ward of the State." Apparently, that means I belong to the State. After all I've been through with the social worker, at Jamie's house, at the foster house on Kilby Street, being a Ward of the State is safer. It means when bad things go down, I'm still free to go.

"I'm calling the cops. You belong with us here. This is where you will stay."

It isn't appropriate.

You think you are too good for this family.

Just like your mother.

I take a deep breath and run for the door, open it, slam it behind me, and book down the street. It's still warm out, the sun like a drop of honey in the cloud. I run as fast as I can until I get to the end of the block, and then make a right onto Route 20.

Chapter 46

A Great Big Mulligan

Year: 1991, Mal—17 years old

I have the vaguest sense that I'm heading in the right direction, toward the Hale's home in Charlton. For a while I was in a kind of a fugue state, unaware of what I was doing or why. But now each step I take away from that house brings me more confidence that I'm doing the right thing, untangling myself from a place where, once again, I was never truly wanted.

Cars pass by doing maybe fifty miles per hour, slow enough that I can feel them pass but loud enough that I can't hear the muffled men's buffoon voices that always scream out the windows. I pay attention to the things I see along the road as I walk: twisted up beer cans, a dead turtle, a snake.

"Mulligan," my mom's friends at the bar sometimes said when somebody messed up a story or spit out a shot of tequila. It means do-over. It means you may have started off in the right direction, you may have tried really hard, but you fumbled and it was time to wipe the chalkboard clean and start all over again. The time I'd been in Auburn had been a Mulligan, and I'd almost pulled it off. I had reinvented myself, gotten cleaned up real good as my father would say. I had all the things normal kids had: a best friend, a boyfriend my own age, good grades. I was doing it right.

It wasn't that I'd failed at that Mulligan. My past hadn't come back to trap me, like it sometimes did. Rather, it was as if Marybeth was a kid trying to sneak up behind me, push her knees into the back of mine, and knock me down. I wouldn't let her. I had worked too hard and too long for it.

"Hey baby," some giant fool says, rolling up slow beside me before he veers into the convenience store parking lot. I slow down, and after he disappears I stop, putting my hand on my chest to catch my breath. My calves ache, so I know I've been walking for a long time.

I try to focus, formulate a plan.

Of course I can't keep walking forever.

At the same time I can't turn back.

I touch my side pocket, feeling the quarters and dimes I'd shoved in there. I turn into the convenience store and spot a pay phone. Time to call Aunt Laney.

Chapter *47*

Mosquito Bite Magic

Year: 1991, Mal—17 years old

"The lake house" was my Aunt Laney and Uncle Ron's summertime refuge. It was a simple yet charming lakeside cottage nestled in the woods of Charlton, Massachusetts. Charlton is about fifteen miles southwest of the Main South section of Worcester, but it might as well be on a different continent with plenty of mosquitoes and quiet to go around.

I left Marybeth's house with nada. Zilch. Only the clothes on my back. It's a familiar feeling. But after a trip to TJ Maxx I was good to go with underwear, bras, a toothbrush, and some other basics. The girls, Amy and Kendra, were more than happy to dress me up in clothes that brought me back to Cherie Levasseur—acid-washed denim shorts with a bubblegum pink spandex liner, an off-the-shoulder top that was black with fluorescent geometric shapes on it, reminiscent of Flash Dance, and of course a clear glitter banana clip to complete the look.

That summer was magical. We spent the days bobbing in and out of the lake, jumping off docks, and going for slow boat rides around the lake in the evenings. I never had so many mosquito bites in all my life, and I loved it.

The plan was that I would spend that summer with the Hales—my

Aunt Laney, Uncle Ron, and cousins Amy, Kendra, and Robbie. Once the summer came to a close, they would head home to Connecticut and I would head back to Auburn and Aunt Marybeth and Lisa. But as summer started to set, we all realized that tensions with my Aunt Marybeth weren't easing.

August was here now and the anxiety of going back to Auburn was building. I think there were even attempts by Aunt Laney and Uncle Ron to talk through things with Marybeth and come to some sort of resolution on my behalf, but to no avail. After a private family meeting, the Hales extended the ridiculously generous offer for me to come home with them to Connecticut.

I had mixed feelings. A move to Connecticut would mean I wouldn't see Dan as often, I'd be leaving Lisa behind, I'd be making Marybeth even more angry than she already was, missing out on senior year with Kelly Rae and the rest of my friends at Auburn High, and I would be the new kid again at what would be my third high school. But the thought was exciting, too! The Hales were warm, welcoming, and they were the kind of family that I only knew of on TV—The Cosbys, The Brady Bunch, and Family Ties. I had never known a family like that to exist in real life.

So we agreed. The Hales would end that summer with an extra family member—me. And I'd be starting yet another new chapter.

The wren's lousy street rep may be primordial. They were first found in caves a long time ago, and so they were classified as being part of the Trylodytidae clan, which comes from the Greek word tyloglodytes, aka cave dwellers. Surely this could explain our family's habit of half burrowing down in the wet, cold, dank streets of the armpit of New England, never quite getting too accustomed to the sunlight.

But the wren's family extended so much farther than the place where they were first discovered; they had spread across North America, south toward Europe, and north across a prehistoric land bridge into other parts of the ancient world.

Now there are wrens on every continent on earth, and scientists have counted nearly ninety species. Many of them are kinder, less batty birds like the elegant scarlet-headed Carolina wren, or the lemon and lime colored New Zealand rock wren who, aside from his aboriginal name, which means the complainer, utters only a paltry three note stores of song and is an otherwise peaceful and innocuous bird.

Some housewives appreciate the house wren for the intensity of her song, her ability to rear her young on her own, and uncanny ability to bolt and rehome. And there are surely some men who appreciate the male wren for his chest-thumping antics, his polyamorous prowess, and the remorseless way he pirates babies or hijacks his enemies' nests. More people loathe them in a way they can't quite dignify, though, in some old and primal part in their hearts. In this way they regard them like human sociopaths, people whose actions are so bad, so alien, that people who aren't wired like that can't understand. Trying too hard to process these behaviors can drive a person mad.

Yet there are wrens out there who are absolutely adored, held in the highest esteem like gods and goddesses. The superb fairy wren in Australia sports beautiful bright blue feathers when it's mating and has been known to woo by plucking colorful pink and purple flower petals and presenting them to a lady. They're just as promiscuous as the house wren, and will defend their turf, but they aren't known for committing infanticide by spearing eggs or dropping their enemy's babies off a ledge. They are no bloodthirsty pirates, no thieves in the night.

If threatened by a much larger predator—say a magpie—the fairy wren will simply stand its ground and sing, loudly. Nobody knows exactly why the males do this; most believe it's a way of showing off his guts, an effort to impress the ladies. Beautiful, gentle, bold, brave; the fairy wren's delicacy has earned it the sweetest reputation and a host of passionate fantastical monikers. There is the lovely fairy wren, the splendid fairy wren, the blue-backed fairy wren, and the red-backed fairy wren.

I'd like to imagine I belong to a more elegant species, that maybe my lineage was grander than it could appear. When I grew older and started to circle farther and farther from Main South and learn of all the other colorful birds that were out there, their song like chiming crystal glasses, their colorful plumage, I realized that even though I may not be as colorful, I had a talent for blending. I could emulate them. Eventually, after I stopped trying to outwit them or to match them call for call, I stopped being jealous of them, no longer cringing if they seemed to recognize where I came from.

Still, I was an anomaly not only in my family but among my own kind. People from Main South rarely left the neighborhood, let alone wanted to see Paris or go to college. Every once in a while I wondered whether something strange happened while I was a fledgling; had my father wooed my mother on his way from some other bird's household? Had I been found in the marsh after I'd been plucked from a nest?

Chapter **48**

An Embarrassment
of Riches

Year: 1991, Mal—17 years old

While the lake house in Charlton was charming and simple, the Hale's home in Woodbury, Connecticut is beautiful, huge, and almost stately—like the home that a Senator would live in. It's like no other home I've ever known before. It has a staircase with carpet that's so thick, your toes sink into it when you walk. Everything is clean, and everything has a place. Everyone cleans up after themselves, even bits of food or little paper scraps that find their way to the floor from the counter. You won't find any peanut butter-coated knives on the floor here. The Hales actually pick things up off the floor as they pass by.

Every day I see something new and amazing. There's the garage door opener that makes the door outside lift up and down and which protects the cars from the sun and the wind and the snow. There's a mailbox that sits on the street, and the drive-by mailman shoves mail into it as opposed to using the string of metal boxes attached to the side of our triple-deckers.

The thing that amazes me the most is when I sit down at the kitchen island for complete meals that magically appear out of overstocked cabinets, and a giant refrigerator with a machine that makes ice and has silver drawers. There are napkins I use to wipe the sides of my mouth, and when I spill my drink there are paper towels to wipe it up. I hadn't grown up with any kind of paper products aside from toilet paper, which we used to wipe our privates, prop up uneven table legs, plug up mouse holes, and for any kind of spillage that occurred anywhere in the house. It is such a luxury. I even feel a little irresponsible trying to decide which paper product to use for a given mess.

"How was field hockey today?" my aunt asks.

"Oh, it was fine."

"You want more ravioli?" she asks as she scoops more onto my plate without waiting for my reply.

"Yes, please," I say and smile. I've learned that raviolis are my absolute favorite food in the world. I don't know if it's the field hockey practices, the fact that I'm growing taller, or the fact that I'm still having trouble believing the freezer is bottomless.

"I think you have a tapeworm in that stomach, Mal!" she says and laughs.

In many ways this polished world will always be dreamlike to me. It isn't just the new things I notice. It's an overall courtesy, a measured attitude, a calm that exists in my aunt's house but extends out into the neighborhood. People have disagreements but they don't scream at each other, and they certainly don't hurl each other around like mud wrestlers or duke it out on the street.

Every once in a while, when I am not thinking about it, I imagine my parents here. I stand in the back yard looking at the flowering bushes and imagine my parents rolling around on the lawn—my mother screeching, me jumping on my father's back. I open the fully stocked fridge replete with its silver freezer drawer and the frozen cuts of beef, the veggies with the dates markered on sealed Ziploc plastic bags, and remember what it was like when my mom came through the door with the cardboard box and our government rations of cheese, powdered milk and cornflakes, how we converged on that box like honeybees circling nectar.

I don't know why, but I don't miss Kelly Rae at all. I don't miss Auburn High School. It's almost as if that world never existed. Sometimes I can feel Lisa with me again, though, the way she batted the olives on her fingertips or smiled when she threw down the right hand in Rummy.

We haven't talked since I left. I worry about how much I hurt her.

Chapter

Guest of (Dis)Honor

Year: 1992, Mal—18 years old

Dan and I are sitting on the couch waiting for my aunt to come bring us the snacks that she always brings out for guests. Dan has been here so often I don't know how he is considered a guest anymore. Still, I keep myself at a cautious distance from him, not even letting the edges of our hands touch.

"Hey, Mal and Dan," my aunt announces before she comes through the door with two cans of soda—Diet Coke for me and a Root Beer for Dan. She hands them to us.

"Thanks Mrs. Hale, you didn't have to go all out for little old me," Dan says.

My aunt laughs. She and my uncle adore Dan, believing that somehow he is the anchor of stability that's kept me from going off the rails these past few years. They aren't wrong. Dan is probably the most normal thing I've ever done with my teenage social life. He's outlasted all of my friends and most of my family.

"Nonsense. You're our company. We're happy to have you visit."

I open the can, appreciating the sound the bubbles make as they rise.

"Did you hear the wonderful news?" my aunt asks.

228

"Oh, you mean about Dartmouth. I sure did. Couldn't be more proud of my girl."

I take a sip of the Diet Coke. I wish everyone would stop talking about Dartmouth. I'm not saying it's a bad thing I got in or anything, but the tuition is double the cost of the scholarship I got. There's no way I'm going because there's no way I'm going to be able to afford it.

I don't know why the Hales are perpetuating the myth that I'm going. Even if they offered, there's no way I'm letting them pay. Not to mention, Dartmouth is a total reach school for me. I can't even believe I got in. Even if there was some miracle of a way to afford it, I'd be so in over my head.

"Is your car still in the shop, Dan?" my aunt says, her voice carrying a slightly higher pitch than normal.

"Yes ma'am. I apologize. That old thing out there is my dad's car. He let me borrow it for the occasion. That reminds me. I have something for you Mrs. Hale," he says.

He stands up and goes over to the Varsity Jacket he has draped on the chair, and reaches into the inside pocket. He pulls out a box of perfume.

I bite the inside of my lip. Of all the things Dan does, what cracks me up most is his idea of a gift.

"It's Opium. The ladies love it."

"Dan, you don't have to do that. That's too much!"

"Nonsense. Mrs. Hale," Dan says imitating her voice from earlier. "We get a good discount at Filene's and besides it's the least I can do for all your hospitality this year."

I refuse to look at Dan. The truth is, I don't know exactly how Dan makes all the money he does to put himself through community college, to help support his family, and pay for his car. He's told me just enough that I know most of the little packages he doles out, like Mrs. Hale's newest perfume, he somehow gets from the store and resells. They're the kinds of objects my dad says "just fell off a truck."

"Oh, you are too much, Dan. Thank you!"

Aunt Laney makes a great production of opening the perfume box. She pulls the bottle out, takes off the cap, spritzes it on her wrist, waves her wrist in the air, then puts it up to her nose.

"Oh, smell, Mal!" she says and puts her wrist up to my nostril.

"Oh, yeah. Nice. Good taste, Daniel," I say.

My aunt looks at us, smiling in that warm way that she has.

"Well, I'll leave you two alone to talk. I'll be upstairs if you need anything."

"Okay, Laney."

She leaves the room. We listen until we hear footsteps on the tiled floor, up the stairs, on the plush carpeting, and the door closes to her room.

Dan leans in and kisses me. I let him for a second, then push him away and look toward the doorway.

"What's up with your car anyhow?" I ask.

Dan's face tightens, then he smirks.

"Oh no, did they finally repo it?"

"Not exactly."

I look at him strangely. He's laughing inside as he takes his fingers, sweeps the bangs from my face, and kisses me gently on the forehead.

"Seriously, Dan, what did you do?"

"Let's just say I was smart about it. No way I am going to let the company take it after all that work I put into it. So I sort of, you know, fortified it with the insurance."

I look at him, squinching my eyes, studying him.

"Better you don't know. I don't want to make you an accessory."

"Accessory—like a bracelet? Oh, you mean an accessory, like, to a crime."

"Yeah, that. Not a crime exactly. Let's call it an incident."

"You know why I like to hang out with you so much? You make me look good. I'm practically a saint in comparison," I say.

"You are a saint."

"Oh, come on, just tell me. I don't need all the details. I'll keep my mouth shut."

"Let just say one night my beautiful car was the unfortunate victim of a small explosion. Mal, let me tell you, my baby died a beautiful, amazing, fabulous death."

He leans into me and I kiss the top of his head. We rest there a while. Slowly, the parts move through my mind. Dan's father probably won't let him use his car forever. Who knows how long it will take for Dan's insurance scheme to pay off. He'll probably come visit me less.

The letter from Dartmouth resurfaces in my mind.

It occurs to me it's very possible that in less than four months I'll be going to college. And when I go, for the first time in three years, Dan won't be coming with me.

Chapter 50

Song of Myself

Year: 1992, Mal—18 years old

I'm wearing my favorite Kelly-green sweatpants and made a point to comb my hair. I'm sitting in my English composition class trying to pay attention. Professor G is tall and thin. He's wearing jeans that would make me think he was trying to look cooler and hipper than he is if it wasn't for his incredibly white buffy beard and bedraggled hair. Some of the other students call him Father Time. The nickname softens me toward him, somehow.

In my pack I have the essay I turned in to him, with his handwriting scrawled across the front.

Elementary writing, he'd written before he'd hooked me up with the tutor.

It was humiliating, especially when I sat down with the befuddled tutor who had nodded solemnly when I told him I'd gone to several schools growing up, as if to offer up an explanation for my atrocious grammar and overly simple sentence structure.

But I kept that first paper in my pack as a reminder to keep trying. And I'd already improved. I'd written several essays that had gotten B's and on which Father Time had written compliments like *Good work. Intriguing and compelling story. I'd like to learn more about this character.* Reading those comments is kind of strange, because of course the "character" is me.

I look through the window toward the Green. The low afternoon sun shines on the reddish-brown stone of the buildings and the cleanly swept sidewalks. The trees are at their peak, all the maples and oaks flushing red and yellow. The leaves are already falling off the tree, dancing in the air before they land, slowly, on the perfectly manicured lawn.

There's something about the beauty and calmness of this place— the old fine buildings steeped in academic history—that anchors me. I've never been any place so proudly and perfectly focused on academics before. I mean, education has always held a special place in my heart, but this is different. Pre-Dartmouth, school was having breakfast and lunch each day. It was structure, security, a safe place, and occasionally a teacher who took you home with her when you had no place else to go; a teacher who cared enough to gently tell you your sneakers smelled really bad. And I loved it.

But Dartmouth is different. It's truly academia. I can't get by on general logic, common sense, and memorization. It requires real work and truly critical thinking. It doesn't come easy to me. In fact, it makes my head hurt. It's scary as hell, but I love that, too.

I'm so lucky to be here. I'm feeling way in over my head, but everyone came through for me to make this place happen. And the people here make me want to be a better version of myself. I have my scholarship from the State of Massachusetts, a generous aid package from Dartmouth to cover almost the other half of expenses, and the Hales to pick up the rest. I was terrified to come here, but it's an opportunity I couldn't pass up. It's not every day that Main South kids get to go to an Ivy League school.

Today I'm slightly hungover, the result of a losing game of pong I'd played half the night at the Sig Ep house where I'd gone and hooked up with Bill, a senior. These things are proof enough for me that I have arrived at this Ivy League school. Not because the fact that Bill wanted me was validation, but because, in a way, it means I can be like everyone else—or at least blend in.

In the past, I always had to be responsible for myself—to act older than I am in order to take charge of my life. The first time I'd done that was when I'd walked across that little bridge on my way to school from Steve's apartment on Chelsea Street; that decision landed me in the foster home, then Mrs. Eressy's couch, Cherie's closet, and Robyn's bathtub. Let's just say there was a lot of fallout from that decision, which eased when I finally went to live with the Hales. But before college, there was always that feeling of trying to get some place where I belonged. Now I belong only to me. I don't have to pretend so much as decide who I am going to be.

Father Time is reciting a Walt Whitman poem, sections of *Song of Myself*. He's swept up in the beauty of the words. I look around. A girl with beautiful curly red hair the color of the leaves and a bored expression on her face notices me watching her and raises her eyebrows. I smile and re-turn the favor. She turns back to her chair.

I watch Father Time—the way he doesn't look at the book but recites the poem, enraptured, with one hand on his chest as if he is standing on some woodland Shakespearean theatre company's stage, pouring his heart out to a traveling theatre audience. I feel a warmth inside, like the pale autumn sun that lights up the trees, as I remember what I'm going to ask him.

After class ends, I pretend to be messing with the books in my pack until the students spill out of the room. Then I walk up to the desk where Father Time is organizing a messy pile of papers.

He looks up.

"Hello, Marilyn," he says in the dignified way he addresses all the students.

"Hi," I say. My courage has somehow fallen from my chest to my knees.

"Your work is improving. Are you still working with the tutor?"

My words are fish-hooked in my throat.

"Yeah. It's great."

I look toward the open door—the students pushing their way down the hallway, the old school clock on the wall.

"I liked the poem. The one you just read."

He looks up at me, beaming. Then he looks back toward his papers in the distracted way he does mostly everything.

"Whitman. I think so many of us have lost that kind of passionate fervor for life. I think sometimes that's a trapping for those who've grown up with too much, who never had to struggle much. Do you agree, Marilyn?'

"Um. I guess. I think I know what you mean."

He looks up at me, his pale blue eyes focused on me almost like I'm a colleague he's anxious to share an insight with.

"You're determined. I enjoy reading your stories. It's wonderful to see how much your writing is improving, but it's just as enjoyable to read your stories. You haven't had an easy life."

He looks at me that way again, then looks back down at his papers.

"If you didn't grow up with privilege, if you had to fight for it, that means you've earned it, that you deserve it, even more than those for whom it's always been theirs."

I stare at him. Chills flood me, and I get that tugging feeling in my chest like I am ready to cry. It's a feeling I got only a few times before in my life. It's this little space in time that feels so defined, so tangible but it's hard to find; like a secret room that hides behinds a bookcase. You feel so lucky when you magically stumble upon it.

What Father Time just told me was that I belonged.

I think about the eloquent way I had phrased the question in my mind, rehearsing over and over again in my dorm room.

"That's kind of what I wanted to talk to you about. I had this really strange idea. Forget it. I mean it's probably crazy. Forget it."

How can I be validated yet so unsure of myself all in the same moment? He is staring at me, interested. His face also expresses confusion.

"You know, I was just thinking someday I might write like that. You know, about my experiences. I don't know why I even thought about it. I mean, of course I'm nowhere good enough."

"It's always helpful to write about what we have read, to connect with the other academic greats, the great poets and philosophers who took pen to paper and poured their souls out to connect with other human beings in this difficult world throughout the ages."

I look at him, dumbfounded. The claws turned inward for not having explained what I was talking about.

And it *was* a crazy idea. Who would be interested? Why would I even want to go back there?

It had made so much more sense in my dorm room.

Chapter 51

The Wrong Way

Year: 1992, Mal—18 years old

I'm sitting in my dorm room looking through the window at the night sky. The streetlights are on. Davey and Lisa haven't arrived yet. I've changed back into my sweatpants.

I'm feeling torn. I'm relieved they haven't come, that their presence hasn't outed me—plopped Main South at my doorway like a hefty bag full of tin cans. I'm ashamed for feeling this way. At the same time, my heart aches a bit. While it's true I haven't really been close to Lisa or Davey in years, that I barely know them, there's an inexplicable Wrenn undercurrent that flows through us and binds us together..

I'm lying on my bed on my back, my arms crossed over my chest, when someone slams open the door to my room.

"Mal. Phone call for you," a girl says. She's a freshman like me, but I don't remember her name.

"Okay, thanks," I say and bolt up, a headrush making me dizzy as I stand and make my way from the room.

The payphone is dangling in the air by the chain when I pick it up. "Hello?"

"It's her, it's Mal." I hear someone screaming like a lunatic, followed by the sound of air and people laughing in the background.

"Lisa?" I say.

"Yeah, it's Lisa," she says in her high-pitched voice. Then she starts laughing again.

"Are you okay?" I ask.

She laughs harder.

"LI—SAAA!"

"Yeah, sorry. I'm fine. I was just calling to let you know we aren't going to make it there tonight."

"That's okay. Where are you?"

"Back in Worcester."

"What? You guys decided not to come up?" I feel a great sense of relief wash over me, but simultaneously a tinge of sadness.

"Nah, we tried. We got close."

"What happened?"

"That's a long-ass story. You sure you want to hear it?"

"Why ... no...."

"Man, where to start."

I hear her yelling something to the people in the room. I picture lights out in a living room, a shag carpet, the dim blue light of a television, Budweiser cans being sucked and crushed.

"Whose house are you in?"

"Jimmy's. He has the phone. I thought you'd be worried."

I nod. It's considerate of her.

"So, the first thing that happens is we take 290 and we are taking it, so you know we're taking 290 in the wrong direction, accidentally, you know. And then we are on the Mass Pike. We're like two hours going in the wrong way. We're at, like Bridgeport, Connecticut or somethin'."

I put my hand on my forehead and cradle the phone between my shoulder and ear.

"And then, you're never gonna believe this one, guess."

"I have no—"

"We run out of gas."

"You run out of...."

"Gas, yes, yes we run out of gas! We had just enough, and we have no money like I told you, and we run out of gas. The car just kind of jerks shut and I'm like, well, you know, but it takes me a few seconds to realize the car stopped because we have no gas. You know the gas meter on that car was kind of funny the whole time."

"God, so what did you do?"

"So, Davey, he says to me, 'Well Lee, guess you better get out and start hooking!'"

She's laughing hysterically. I'm picturing the twins as they were at five years old, with Lisa clutching Davey's sticky hand.

"So, I'm like, If I'm gonna do this, you better go hide your ass in the bushes."

"Lisa, what are you talking about? What did you do?"

"Oh, not for real. I was just flirting and stuff."

"What do you mean? Flirting with who?"

"Some patrol officer guy came by and asked what's going on. So, I tell him, you know, real sweet-like, I ran out of gas. I need money. I left my wallet at home."

"You left your wallet. Did you even have your license?"

"He didn't ask," she says quickly.

I suck my breath through my teeth, look down the hallway where my RA is using her keys to get into her room, then slams the door behind her. "So he tells me it's going to cost like ten dollars a gallon. I'm like whatever."

The RA bounds out the door again, slams it, and books down the stairs with a gym bag in her hand.

"He was a nice guy though. He said he was gonna help me. And he does, he goes to some gas station at the next exit and comes back with one of those gas container things, but it wasn't enough to get to you."

"Wow, Lisa."

"So, the cop leaves and Davey comes out and he's like, 'Nice work, Lisa.' And I'm like, 'At least I got us enough gas to get your ass home!'"

"So, you went back to Worcester?"

"Duh, we didn't have a choice."

"Holy crap."

"Mal, are you mad?"

"No, I'm not mad. I just don't understand how you could start off on a trip with no money."

"Well, we went the wrong way."

"But even if you hadn't...."

"I know. It was dumb. We never took a long trip like that. We didn't know how far gas would take us. All we knew is that we wanted to come see you."

Chapter 52

Claiming A Life

Year: 1996, Mal—22 years old

I'm on a bench on the lawn in front of the hall where I have the interview with the corporate recruiter in ten minutes. I feel like a ridiculous doll in the wool skirt suit Aunt Laney bought for me at Macy's. I like the colors though, which she'd called jewel tones: burgundy, emerald green, and gray.

At the same time I'm excited. It's the excitement of what I'd imagine it would feel like going to some kind of posh cocktail party, a place where sophisticated people with important jobs and fancy jewelry clink the ice in their glasses and laugh in muted tones.

It's my senior year. It's been a while since I've felt insecure about my right to be here, in an Ivy league school with the sons and daughters of senators and lawyers and owners of big banks.

It's been a long road, from the time my guidance counselor at Auburn High nominated me for the scholarship that would pay for half of my college tuition, until someone at Dartmouth accepted me and believed I had "potential." Here I sit on a manicured lawn at Dartmouth, the scrappy, grubby tomboy from Main South, who's just dug the dirt out from underneath the nails Aunt Laney had insisted I get manicured while waiting to talk with recruiters from Andersen Consulting and JP Morgan.

I remind myself that I deserve it, that I belong among all these people who accomplish great things, and that I will accomplish great things too. I remind myself of what Father Time had implied, that the fact that I didn't grow up in a privileged home or go to private school like many of the students—that I had to earn that privilege—meant that maybe I belong here even more, that I deserve it.

These companies represent one of the final rounds of the gauntlet. Working for big corporations is certainly different than the work that my parents did. There were so many times during my childhood when my father managed to talk someone into using him on a day job painting cruddy houses or driving a truck, when he'd come home two or three days later and sing drinking songs late into the night after he'd been fired for insubordination—which I later learned had something to do with his big, dirty mouth.

I remind myself that I have as much right to a normal life as anyone else. I can make better goals.

At the same time, I don't know exactly what I'm here for. The companies are hiring people for "corporate consulting." I have no idea what a corporate consultant does, just as I don't know how a geography major can become one.

If there's one thing I learned though, it's that you can claim a life that doesn't resemble your own just by believing in it. It's something like dreaming. It's more than just getting bounced along on the street like a tin can that somebody will eventually redeem for a nickel, the way that everyone where I come from just seems to exist to survive. It's something different, and I've always had the odd ability to do it. I haven't dug myself out of homelessness and gotten to attend an Ivy League school because I didn't believe in the possibility, even though it was probably far-fetched.

I've been able to imagine myself wearing fancy suits and walking around boardrooms on carpeted floors in low heels, standing around a water cooler with colleagues and laughing at smart jokes, looking out big windows onto the city of Boston. I can envision myself on the phone selling something to customers, smartly typing sixty words per minute at my desk. And although I had no idea what our jobs would entail, I can vaguely imagine the purpose, the importance behind it.

I stand up, brush off my crazy suit, and start walking across the Green.

Chapter

53

Sense of Place

Year: 1996, Mal—22 years old

I go back to the River Cluster, the dorms where I was stuck as a freshman, and down the stairs to get to the Connecticut River. I sit on a rock overlooking the river, enjoying the warm spring air on my face and the near clarity of the pebbles underneath, coppery and gold in heavy sunlight. I appreciate the river's rhythm. The water rolls. The currents shift slightly. Birds call out in the trees beneath the wind.

The river makes me oddly nostalgic. When I lived in the River Cluster as a freshman, everyone had joked that it was so far off campus it was actually located in Vermont, in another zip code from the rest of the college. It was a nice way for me to ease into living on campus, in a world full of people who had grown up differently and where I wasn't yet quite sure I belonged. Although, like most of the people in the dorm, I didn't walk down the staircase and up the bank for a quarter mile to get to the river that often. The few times I'd done it had stuck with me.

The meeting with the recruiters wasn't completely awful, but I know I didn't get it. They asked me questions in words that sounded like a foreign language. I was distracted, too—it felt like gravity changed once I was in there, like I was an actor on a stage who realizes they've forgotten how to drink a glass of water. But I managed to participate as well as I could, to get out of there with smiles and polite handshakes all around, and when I stood up my skirt wasn't stuck in my undies.

It was enough, I think, that they treated me with a combination of enthusiasm and disguised boredom, the same way they likely treated ninety percent of the students who came to the interviews.

And that's okay, because it was only one option, even if it's my only option right now.

I still didn't know exactly what it was they were recruiting for, but whatever it was, it isn't where my heart is.

In my lap I have my textbook for my Sense of Place class. I'm a geography major, but not the physical side of geography—the social science side. I took the class because it looked interesting, and I'm surprised by how much it resonates with me. Half the time I sit in the class and I'm practically crying. A sense of place is basically the personality of a place, its identity, how it feels to the people who visit that place or who live there, even how it feels to the animals there.

I open the textbook to the current assignment. The chapter talks about how deep human connections can be on a physical and neurological level—that a sense of place is essentially a bridge between the person and the world. "It is a living ecological relationship between a person and particular place, a feeling of comfort and security," I read. "It seems commonplace that almost everyone is born with the need for identification with their surroundings and a relationship to them. So, a sense of place is not a fine art extra, it is something we cannot afford to do without."[1]

Although the course resonates with me on an intimate level, I'm most in awe of it on a larger, more all-encompassing, almost cosmological scale. I can see how it applies, broadly, in the various places I've lived. For example, I could feel a slight yet profound geographical distinction as soon as I crossed the border from Connecticut to Massachusetts.

In Connecticut everything felt more groomed, from the placement of trees to the streetlights along the highway. Things were well maintained, including the people, with their proper clothing and terse accents. Massachusetts, on the other hand, was haphazard, wild, from the trees to the random road construction—even the concrete of the highway felt grayer. My Massachusetts was Connecticut's rough around the edges, tough guy

[1]*The Geography of Nowhere: The Rise and Decline of America's Man-Made Landscape,* by James Howard Kunstler.

cousin, wearing a flannel shirt and speaking with a rolling accent that was partially swallowed up by the air.

The course leads me to understand Worcester differently on a personal level. Ever since I left, Worcester has returned to me, like a memory but on a sensory level. Memories of a scent surface, barely detectable: the snow, weeds, twisted metal and dirt. It reminds me of the time I spent with Lilac, on those long afternoons we hung out under the porch smoking pot. The scent of over-boiled hot dogs and syrupy baked beans in the cafeteria return and remind me of the Mustard Seed Soup Kitchen. When some guys burned some plastic jugs in a campfire behind the frat house, it reminded me of two things—the time when I met Dan at our campfire at the Rez, and the unnatural scent of whatever drugs my mother and her friends smoked.

It's surprising that the memories the scents trigger are so strong and almost present, as if I can touch them; whether they're pleasant or unpleasant memories, they seem relatively neutral to me. Either way, they make me nostalgic. It turns out that Worcester is a place that's hardwired in me, and on some level I belong there even if I didn't believe that I did.

The book talks about how a sense of place is different between people who lived in different centuries, where there was primitive technology and they were isolated on farms and the like with the few hundred or thousand people in their towns being their only context. Being marooned like that makes their relationship with place even deeper, more intimate. The book says that people who live now and are connected to a wider world through technology, phones, and airplanes tend to have a more washed-out connection to place, but crave these connections on a deep level many of us aren't even aware of.

My mind returns to Worcester. Few people who lived there ever left there. Worcester is the only world they know. Almost everyone I know talked trash about it, blamed it for their crummy lives and circumstances. In Main South it wasn't unusual that our family didn't own a phone or a car. I wonder if that's maybe part of everyone's problem there. It's a place where people have become stuck between centuries.

Maybe the sadness of the places keeps them butting up against their own worst moments. Maybe you have to be away long enough for it to stop hurting like that in order to get over it.

I skim down to the negative experiences of place. The book talks about women who are abused or countries where genocide occurred can make people feel stuck in the place. It can also contribute to a "poisoned" sense of place in which people wind up being hateful and having resentment toward people in other places, which could also be the case in Worcester.

Maybe this is why people from Worcester often shun people who have left, as if for all intents and purposes they no longer exist.

But then my mind turns to my Aunt Laney's house in Charlton. The quiet air dotted by the sound of fish coming to the lake's surface for a bite of water bug, the way that quiet air simultaneously whooshed through the trees, and the swarms of mosquitoes seeking me out all left me with a very different sense of place. How can a physical place that is merely twenty miles away from Worcester have such an amazingly different personality?

PART 9

Losing Our Male Wrens Again

Once upon a time somewhere in the green hills on the South Coast of Ireland, where leprechauns plucked wishing flowers, just down the hill from where the red-headed barmaids served pints of genuine Guinness to sailors who cried about their lost loves, all the birds of the land held a contest. They wanted to see who among them could be the king of all the birds. Whichever bird flew the highest would win this distinguished title.

There were some contenders among them. We're talking the Marvelous Marvin Haglers of the bird flying world. There were the raptors: the peregrine falcons that could fly a hundred and fifty miles per hour and snatch a rat from under a knoll; the eagles with their long wing span who could block out a competitor; the owls who could crush skulls with their talons. Then there were the wicked smaht birds: the ravens and crows who could trick a human by imitating a car alarm or their baby's cry. And there were all the others: the swift and the fierce and the sad, the mallard duck and the blue jay and red robin and yellow finch, and even the giant heron with their clumsy, oafish, prehistoric legs.

Most of the birds were hopeful, as birds don't get anywhere in life by being bashful. They'd all developed tricks over time to fool intruders like faking their enemies bird song, making dummy nests, or even when all of the blackbirds gathered in giant gaggles together all at once, like magnetic filings, and swooped up into the sky and down in a farmer's field of corn or wheat and back up again.

They all had their powers. The males knew how to primp and preen and distract others with their beauty and chest beating. The females were smarter and fiercer but knew the men were kind of dodos and that they would get more accomplished if they didn't show off.

Deep down though, many of the birds were realists. They knew they couldn't fly as far or fast as the raptors and didn't think they'd be king. Some figured maybe they would be runner-up, get a second-place blue ribbon like I got that one time for reading.

The contest began. The referee blew a secret bird whistle and all of the birds took to the sky. At first it was really exciting with all the birds flapping and yelling. Then things started to slow down a little. The birds all had great heart, but of course, after a few hours, the smaller and clumsier birds had to give up and find a spot to land. From the ground, they pecked around for some seed, but most were masking their exhaustion. They waited with great humility to see who would be King of the Birds.

Eventually almost all the birds came down from the sky. From high up they heard the eagle, who screeched with the squeaky, feminine eagle voice that didn't match his size—a voice that embarrassed him sometimes—proclaim himself king of the birds.

Just then, a small wren hopped down off the back of the eagle. "No, no," he cried with his ferocious voice, "I am the king of the birds. I hitchhiked on the dumb eagle's back and I flew higher than he flew and peeked through the clouds." The wren's otherwise impressive voice shook a little. The wren isn't exactly used to confronting his opponents directly, especially those as large as an eagle. And he hadn't meant to call him dumb. The words just slipped from his beak.

They both flew down. The eagle was humiliated. He went off in a huff and sought support from the other raptor birds. All the birds of the land waited until they had broken up their little raptor pack. Then they came over and told the wren he had cheated.

The wren turned into a geeky punk and told the raptors he was using his wits, something they lacked. For a while the raptors seethed, the owls turning their heads around two hundred degrees to freak him out with their stare.

Chapter 54

The Mortician's Play-by-Play

Year: 2018, Mal—44 years old

I'm on the phone with Lone Wolf. The iPhone is a strange thing now. I hold it, feeling the weight of it, and remember how we didn't even have a wall phone growing up. I'm standing in the kitchen in my suburban home in Duxbury with its one-cup coffee maker, a collection of steak knives in butcher block holders, and a mailbox at the end of the drive-way. But a part of me is still in Worcester in some rough kitchen, in some undefinable house with an address I may eventually add to my eviction list, roaches scurrying past food congealing on plates and bowls in the sink and only some ketchup packets in the fridge. Part of me is in one of those apartments with the television perpetually blaring, with my mother's friends stuffed on the couches, with the scent of something caustic like burning plastic smoldering in thick brown paper wrapped in somebody's hand.

"So, like I was saying Marilyn, it was a tall order getting your brother David ready. To make him viewable," Lone Wolf is saying.

I move to a chair and sit down. I still don't know if I made a mis-take, agreeing with my family that it was important to be able to see Davey

248

before he was cremated. Deep down though, I knew I had to see him. Something about it is important to me.

If there's one thing I can give Lone Wolf credit for, it's talking to the medical examiner's office and convincing them to allow him to attempt to make my brother semi-presentable before the cremation.

I'm beginning to feel that Lone Wolf has some of the same qualities as my parents. He's kind and well-meaning but winds up inadvertently bungling things up in a way that seems perfectly reasonable to him, and then he explains it to me as he would any member of the giant, dysfunctional community in Worcester. I'm on my third heart-wrenching call with the man. Maybe he's just being cautious by giving me a play-by-play account of their work. It could be he just wants to warn me about the physical condition of my brother's body.

Through the phone I can hear Lone Wolf's side conversation. "Okay, we're going to have to adjust his jaw," he says.

The feeling of shame returns to me. I think back to the days when Davey still lived with us—just Mom, Davey, and me. In some way, I felt like my mother and I were always picking on him because he was the boy and we girls kind of stuck together. Did this influence my mother to kick him to the curb, sending him into foster care when he was eleven? I don't remember Davey being a particularly mischievous child. But without my dad, I think my mother was in over her head and even more out of control than we all were together as a family.

It wasn't long after Davey disappeared that I disappeared too.

"Paul, Paul. We need two or three sutures over here, over here on the right side."

I'd lived with dysfunctional people long enough to understand you can't really talk sense into them unless you somehow give validity to their completely messed-up view of the world, that you have to do everything in your power to sympathize with that view if you wanted to get anything accomplished. You had to occasionally give whatever they were saying credence, even if it was killing you.

"We're going to do our best to fix his nose now," he says.

And you have to know when you reach your limit, and how important it is to cut yourself off.

"Lone Wolf, I really can't tell you how much we appreciate what you're doing for our brother, for our family. I have to go pick up my son now, though. Thank you so much for the call, Lone Wolf."

"My pleasure, Marilyn."

"Okay. So, we'll come on Saturday. He will be ready then, correct?" I ask.

He pauses a few seconds, his breath thickening on the phone.

"Yes. Saturday. As promised. We always keep our promises. I won't be there Saturday, because unfortunately I have other obligations. But I want you to call me after you view him. You have my cell phone."

Chapter

Davey Resemblances

Year: 2018, Mal—44 years old

We stand in the funeral home, staring down at the gurney where Davey is laying. I fixate first on his beard; full, unkempt, dark brown with patches of red and white in it. I've never seen him with a beard before. His mustache curls over his lip, also brown with patches of red. His hair had darkened to a deep walnut color with reddish tones, like my father's, and his hairline had receded. His jawline, which Lone Wolf had told me they'd struggled hard to bring forward, resembled my father's slightly. His cheekbones looked like my father's cheekbones too. I find this surprising, because Lisa was always the one that looked like my father. My brother used to resemble my mother, and I was the mutt.

The rest of his face is damaged. I see that Lone Wolf wasn't exaggerating the amount of work that they did to fix him up—the way he said they had to rebuild his nose pretty much from scratch. But they obviously didn't know, or couldn't appreciate, what he truly looked like beforehand. His nose and lips look like the features of an entirely different man. He just isn't himself.

I gasp quietly. The totality of how a life can be erased so completely hits me hard. I feel so sad for him—all of him, the Davey with the cowlicks and this Davey with the red and white beard and whatever is left that resembles him in that face. Again, I wonder how this happened. Could it have been prevented? Apparently, he was on some medication with side effects of paranoia and hallucinations. If he wasn't on the medication, would he have jumped? Surely he wouldn't have made that decision, otherwise. Did he even make that decision at all?

I look at what's left of my wily family. My mother's eyes are still dry and her expression appears almost bored. I know there's something deep down in her that grieves or will grieve when it hits her. It has to hit her, eventually. All the men in our family are gone.

I examine Lisa again, Davey's soul shadow, his twin. They shared a womb. That different connection has to be there, hardwired somewhere within her. It doesn't matter if they didn't physically see each other often. It must be worse for her to see him disfigured like this, to know he's been ripped from the earth.

She stands there. Her body spasms quietly while tears roll down her cheeks.

As the car moves, feeling returns to my body, my legs, my shoulders, and my neck. My jaw loosens. The sky is still gray, but the clouds are almost translucent, giving us permission to breathe.

"You okay?" Greg asks quietly.

"Yeah," I whisper.

Greg's type-A nature, which can at times drive me up a wall in regular life, has been incredibly helpful since Davey died.

"No, Greg, don't turn down there. That's Kilby Street," my sister calls out.

By now Greg, who has become a skilled first responder, gracefully careens the car away from Kilby Street and makes a right onto another road.

"Bunch of spics down there," my mother says.

"Cheryl. We don't use that kind of language in this car," Greg says.

"What, there's nothing wrong with it. They don't mind you call them that. Some of my best friends were Puerto Ricans," she says.

I smile awkwardly, watching the crinkle in Greg's forehead deepen.

"Where are we now?" my sister asks.

We drive down the streets. A heaviness weighs on my eyes. I know how easy it is to get disoriented here, to wander the streets in loping, coyote circles. Everything is exactly the same. Lopsided triple-deckers with faded paint and sagging porches line narrow streets. There are makeshift, milk-crate-sized yards. Everything is gray or dirty white.

We're nowhere, I think.

My mind returns to my geography book in college, the idea about the sense of place. I recall the neutrality of the sensory memories that returned to me from Worcester, how they had made me feel more connected to it, even nostalgic. I could be like that as long as I was far away from it.

The book spoke of spots where lots of people had died, or been hurt, and how those places can be toxic somehow—yes, poisoned, they called it poisoned—a poisoned sense of place. People get stuck there, it says, repeating the same patterns, getting mangled.

It's true. Every time I come back it's because somebody's been mangled.

"He had some of dad's features. His cheekbones, his jaw. It surprised me. He still had your thick hair though, Mom."

Nobody responds but Greg, who squeezes my forearm. In the back seat, Lisa makes a slight whimpering sound that she tries to keep to herself.

I remember my dad, just the edges of him, the way he looked sitting on the chair watching the television, rubbing the scruff on his face while he took in the antics of the Road Runner, his whole body shaking with laughter. Even when he was drunk, that laughter was sweet and boundless; it drew people to him and took some of the pressure off their foul moods. I remember his large hand, or so it seemed back then, touching me on the shoulder that day we'd found my hamster, or touching me on the chin when he put the string around my tooth in order to pull it. He was there, present, until the day when he wasn't.

I remember the last time I came to Worcester after something bad happened, it was to visit my dad.

Chapter **56**

Another Mangled Man

Year: 2000, Mal—26 years old

The strangest part about looking at my father lying unconscious in the ICU, his body mangled with tubes shoved up his nose and a trach in his throat, is that his ravaged face is so familiar to me. This is the same toothless man who showed me how to fix his car, who took me to McDonald's for cheeseburgers, and who marched me back to school that time I cut class. It's been a decade since I've seen him last. In fact, it was that day at my Aunt Marybeth's house when he hadn't noticed my new haircut.

My fiancé, Tom, who's sitting on the chair underneath the beeping machine, is less familiar to me. The thing that's strangest about him is that he's been crying. In the fluorescent light of the hospital room, I can see there are tear stains on his face. His tear-stained face confuses me. It seems unfair that Tom is able to cry for my father when I don't seem to feel anything at all.

I look at my father's thin body, wrapped in the blanket. His head is tipped back awkwardly on the pillow, on the exact spot between his C-1 and C-2 vertebrae, where the bullet caught him. Again, I touch the spot on the back of my own neck. Up until now I hadn't known it existed.

The machines make a labored breathing sound for him, like someone suffocating in a movie. It's dark but I can see his ravaged, concave face lit up by the machines that are flashing and beeping, like a map made by a cartographer plotting a spaceship's flight path.

We don't know if he's going to live.

I'm disoriented. The feeling is old, yet familiar, the way I used to wake up sometimes when I was a kid in a new apartment and had forgotten where I was. It always shook me for some reason, and I'd go over the places we'd been like a prayer in my mind—the shapes of the rooms, hand-me-down blankets on rented beds—until I pinpointed the correct one.

If my father was conscious, I wonder if he'd feel the same way.

"Stubborn son of a bitch." The nurse starts to tell me the story again, her voice slow and somewhat demented-sounding, like she's telling a sick fairytale to a child who's prone to bad dreams.

It's a strange situation, having people talking to you about terrible things that have happened to your father, viewing through the lens of a traditional father-daughter relationship. They assume that my heart must be absolutely crushed right now. But it's not. And this is a man I hardly know.

She is trying to be kind. She doesn't know how cold I am. She has perhaps mistaken my blank expression for ordinary shock. "In the ambulance, he'd been pronounced dead already. I don't know how long he was down, maybe a minute. Then your daddy here just shot back to life, just like a zombie. Scared the crap out of the medics."

Tom laughs awkwardly.

It doesn't surprise me, really. My dad had a reputation in the bars of shooting upright after he'd been cold clocked, swinging at the air with his eyes closed.

It was probably more habit than anything else. He probably wasn't fighting because he wanted to live.

I look at his scrawny ribcage and neck, at his off-colored skin. I look toward the accordion tube on the machine squeezing breath in for him, at the saline bag dripping, and see not what is being pumped into him but everything that is draining out: a lifetime of booze, cigarettes, and coffee. I imagine what a toll it must be taking on his well-pickled body, detoxing from everything all on the same day.

No wonder he won't open his eyes.

A large, clammy hand plods down on my shoulder. I shudder.

"Honey. The cops are still in the hallway. They are waiting to talk to you. Patiently."

I stand in the hallway where the two large cops hover over me. One has red hair and is mealy faced, and the other is dark haired with elephant-sized paws. They're talking softly to me, with that nearly familial way that all people in Worcester share with each other, and that the cops in particular always used when speaking about my father.

"Your dad he's what we cahl a frequent fliah.... But I always liked him. He was, uhm, is, a real sweet guy."

The other cop laughs, then stops abruptly.

"Rah sense of humah, that David Wrenn. He had me in stitches a few times. Batty but ah gahd soul. Spirit in him," it sounds like he's saying.

Is it possible being away for so long has stripped me of the ability to understand the accent? The idea makes me happy.

"Spitfihah, a real sweet guy," the first cop repeats.

It sounds like they regarded my dad as some kind of mascot, the cop pet.

"This is what he had on him," the first cop says and hands me what appears to be a brown paper lunch bag. My hand reaches out and takes it, robotically, without me telling it to. I curl my knuckles and clutch it, managing to pierce it despite my chewed-off fingernails. Looking at the lunch bag I see in black block letters **WORCESTER POLICE EVIDENCE** with black lines that have the contents of my father's life detailed on it:

CASE #9 INVENTORY #IOOC6702
CONTENTS—1 Brown Wallet w/ Personal Papers
DATE AND TIME OF RECOVERY—6-24-2000 at 13:15 hours
VICTIM—David Wrenn
TYPE OF OFFENSE—Shooting

"We are real sahry this happehned. He didn't deserve it," the mealy-faced cop says.

"I'm sorry. Excuse me. But what happened, exactly?" I say, my words like polished stones. I search their faces for some trace of judgement toward me for something, for leaving Worcester maybe, for letting my dad rot here. I find none.

"The report is inconclusive. But from what we heah from corrobah-rahting witnesses, your dad was at a bar in the projects ovah on Pleasant Street. It was the middhl of the dayh."

"The projects?" I ask. This fact alone is enough to show my father had hit his personal rock bottom, that he had traded his racist beliefs for rotgut.

"Who comes to rob a bahr in the projects in the middhl of the dayh....
Crackheads, I guess. The registah barely has any cahhhhhssssh."

"They were wahving that gun around in the air."

"It's fuzzy then, but your fathah somehow for some reason, he stood
up. He was maybe a little anahyed that those guys were rahbing the place."

The other cop snickers. I suck my stomach in.

"Anyhow, he just says then, he goes, 'I'm outtaah heah.' Just like that,
'I'm outtaah heah.' You cahnt blame him, I guess."

I challenge the cop who snickered with my eyes.

"I don't understand."

"Fah as we cahn tell, he spooked them. They were prahbably jitterhy
anyhah. One of them gets an itchy finger and David Wrenn, uh your da, he
gehts shot."

They stare at me, waiting for a reaction. I don't know what they are
expecting from me—validation that they told the story right? Maybe they
want me to laugh at the punchline.

"Okay," I say.

"We didn't get them yet. The robbahs. But I promise, we will."

I look inside the brown paper lunch bag to find what's left of my father's worldly possessions—the only clues I have about what his recent life
had been like. There are two Pall Malls, which means he was so broke he had
to bum or buy single cigarettes and they didn't even have his brand. There's
a wallet with his taxi driver's license, no doubt evidence of some kind of job
scheme that perhaps lasted longer than most. And, to my surprise, there's a
photo of our family when we were all together. The twins couldn't have been
any older than three and I was four. My parents appear ageless to me, their
slow, sparkly expressions filled with hope.

Chapter

Perfectly Unsettled

Year: 2004, Mal—30 years old

Four years have now passed since the shooting. Tom and I have since married and have a brand-new, beautiful baby boy named Jack. Life had carried on over these four years in some sort of weird new normal that includes weekly trips to visit my father in a long-term rehab setting. He's a quadriplegic now, and a ventilator does the breathing for him.

I sit in the rocking chair, my son Jack curled up on my chest, in the tiny, buttercup-yellow, arts-and-crafts-style bungalow with the wrap-around porch Tom and I now own in Scituate, a little waterfront community South of Boston.

I look down at this tiny creature I'm rocking, part of my hand cradling his neck. His head has turned red from his crying. I kiss him on it.

I haven't slept in days and the hormones pretty much make my skin feel like it's inside out. This baby boy is my whole heart and world now, and yet I'm so uncomfortable, so unsettled. I'm somewhat angry, if I'm being honest. I'm not mad at sweet little baby Jack, of course—it's more the circumstance, the past that brought me to this vulnerable child I don't know how to take care of. I feel so unsure of myself. I'm more aware than ever that I didn't have an upbringing that I can use as a model for Jack.

I'm mad at everyone, too. I'm mad at Tom because even though he's dutifully changed diapers and rocked Jack to sleep for the first couple of weeks, he got to go back to work.

I'm mad at my father for getting shot, for catapulting me back to Worcester and back into his life after I thought I had broken free of it all. I remember my father's face mangled in the darkness, the IV tube shoved up his nose.

I try again to piece together the cop's story, to imagine my father in the bar when the robbers came in. He'd been sitting there nursing something, the cheap watered-down rotgut the bartender was pouring him all day. What could he have been thinking about: slow dancing to "Love Me Tender" with my mother, fantasizing a giant plate of eggs over easy with salt, pepper, and ketchup?

I imagine the guys coming in waving the gun. My father had probably sobered up enough to recognize something serious was going on. Clearly his sense of reasoning, the ability to execute a real plan, was gone though.

"It's fuzzy then, but your fathah somehow, for some reason, he stood up. He was maybe a little anahyed that those guys were rahbing the place."

My father startled the robbers—this bow-legged, copperhead barfly who'd just stood up.

"'I'm outtah heah.' Just like that, 'I'm outtah heah.' You cahn't blame him I guess."

They shot him.

The cop's storyline disappoints me. It shouldn't matter how he got shot, but the little girl in me wanted to believe he was some kind of hero, that he was shot trying to save the day.

They never did find who did this. Something tells me they don't try that hard to solve the cases of public nuisance victims.

The only way people get out of Worcester is in a body bag.

People used to say that a lot in Main South.

I remind myself that truth isn't mine, how fortunate I am. I had gotten out with all my limbs intact. I was lucky to go on to college and even to graduate school. I had found a good man and had a beautiful baby boy. I was starting to build a life for myself, one with stability, safety, and normalcy.

Had I really gotten out clean though?

The baby stirs.

Shhh, hush it's okay, baby Jack, I whisper in my practiced voice.

I remember Tom's face in the hospital room after he'd cried. He was deeply confused by my nonreaction. He's looked at me that way more than once since we've been together. It's a very specific expression. It's as if there are moments when he recognizes his suspicions about there being something missing in me are confirmed, but he doesn't want them to be. It's a sweet, almost endearing expression; it makes me feel almost sorry for him. At the same time, it breaks my heart.

I look around the cottage. It's tiny but neat and well cared for, and it has everything a person could possibly need. Tom has gently nailed framed photos to the wall: of our wedding, Jack and me in the hospital after he was first born, even me in my cap and gown after college graduation. The appliances in the kitchen are shined with Fantastic. The salt air coming through the open windows makes the curtains billow. I'd wanted it all so badly: a comfortable and pretty place, a good man, a beautiful son.

It just took a few hours in Worcester for me to feel like a fraud.

I resist the urge to pull my hair back from my eyes to avoid disturbing the baby. I push my legs down deeper into the footrest and rock slowly, just barely, in a way that I hope will soothe us both.

It's always been this way with Tom—me standing between narrowing panes of unsmeared glass, feeling exposed. I've tried so hard to be some variation of the me I've been fantasizing about since that day I crossed the bridge on my way to school, since the day that first essay was accepted, and all those years I spent looking up the definitions of words in my English books. When I was twenty-three years old I thought I'd finally become her, with my smart-pressed suits and my clean fingernails, when I'd landed my first job in the corporate world.

And that's where Tom and I first met—at work. Tom had been a part of that world long before I had. He was a nice guy; responsible, gainfully employed. He was everything I thought was a smart, sensible choice for a partner. I felt safe around him. There was something sweet and concerned while he looked at me working that made me feel both validated and protected. It was as if Tom was the final detail I needed to cement and build my own life.

Chapter 58

Lucky?

Year: 2004, Mal—30 years old

I stand in my father's room clutching a large, white dogwood blossom picked from the tree outside. I use my other hand to balance baby Jack against my body. He's quiet, heavy on my hip.

The drapes in the rehab are open. Corn-colored light exposes pale red shadows on my father's cheek.

My father. David Wrenn. His tiny head is elevated on two cushy pillows. His deep auburn hair has grown long enough that it spreads onto the starched white.

My father is a head.

That is how I think of my father now, as the only part of his body that works. My father is a head. My father is a head with ears that can hear and a mouth that will never again eat food from a spoon and cannot speak. That mouth is still mostly toothless.

"Hi Dad."

I bend down slightly, hoisting Jack's tiny body while shifting him toward his grandfather. I let the flower drop unskillfully onto the small rolling tray.

"The baby," my dad says. No words leave his mouth. His face contorts

261

as he stretches them out. I can still "hear" the words though, spoken in his thick Worcester accent and the exact tone of his voice that imprinted on my brain when I was a child.

If the nurses heard him, they'd probably make fun. That accent embarrasses me, but it also makes me nostalgic.

There's something unnerving about seeing his scrawny, leprechaun body so inert, to accept that those quick and jerky limbs that had prevented him from being cold clocked in bar fights will never move again.

All those years in and out of rooming houses and homeless shelters, and yet, here he is, in a warm bed and with a full belly. And he can't feel any of it. Is he lucky?

My dad's expression looking at Jack is amused, even juvenile. It's the same way he looked when he watched cartoons in one of our many living rooms growing up.

"I brought him to see you. He wanted to come see his grandpa."

The sound of my own voice in this place, on the other hand, makes me cringe. It feels false.

It's become my job to come visit my father, to bring him flannel shirts and Elvis CDs, small comfort items to compensate for his only real belongings—a photo of our broken family and two Pall Malls in the paper bag the cops handed me at the hospital.

I close my mouth and try and breathe through my nose. The rehab home smells like urine and antiseptic soap, a distinct scent that makes my tongue feel hairy.

I check Jack again. He's quiet. His color is normal, his cheeks pink like they're supposed to be. I laugh. I've stopped recording every bowel movement, nod to sleep, or how many ounces of formula he drank, in my graph paper notebook. But the feeling that I'm doing something irreparably wrong, like I'm missing that parental instinct, never goes away.

My father is still young, only fifty-four years old. He hasn't aged. There's a sweetness in the way I remember him, like remembering warm wind in autumn or the scent of the ground warming in spring.

Strangely, he is the goodness in my childhood.

I follow his eyes to the thirteen-inch, old-school tube television on his nightstand.

"Sox playing?" I ask.

Behind the curtain, my father's roommate is cursing the birds.

"Sox playing?" I repeat.

"On a wickeed winning streak," he mouths, his feisty Irish temper intact.

"Yeah, look at that, eleven to four. What's this, game number eighty-six?"

"Eighty-seven," my dad says.

I smile. My father dropped out of school in the sixth grade. He's by no means a dumb guy. He has a wily kind of smarts and can talk most men under the table, but he's never been academically focused. He can't read books or the newspaper, except sometimes the funnies. There isn't any message he's dying to communicate to us that will keep him alive. But he still loves his Red Sox games.

It is a small miracle the Red Sox are doing so well this season, just three games behind the Yankees.

The head can turn, be propped up. It can root for the Sox.

The Red Sox are my dad's religion, like lighting a candle at church. It's the same for all the guys who never left Main South. Lying there watching the Sox is almost as good as sitting at the bar in the mid-afternoon with his neighbors, spellbound. When they scored it was as if he was cheering with them, loudly, squeezing each of their shoulders.

"How's Pedro pitching?" I ask.

"Lightning," I think he mouths.

"Good," I say.

My father is wearing a johnny. The clothes I bought him are more symbolic than anything else. I examine his nails, which are ragged but have been trimmed recently. Thank God. I don't have it in me to harass the nurses today.

I hoist Jack up in my arms and sort of rock him. He's remarkably quiet. Of course, this worries me.

I don't know if my dad is proud of me for going to Dartmouth or for getting out of Worcester, or if these things just serve to make me foreign to him, like all those other people in the world he hates because he feels that they judge him. I do know my dad is proud of us for having the baby.

A nurse walks in, hovering, not saying a damn word.

I can see her disapproval in the way my father's eyes clutch the television.

"Thank them for trimming his nails for me."

She nods and glances at the television, then winks at me.

"Red Sox winning yet?" she asks.

"It's a close call."

"He says that it's close," I say in my cheeriest voice, noticing the slightest smirk on my dad's face. He looks at me and winks, the same way he did when my mother occasionally talked about her wealthy relatives over the years.

The nurse goes up behind my father and props his pillow a little.

"Are you doing okay, Mr. Wrenn?" she asks in a cold, business-like tone.

My father blinks his eyes. Only I can tell he's annoyed.

"Course he's okay. He's a fighter," I say, crooning.

The nurse doesn't respond, but stands there, still hovering.

Quadriplegic. Paralysis. Nonverbal. Those were the words that they used. Did those charts carry, lodged between the Latin-based language undecipherable to non-doctors, the story of a man who was shot, unheroically, in the crossfire of a haphazard robbery by crackheads while he was day drinking in the projects?

"He chose to live. They pronounced him dead you know. In the ambulance."

The story spills out of me.

"But this stubborn son of a bitch shot back to life in the ambulance. He wasn't ready to go yet."

Am I imagining a trace of a smile on my father's face?

I wondered if he would have reconsidered if he'd known the body he was shuddering back into, the body of a man who would be numb beneath his Adam's Apple, who would never be able to speak again, who would be on a breathing machine his whole life.

I look at my father—his piercing green eyes, his small, sharply angled jawline.

Still and clean, two things he's never been before.

I don't know what's left of him now that he's gone from Worcester, now that he's in this place. Every ounce of my father's spirit, his impulse toward survival, comes from his ability to move around physically—to leave the house when the landlord or the cops come knocking, to flee the bar after he'd kicked someone's ass or someone kicked his ass, to skirt the edges of the college campus collecting cans. In this place, he is trapped.

"Oh, we know your father's a fighting son of a bitch. We have a bet going about how long he'll go before cursing one of us out."

I'm not imagining it. He's definitely laughing.

I let out my breath, rock the baby. He's sleeping. Somehow he is lighter to me than usual. I want to laugh too.

"Oh yeah. What's the spread?"

"Double or quits. Pretty good odds. I've got my money on three hours. What do you say, David?"

"Fuck you," my father mouths.

I laugh. The nurse slaps her hands together.

"Looks like I'm the lucky winner."

I look at my father. He winks at me again. His eyes look teary, soft, like a little kid who has just woken up from a nap.

I hoist Jack up higher.

"Well, I will leave you alone with your sweet grandson," the nurse says.

I clutch the baby. The nurse sort of kisses her fingers and then touches Jack's head with them, like a priest.

The door closes behind her.

I move the chair over to the side of my father's bed. I follow his eyes to the television set. It's a pizza commercial, smiling people chewing cheese.

"Dad, we're going to have to leave soon. Jack needs to eat."

He blinks his eyes, slowly, butterfly-like for a few seconds to let me know he understands.

"Dad, I wanted you to know something. I just wanted to tell you, you know everything that happened back when Davey, Lisa, and I were kids? It's okay."

He doesn't move his eyes at all. But I can feel him focused on me.

"What the fuck are you tawalking about," he says, his mouth dragging.

"I mean, you know, for the bad things. It's okay."

He turns his attention back to the television set, as if it was one of the living rooms in one of the successions of old triple-deckers in Main South we were being perpetually evicted from. If he could still use his arms and fingers, he would have aimed the remote and turned the volume back up.

PART 10

Saying Goodbye

Wrens don't do well being still. They're kinetic beings. Air under their wings, swooping acrobatically from branch to branch, and terrorizing the other birds is the way they process the world. Movement infuses their crafty brand of intelligence, their royal status, their complicated song. If they don't keep themselves busy doing nonsensical things—building dummy nests, sticking their flags all over new turf they won in their gang wars, making themselves hoarse trying to attract a new mate, wrecking and rebuilding their homes—their spirits go dormant. They lie in bed like their ancestors did in that mouse hole, fear slowly burning a hole through their hearts. Everything that makes them special is stuck and their curiosity, their hidden beauty, is barely perceptible.

After I was away from Worcester for a bird's life cycle, completed grad school, and began to engage in the world with some joy, like fairy wrens picking up pink and purple flower petals, I still was hard-pressed to articulate stories about the family and the place I'd come from.

Sometimes I'll hear an otherwise-refined person talk trash about people on welfare or food stamps and something deep in my throat begins to grumble.

I want so badly to speak up, to explain that mooching off the system, being trapped in that world where your craftiness comes to define you, isn't something the wrens do because they are lazy or bad hearted. It's more that they spent their fixed lives trapped in a cacophony of sound and confusion, that flying from limb to limb until their energy is spent is the way they believe they're hardwired to survive. It bothers me that I didn't inherit my father's ability to yell back—that as hard as I tried, I was never able to learn any of his songs.

Chapter

Summing Up A Life

Year 2004, Mal—30 years old

I'm surprised that the cavernous church where my father's service will be held is so warm, with gas that had been ordered and paid for, as if all the heat in Main South has somehow been pumped into this place people visited for funerals and the occasional Sunday.

We're in the front row. Tom is shifting uncomfortably, picking the lint off his dress pants. Next to him are Aunt Marybeth and Lisa, their faces sunburned and stunned. Next to them are my mother and Davey. I hold my carriage high, the way my Swedish Nana had carried herself, but the breath barely enters my lungs.

Soon I'll stand up and deliver a eulogy for my father. Marybeth was the one who asked me to do it. She was counting on me to stand at the front of this huge, wide-open space and fill it up with words—kind words that would make everyone look back longingly on the life my father lived and the person that he was. I had lain in bed for weeks trying to come up with the right words, racking my memory and looking for the good things.

Slowly, it dawned on me that our relationship was more fraudulent than I had understood. My compassion toward my father over the course of those four years he'd been laying in the rehab mouthing words and blinking his eyes ran deep but was connected to the romanticized father who had taught me to turn over a car and brought us Happy Meals during our childhood. I'd blamed my mother for everything that went wrong in our lives, but I had seen his drunken antics: all the shoeless nights and black eyes, the screaming, and the trips in the paddy wagon had been something that was "just him." In my mind I had equated it with an endearing quality.

And he was, in some twisted way, endearing. I can't hate him, but I also have to admit to myself that I didn't really understand him.

I turn around and examine the pews in the church, mostly empty with the exception of the last row where a few people I don't recognize sit. I look at the old guys among them, one with fresh shaving nicks on his cheeks and tugging on the tie of his ill-fitting suit, and search their eyes for memories of my father. Were any of them the ones who had run with my father toward the end, or were they neighborhood fixtures I didn't remember—long defeated families who had never left Main South and felt obligated to be here?

We're his only real relatives. I know that for sure.

"I couldn't find Joe Ballote," Aunt Marybeth had told me.

Hearing that had made me feel unreasonably sad. The only constant I had known in my dad's life was Joe Ballote—both Joe Ballote, Dad's friend, and Ballote the hamster.

I unbutton the top button of my dress shirt. I don't want to be here in Main South, on the streets I had vowed to leave behind. Just returning here makes me feel like I have a film of dirt or something on me, that my body is crooked. I'm mad at my father, not so much for dying as for making me return to those streets, to this church.

My father wouldn't have wanted to be here either.

A memory comes to me. It isn't of my father but me and Davey, sitting in this same church on Sundays in our raggedy clothes, our legs still so short that they hadn't reached far past the benches.

Our parents had sent us here on Sundays, alone. I remembered them both sitting in Hollywood Street, the apartment clogged with the scent of stale cigarettes floating around in a half inch of water. Outside on the street, Davey had pressed his sticky hand into mine and we'd walked: down Hollywood Street, take a left on May Street past the Pennywise Market, and then making a right onto Main Street where St. Peter's Catholic Church is located.

Of course, we'd always arrived after mass had started, when the priest was chanting in Latin or the big gold incense ball was sending smoke to fill up the room. Davey and I both had felt dwarfed in that church. In those days it had been packed with people, many of them strangers, who'd hidden behind their crooked window-shades most of the week.

It occurs to me that's what I'm doing back at church. I'm bringing everything I held onto of him after the rehab—his Elvis records, his ratty photos and even his ashes—to the altar. It's my job to invoke whatever cruddy pieces of memory exist, the lottery ticket stubs of his soul, back to St. Peter's church in Main South to attempt to do his life some sort of justice. To make peace.

I stand at the podium and look out into the massive church, seeing a man licking his hair back into place, a child shifting in a woman's lap, and everyone's chins cocked up toward me. The brightness of the lamps makes me squint. I hold my thighs tight together to keep my knees from buckling. I stand there, waiting, until I work up the courage to speak.

"Thank you," I start.

"Thank you all for coming out to pay your respects to my father. I know he would have appreciated it."

The silence in the room is thick and expectant. I have a hunch what people are expecting from me. The regular people want me to explain my father to them. Others—the hardscrabble men like my father had been—are waiting not just for words but for expression, emotions that would prove he was a good father, that he'd had an impact on me. They want me to legitimize him, to turn him into someone who mattered, not just for me but for them. If his life measured up after he was delivered to those pearly gates, their lives would matter too.

I don't have those words though. It occurs to me as I look around the echoey room, horrified, that I don't have the emotions either.

"David Wrenn, my father, was a good-hearted man. He had a good heart. He did. He … umm … was always a lot of fun."

"Uh-huh. Yes," someone in the back row is saying.

"He loved Elvis and the Red Sox. He worshipped those two things as much as anything."

"That's true."

"He had this way about him. Some would call it almost childlike. But it was more, I don't know, innocent. There was an innocence about him in the world. It was his way. He had a terrific sense of humor. He may not have always been the smartest man in the room, but he loved to laugh and have fun, and he wanted the same for those around him."

"Amen."

"That was the message in his heart. He wanted everyone around him to laugh and have fun, and he only wanted the best for them in that way," I say.

I stand, staring, willing more words to come to my mouth.

They don't.

Slowly, I walk away from the podium, making sure I don't trip on my way down the stairs.

PART 11

Finding Mal

The raptors couldn't handle the humiliation of losing their crown to a piddly wren, and so they challenged the birds to a rematch. They decided this time they would crown the bird who could swoop down the lowest in a contest.

The wren agreed, chuckling a little inside because he had a distinct advantage over the other birds, being wily and having pillaged many of his competitor's nests.

The contest began in earnest with all the birds flying with their bellies scraping the ground. The little wren found a mouse hole, deep under the mossy green earth, and he used his wren skills to empty it out and then crawl inside and pull the moss down around him. After enough time had passed, the wren screamed out that he had won. He was the lowest bird, so he was the king.

The raptors were mad. They had to admit the wren was the winner, but they were determined to make him pay. They told him sure, he was the king of the birds, but only as long as he was alive. They told him they were going to get him.

And we all know that although the wren can commit violent atrocities, he's mostly able to do so only by sneak attack, by gliding stealthily through the darkness or committing real psycho acts that the other birds never suspect will occur. He knew he was only the size of the raptor's eyeballs, of the wrist bone in the talons that could crush large animal's skulls.

The poor wren king did the only thing he could do. He stayed in the mouse hole. He waited. Hours passed and the eagle stayed outside the hole, just waiting for him to come out. When dusk came, the falcon stood watch; at nighttime, the owl.

Several days passed until the wren decided he needed to get out of there. He just couldn't sit still all the time. It wasn't in his nature.

He waited until the crack of dawn, when the sun would startle and annoy the owl, and slinked out, darting between leaves and in the shadows of tree roots. And in this wily way he escaped. He saw the opportunity and he took it.

This is perhaps one explanation for the reason the wren lives as he does, slaughtering any would-be enemy birds to establish his rep; always on the move, flittering uncertainly from place to place. For although he has the kind of street smarts that have earned him the title of king, he holds the title in secret. The raptors are still angry with him because he caused them such shame. No matter what he does, he always remembers the long days and nights he spent hiding in a mouse hole, peeking out at the dawn at those yellow eyes.

Chapter **60**

Finding Mal

Year: 2018, Mal—44 years old

We've been driving so long it feels like we're going backward. Or maybe it isn't that we have been driving so long as much as we have been driving around the same blocks, traversing the same tattered streets, the same tattered triple-deckers.

I want to leave but I can't. Not yet.

It's possible we've overstayed, that old Main South ghosts are clutching at our jackets.

It's more than that though. After this journey, I likely won't be coming back to Worcester. There are just a few things I still have to do to come to peace with this place, to lay down the bones of my memory.

"Mal, you here?" Greg asks quietly.

"Yeah," I whisper.

I examine this man, my husband Greg, his big steady hands on the wheel. Even if we're still coasting on this highway, Greg is my anchor. I trust him in a way I've never trusted another person in my life.

"I was thinking, you know, how insecure I was when my father was shot. What a different person I was. How afraid I was, you know, just to be myself. How I couldn't have possibly been that person with anyone else before in my life."

Greg smirks in that cute little boy way he has when I'm complimenting him. He turns toward me, his eyes mirroring me with grace and compassion.

"You are here, Mal," those eyes say. "You are loved."

Greg eased me into being comfortable with myself. At first, he did this exclusively by example.

It was the quality that had attracted me to him in the first place.

Tom and I had been divorced six years when I first met Greg. During my marriage to Tom, I started to see that while he was a good man, a fine husband, and a loving father, I needed to find a soul matching mine. One that really spoke to and understood me.

Those six years later, I was at a restaurant with a girlfriend in Plymouth on a sweet June night, overlooking the ocean. Greg sat down at an outdoor bar a few seats away. I remember noticing he smelled fresh, like the lawn he'd been mowing, and his face was still glistening with sweat. I'd watched him. He was just so at ease with himself, eating his dinner and nursing his glass of wine. I felt like I'd known him before.

Somehow, I mustered up the courage to talk to him. We spent the whole night sitting at that bar, just talking. We haven't stopped talking since.

The best part about Greg was that he was never embarrassed to be with me. His emotions toward me whether we were in public, around his friends, or in private never wavered. He reminded me that it was okay to be comfortable with myself, that there was nothing wrong with me as I am. It was so different from the way anyone else had ever treated me. It helped me process it all, stop feeling all that old shame.

I put my hand on the wrist that was on the drive shaft, held it. His muscles relax as I squeeze it.

"Remembering your dad?" he finally asks.

I surprise myself by starting to choke up a little.

I nod my head yes.

"It's okay," he says simply.

I turn my head to the window, making a fist and wiping the tears off. Lisa and my mom are so quiet in the back seat I'd almost forgotten they were there. We roll by a house I recognize, a huge, sandy-brown house with a wide lawn. The old school bus they used to drive across the country is gone, but the lawn is covered with enough stuff to fill a flea market. There are magazines piled in crates. There's a toaster and a kid's old wagon. Piles of junk wind from the yard all the way up the wraparound porch. There's a wooden chainsaw carving of a wizard with long hair and a robe, that looks partly like Father Time and partly like Wally. A black cat winds around the side of the house.

"This was Lilac's house," I say. "Obviously her parents still live there." The laughter starts bubbling up and I tap my fist on my chest to keep it together.

Memories flood back at me: me and Lilac sitting in her room while she pierced my ears, the cold potato on the back of my lobe, the scent of pot, gloppy peanut butter, and carob cookies wafting through the room. Me and Lilac laughing hysterically, loading up the shopping cart with cans.

It wasn't all bad. There were moments. I was happy, I think. The thought surprises me. That was just as real.

"Mal, let's go see if they're there," my sister says.

"Do you want to stop for a second?" Greg says as he slows the car.

He rolls down the street slowly and I squint into the yards, counting the houses until I see it. It's a wide vacant lot between two triple-deckers. I examine the spindly trees that are planted there until I find a larger spruce.

"Stop," I whisper.

He does. I stare. A warmth floods me and the muscles in my shoulders draw back. My body relaxes in a way it never has. I feel everything around me: the thick nighttime silence, the cool blanket of snow. I imagine it now just as we did all those years back. Lilac and me lay side by side, our legs extended straight on our sleeping bags, our chins tipping up toward the sky. There are soft smiles on our faces. There are stars. Through the canopy of pine needles we can hear the night birds.

EPILOGUE

It's now 2022, four years since Davey's death, and since that time I've reconnected with my mother as her health has landed her in a nursing home. The word "reconnected" isn't the right term, really. But I've been more involved in her life as she's not been able to care or advocate for herself. She's only seventy-two now—young by nursing home standards, but it's also surprising that she's lived this long given the toll years of drugs and hard living takes on a person. She's been clean now for more than ten years, but you can see that the damage has been done. Her demeanor is sweet, friendly, even warm. But she doesn't have the wherewithal, or perhaps even the interest, to hold a conversation.

She's been in this nursing home for three years now, happily playing bingo twice a week, making her trips to the dining room for her meals, and occasionally squabbling with whomever her roommate is these days over the volume of their dueling TVs. But something's different these last few weeks. She's declining, and ultimately landed in the local hospital ICU with a severe urinary tract infection that has evolved into sepsis.

She's been here for a couple of weeks now. Each day there seems to be a little bit of progress that's matched by backsliding. She's barely responsive, and it's unclear if she's aware that I'm here. While I've always kept my emotional distance from her, her quietness and stillness give me the chance to just be with her with nothing at stake. Without fear. Somehow it's easier to visit with her now—even in just silence—than ever before.

I hold her hand. It's limp but so small and soft. I study her face, taking in all of her features. Her eyes closed make it easy. I'm amazed and even envious at how luminous and beautiful her skin is. It's as if she spent a lifetime taking great care of herself. The irony.

She never does regain consciousness, and within a few days slowly slips away to death's calling. In the coming days I feel sadness, but I'd venture to guess it's not the same sadness that many might feel when they lose their mother. I am, of course, sad for her. Sad for any pain she might have endured over those couple of weeks in the hospital. But I guess I've already mourned my mother over the years that have passed—mourned the mother I wished I had. My mother's death also has me revisiting my brother's and father's deaths at the same time.

Over the years, friends and acquaintances have shared the losses of their own loved ones with obituaries and stories about the rich, beautiful lives they've lived. Sometimes, there are even impressive accolades and accomplishments to be proud of and celebrate.

My family, like many others out there, was complicated. They lived very difficult lives. They didn't always make good decisions in life—they often made terrible decisions. Our family was fractured, broken even. We certainly weren't close.

I never felt comfortable publicly sharing the losses of my brother and father, partly because there weren't prideful stories to tell or close relationships to mourn. In fact, I didn't write an obituary for my father.

I spent many years and a lot of energy distancing myself from them—trying to build a life and world that was my own, one that was closed off and insulated from the ways they lived. Truth be told, when I first married I couldn't wait to change my last name.

But with the passage of time, even though the relationships themselves didn't evolve, my feelings about those relationships were and continue to be very fluid and complex.

They were complicated people, but they're my family. They are, no doubt, a part of me and who I am, and their lives are worth recognizing and remembering. In fact, while working on my mother's obituary, it really weighed on me that there seemed to be no real record of my father's life. So, fourteen years after his death, I've written an obituary for him, too.

Despite their challenges, they had beautiful qualities. My mother had a friendly, fun, and childlike sweetness about her; my father had a feisty spirit and inherent toughness but also loved a good laugh. And, last but not least, my brother had an everlasting sweet smile, a mild-mannered demeanor, and innately kind way about him. I can only hope that I inherit some of their qualities.

A friend shared this quote that sticks with me:

> *Death ends a life, but it does not end a relationship, which struggles on in the survivor's mind toward some final resolution, some clear meaning, which it perhaps never finds.*
> —ROBERT WOODRUFF ANDERSON, *I Never Sang for My Father*

ABOUT THE AUTHOR

MAL WRENN CORBIN *was born in Worcester, MA and after a turbulent childhood, went on to be a first-generation college graduate of Dartmouth College. After receiving her Bachelor of Arts degree at Dartmouth, she went on to earn her Master of Education degree at Boston College.*

Today, Mal works as a business development professional for a leading financial services firm. Along with her husband and nineteen-year-old son, she lives in Duxbury, a bedroom community nestled between Boston and Cape Cod, along the Massachusetts shoreline.

Raising Wrenns
Mal Wrenn Corbin

Publisher: SDP Publishing
Also available in ebook format
MalWrennCorbin.com

 SDP Publishing

www.SDPPublishing.com
Contact us at: info@SDPPublishing.com